kamera
B O O K S

www.kamerabooks.com

Also from Brian J. Robb in

KAMERA BOOKS

Silent Cinema

POCKET ESSENTIALS

Ridley Scott
Laurel & Hardy
James Cameron

Brian J. Robb

TIMELESS ADVENTURES

HOW DOCTOR WHO CONQUERED TV

kamera
BOOKS

Dedicated to the God of all fanwank, Craig Hinton.

In Memoriam: Barry Letts (1925–2009)

This edition published in 2013 by Kamera Books
PO Box 394, Harpenden, Herts, AL5 1XJ
www.kamerabooks.com

A CIP catalogue record for this book
is available from the British Library.

ISBN 978-1-84344-156-4 (print)
ISBN 978-1-84344-157-1 (epub)
ISBN 978-1-84344-158-8 (Kindle)
ISBN 978-1-84344-159-5 (pdf)

2 4 6 8 10 9 7 5 3 1

Typeset by Ellipsis Digital Limited, Glasgow
Printed and bound by CPI Group (UK) Ltd, Croydon, CR0 4YY

ACKNOWLEDGEMENTS

Several people have been of great assistance in the process of writing (and rewriting) this book. I'm greatly indebted to Paul Simpson for reading the whole thing (several times) as a work in progress and helping me focus my thoughts (as well as catching the occasional factual error: any remaining errors or omissions are entirely my own).

Thanks are also due to Brigid Cherry who read and commented on the manuscript, and to the Titan Magazines' *Doctor Who* 'brains trust' of Jonathan Wilkins, Simon Hugo and Adam Newell for many hours of *Who*-chat (that must have endlessly annoyed our colleagues).

Additional gratitude is due to all those I've known across more than 20 years of involvement in and around British *Doctor Who* fandom, from the Glasgow Braindead gang through to the late-1980s DWAS crowd and the DWB/Dreamwatch group (comprising far too many people through the years to name individually).

Special thanks are also due to Barry Letts, Philip Hinchcliffe and Andrew Cartmel.

CONTENTS

INTRODUCTION

Doctor Who is an amazing television phenomenon. Any 50th birthday is a momentous occasion, all the more so for one of a mere handful of popular TV shows (outside of soap operas) to have made it to the half century and still be on air, as exciting and as fresh as ever. In 2013, *Doctor Who* reached that half-century milestone, just as it was refreshing itself again with the arrival of the twelfth actor to play the mysterious Time Lord title role.

Doctor Who has a unique and endlessly variable premise. At its most basic it is about the adventures of the heroic Doctor, travelling through time and space in his police box-shaped TARDIS, with a human companion along for the ride. With that set-up, the series can be anything, from knockabout farce to gothic horror, deep-space adventure to an internal drama within someone's mind. Adventures can be galaxy-spanning, or take place within a virtual fantasy environment like the Matrix (first featured in *Doctor Who* in 1976), or even somewhere as mundane as Tooting Bec.

Doctor Who began life as a Saturday-evening television series in 1963, and it was back on Saturday night that it triumphed in the ratings in 2013, the show's fiftieth-anniversary year. In between, the infinitely adaptable premise has seen *Doctor Who* stories told through just about every media available, from movies to audio dramas, computer games to Internet episodes. It has spun off a whole host of merchandising, from the 1960s period of 'Dalekmania' to the more recent flood of new series tie-ins.

Doctor Who's genius is that, in the guise of a family adventure series, it is *sui generis*, above being categorised as belonging to one specific genre or another. Often perceived as science fiction, the show is generically all-encompassing, as the past 50 years of adventures (in all media) have amply demonstrated. It's a pop-cultural artefact that appeals to the imagination, and – like the Doctor's greatest enemies, the Daleks – it has been able to survive and prosper, continually coming back after facing almost certain destruction.

Although most notoriously put on 'hiatus' for 18 months in 1985, *Doctor Who* has repeatedly had to fight for survival within the BBC at various crisis points in its 50-year history. Very early on, there was doubt that the show would survive beyond the initial 13 episodes. The impact of the arrival of the Daleks on viewing figures saved the series and allowed it to prosper throughout the 1960s. The next crisis came with the replacement of the lead actor, William Hartnell, by Patrick Troughton, challenging audiences to accept a new actor as the title character. Troughton saw the series through to the next threatened cancellation point at the end of the 1960s, when the BBC were actively exploring replacements for the then six-year-old show. Renewed to run in colour, the five years of Jon Pertwee's stint under producer Barry Letts and script editor Terrance Dicks was a period of consolidation, with steady audiences and strong support from within the BBC. That all changed, however, later in the 1970s, when Tom Baker played the lead for seven years and the show hit its highest viewing figures, whilst also facing a sustained attack by Mary Whitehouse and the National Viewers' and Listeners' Association. Accusations of gratuitous violence brought a premature end to producer Philip Hinchcliffe's run of gothic-horror-style stories, and saw him replaced by Graham Williams, working to a BBC-dictated brief to reduce the tea-time horror and increase the humour. John Nathan-Turner's decade-long run at the helm in the 1980s was a rollercoaster ride for the series and saw it undergo dramatic changes, with him casting three Doctors: Peter Davison, Colin Baker and Sylvester McCoy. The lowest point saw the show pulled off air (again due to perceived gore and violence) and 'rested' for 18 months in 1985. When it returned, little had been done to creatively refresh the by now 22-year-old show. This period culminated in the production team fighting amongst themselves, cutting short Sixth Doctor Colin Baker's tenure. The arrival of script editor Andrew Cartmel and new Doctor Sylvester McCoy saw the series dramatically reinvigorated, but it all came too late as viewing figures crashed to little over three million, leading to outright cancellation in 1989. While reaching respectable viewing figures of around nine million, the one-off, US-made TV movie starring Paul McGann in 1996 failed to lead to a series. It was only with strong executive support from within the BBC that Russell T Davies (a self-proclaimed fan of the original run of the show) was able to relaunch *Doctor Who* in 2005 to critical acclaim and audience acceptance, revitalising Saturday evening family viewing and culminating in the celebratory 50th anniversary special in 2013.

Doctor Who is one of the most written-about TV shows in history – if not *the* most written about. The reasons for this are many and complex, but much of it is down to the participatory fandom that has grown up around the show, and the fact that (despite all its ups and downs) the show has a unique connection to British television audiences. There are books of *Doctor Who* lists, many episode guides (some more useful or insightful than others), several very good production histories (and some not so good) and a growing body of academic literature tackling the original and revived versions of the show. So why add another volume?

This *Doctor Who* book attempts to achieve three key things. Firstly, it's a basic introduction to the series and its 50-year history on British television. Chapter one is an in-depth account of the show's creation and the cultural and social factors that affected its development. However, this book's history of the show is tackled from a very different perspective than most others. The thesis here is that *Doctor Who* earned its place in the affections of British TV audiences because underneath its fantastical adventures was a critique of contemporary social, political and cultural issues, from the 1960s through to the twenty-first century. Fantasy is often seen as divorced from reality, offering an escape from everyday cares. At worst, it is seen as a refuge for the socially inadequate or the desperate. It's a damned genre perceived as having little social relevancy. This could not be further from the truth. The best fantasy – like all stories we tell ourselves – has a subtext that deals with important realities and makes it more engaging for an audience. At its best, this is what *Doctor Who* did with its privileged access to generations of family audiences on Saturday evenings in the 1960s and 1970s.

Taking this idea on board, chapters two to five cover the key periods of the series' history, with a special emphasis on those adventures that reveal an engagement with the social, political and cultural history of Britain. The series arguably suffered in the 1980s (chronicled in chapter five) when it abdicated the key to this unique relationship by turning its back on the mass audience and their concerns to pander instead to the narrower interests of *Doctor Who*'s dedicated fanbase.

And this brings us to the second key focus: *Doctor Who* fandom (explored in depth in chapter six). This began with a number of like-minded individuals who appreciated the show and grew into a series of cliques, some of them actively affecting the direction the series took and others heavily criticising the choices being made.

I'm proud to say that I'm a *Doctor Who* fan, something it hasn't always been easy to admit in polite society. Once upon a time, fans (of anything, but mainly of SF TV shows or film series) were seen as geeky loners severely lacking in social skills, clutching a plastic bag of memorabilia. Like all stereotypes, there are such fans. However, it seems that, now, *everyone* is a *Doctor Who* fan!

I've been part of active fandom for many years. I've edited *Celestial Toyroom* (the officially sanctioned *Doctor Who* Appreciation Society newsletter), and I've written for *Doctor Who Bulletin* (the rebel title that opposed the official view) and edited the later incarnation when it was called *Dreamwatch*. In the late-1980s, I regularly met with *Doctor Who* producer John Nathan-Turner to gather news for *Celestial Toyroom* and attended studio recordings of the series at Television Centre. I wrote a history of the coverage of *Doctor Who* in the *Radio Times* for the official *Doctor Who Magazine*. My connections even run through to the current series, when I visited the set of the new *Doctor Who* (when it was in Newport) and saw the new TARDIS interior before it was made public. I've been several times to the Cardiff Upper Boat studio complex where *Doctor Who*, and the two spin-off series *Torchwood* and *The Sarah Jane Adventures,* are made. It's amazing to still be involved (however peripherally) almost 20 years on.

Active, involved fans from the 1980s became those entrusted with continuing the *Doctor Who* legacy while the TV series was off the air, developing the character's adventures in novels, comic-strips and audio plays, as well as researching and chronicling the making of the original show in sometimes absurd depth. It was due to the action of dedicated fans that the BBC was prevented from wiping any more old episodes in the late 1970s, and many of those same fans were responsible for the recovery and restoration of many episodes now released by the BBC on DVD and CD. The continuation of *Doctor Who* in audio drama by Big Finish has meant that the actors who play the title character never really give up the role. Paul McGann is still playing the Eighth Doctor on audio, over 13 years after his one-shot TV movie appearance. Similarly, Peter Davison, Colin Baker and Sylvester McCoy have all continued to develop their Doctors, long after their time on TV was up.

The third strand featured in this volume is the return of *Doctor Who* to television in 2005 in the newly revitalised series, chronicled in chapter seven. It's a show now run by fans (both show-runners Russell T Davies and Steven Moffat and star David Tennant are all self-confessed active fans of the original series). However, the new version of *Doctor Who* has re-engaged successfully with the mass audience the series lost in the 1980s. The show was refurbished to appeal to everyone, yet it is recognisably still the same *Doctor Who* that went off air in 1989.

Doctor Who is more successful now than it has ever been, and has enjoyed a sustained period of success. When *Doctor Who* was off the air, the memory of the show remained with audiences who'd grown up with it as children, whether in the 1960s, the 1970s or the 1980s. In 1996 the series was dramatically declared the All-Time Favourite BBC Programme in a public vote celebrating the BBC's 60th anniversary, beating the likes of much-loved shows *EastEnders* and *Casualty*. The revived version of the series has won armloads of awards, from BAFTAs and National Television Awards to the science-fiction Oscars, the Hugos.

Crucial to this success has been the revived series' willingness to engage with modern social, political and cultural (even consumer) issues in a way not seen since the early-to-mid-1970s. Unlike in the 1980s, but very in tune with the 1960s and 1970s, *Doctor Who* is once again a TV show that attracts an audience due to its accessibility and the fact that it is easily understood as part of a modern television environment.

The 50th anniversary year saw *Doctor Who* refresh itself once more, as Matt Smith hung up his sonic screwdriver after a hugely successful four-year run as the Eleventh Doctor, making way for Peter Capaldi to step aboard the magical TARDIS space-time machine as the twelfth version of the renegade Time Lord. It may have been seen as another moment of crisis for the show, but the fact is *Doctor Who*'s very strength lies in such change. The show thrives on renewal and every new lead actor or showrunner brings something different and unique to this uniquely long-lived series.   Long thought of as a dead series during much of the 1990s, *Doctor Who* is now guaranteed a future, as long as the series remains relevant to its audience. The Doctor himself is now one of the great British fictional folk heroes, alongside Sherlock Holmes, Robin Hood and James Bond. Each of these characters returns again and again, in new forms and in new media, telling new, but always relevant, stories. Just like them, *Doctor Who* will keep returning, forever.

1. ADVENTURES IN TIME & SPACE

Who created *Doctor Who*?

Reading the credits of the current incarnation of the series will not tell you the answer to that question. If you rely on an early edition of the quiz game *Trivial Pursuit*, which claimed *Doctor Who* was created by one-time Tony Hancock scriptwriter Terry Nation, you'll be no better informed. That assertion has continued to surface, even in the *Guardian* obituary of the first *Doctor Who* producer Verity Lambert late in 2007. Earlier histories of the show often credited the 1960s Head of BBC Drama, Canadian Sydney Newman. The truth, however, is that the national institution that is *Doctor Who* was the product of a committee working within another national institution, the BBC itself.

Hugh Carleton Greene became BBC Director General at a crucial time of change in the corporation's history. Brother of author Graham Greene, he'd been a war correspondent for the *Daily Telegraph* before joining the BBC in 1940. In and out of the BBC throughout the next two decades, Greene held a variety of important posts that allowed him to succeed Ian Jacob to the top position in 1960. He was now running an organisation with a unique history. Founded in October 1922 by John Reith, the British Broadcasting Company (later Corporation) had a responsibility (as stated in the BBC Charter of

1927) to 'inform, educate and entertain' the nation. The BBC was – and still is – funded through a licence-fee scheme, paid by all who own a television. This often left the organisation open to political manipulation by the government of the day. Experimental television broadcasting had begun in 1932. A regular service started in 1936, but was interrupted by the Second World War before resuming in June 1946. The BBC established many of the basic 'ground rules' of television broadcasting, and has often evinced a very paternalistic attitude, resulting in the nickname 'Auntie'.

As Director General, Greene had a clear mission statement: to drag the BBC out of the complacent 1950s (some might say the 1940s) and to ensure that the Corporation's output kept pace with the dizzying social and political change of the 1960s. The big threat the BBC faced was ITV, the independent commercial broadcaster started in 1955, which had found popular success and acceptance as the 1960s began. In comparison with this dynamic young commercial operation, the bureaucratic and hidebound BBC appeared to be a relic from a bygone age. Deference was out and protest was in as the 1960s began to truly swing. It was Hugh Carleton Greene's job to reflect this sea change in British culture in the programmes that appeared on the BBC.

Among the innovative programmes that debuted on his watch (which extended until 1968) were melancholic situation comedy *Steptoe and Son*, gritty police drama *Z-Cars*, and late-night biting political and social satire *That Was The Week That Was* (or *TW3*). All were long-running (except *TW3*, axed amid electoral controversy, although its satiric approach to news and politics lived on through the work of David Frost and others) and significantly developed their respective evolving genres. These three shows all began in 1962. They were to be joined by another groundbreaking series in 1963: *Doctor Who*.

In order to compete with ITV, Greene approached one of the rival broadcaster's key creative figures to become the BBC's new Head of Drama. Sydney Newman had come to ITV from a successful career in his native Canada where he'd started out as a film editor for the National Film Board. After working in American television in the early 1950s in New York, Newman returned to Canada to take up a post with the Canadian Broadcasting Corporation where he became Supervisor of Drama Productions in 1954. By 1958, Newman was in Britain, having been hired by ITV regional franchise ABC (serving the English Midlands and the North) as a drama producer. Newman, brash and forthright like the independent broadcaster he was joining, rapidly rose to become ABC's Head of Drama. He was directly responsible for the creation of *Armchair Theatre*, a weekly show that presented the work of a new breed of 'angry young men' playwrights to large audiences, and gritty drama *Police Surgeon*, which developed into the more fantastical *The Avengers*.

Looking to revitalise the BBC's moribund drama department and under instructions from Director General Hugh Greene, the BBC's Director of Television Kenneth Adam hired Newman to become Head of Drama at the BBC. He took up the post as soon as his ABC contract expired in December 1962. Resented by many in the BBC – due to being younger, better paid, outspoken, and (maybe worst of all) 'foreign' – Newman was quick to make his mark. He split the unwieldy drama department into three units – series, serials and plays, headed by Elwyn Jones, Donald Wilson and Michael Bakewell respectively. All three reported directly to Newman, whose arrival was a sign of big changes to come at the BBC throughout the 1960s.

Donald Baverstock, the BBC Controller of Programmes, met with Newman in March 1963 to discuss the need for a new show to fill an early-evening scheduling gap between the live afternoon sports programme *Grandstand* and the pop-music review show *Juke Box Jury*, which led into the prime-time Saturday evening schedule. The slot had been previously filled by a variety of short-lived shows and serials, including a Francis Durbridge thriller, a six-episode science-fiction serial *The Big Pool* and comedy series *The Telegoons*. Newman and Baverstock wanted a new drama show for the slot, something that could potentially run all year round (with short seasonal breaks) and could attract a loyal family audience, keeping the older *Grandstand* viewers tuned in, yet also appealing to the younger, hipper audience attracted to *Juke Box Jury*. Newman proposed and considered a variety of ideas, including a drama set in a boys' school.

However, for as long as he could recall, Newman had been a fan of literary science fiction. 'Up to the age of 40, I don't think there was a science-fiction book I hadn't read,' he claimed. 'I love them because they're a marvellous way – and a safe way, I might add – of saying nasty things about our own society.' Newman was aware of, and embraced, science fiction's ability to comment on contemporary politics and society in the disguise of fiction about the future. While at ABC he'd commissioned the science-fiction drama-anthology series *Out of This World*, as well as the serial *Pathfinders in Space* and two sequels, *Pathfinders to Mars* and *Pathfinders to Venus*. The *Pathfinders* shows featured juvenile characters as a point of identification for the younger target audience and were co-created by Malcolm Hulke, later a key, politically motivated contributor to *Doctor Who*. Introduced by classic-horror-film icon Boris Karloff, *Out of This World* dramatised the work of key science-fiction authors such as Isaac Asimov, John Wyndham and Philip K Dick, whose *Impostor* was adapted by screenwriter Terry Nation, later to create the Daleks for *Doctor Who*. These previous Sydney Newman shows combined elements that would be central to *Doctor Who*: an anthology-series format, with strong 'audience identification' characters (as the BBC described them) carrying forward from story to story.

Newman's interest in science fiction was fundamental to his thoughts on filling the Saturday scheduling gap, but the BBC had already been actively investigating the possibility of developing a series of literary science-fiction adaptations since early 1962. Always on the lookout for material to adapt, especially literary material, the BBC had an in-house 'survey group' that monitored film, radio and theatre productions for material that might be of use to television. Donald Wilson, then running the BBC's script department, and Head of Light Entertainment Eric Maschwitz commissioned a report on literary science fiction that might be suitable for television adaptation. The report, compiled by drama script editors Donald Bull and Alice Frick, was submitted in April 1962. The pair had read and evaluated a selection of then-current science-fiction novels and short-story anthologies, and had met with some authors, including Brian Aldiss. The report labelled the genre as particularly American and ideas-based rather than rooted in character. Various sub-genres were identified, from simple thriller plots, to technology-driven narratives and 'big ideas' like cosmic threats to mankind and cosmic disasters. Interestingly, one of the sub-genres identified was described as 'satire, comic or horrific, extrapolating current social trends and techniques', a description that could be applied to much of *Doctor Who*'s output over the next 45 years. This was key to Newman's belief that science fiction was a worthwhile genre.

Previous significant science-fiction ventures by the BBC had included the 1950s *Quatermass* serials (*Quatermass*, *Quatermass II* and *Quatermass and the Pit*) by Nigel Kneale and the two *Andromeda* serials (*A For Andromeda* in 1961 and *The Andromeda Breakthrough*, broadcast in 1962); these both fell into the 'cosmic threat to mankind' sub-genre the BBC report had identified. The report suggested that ideas-driven narratives were not enough; to succeed, a new television drama would have to attach the 'magic' of its science-fiction content to 'a current human situation'. Also, 'identification must be offered with identifiable human beings'. This remit would be closely followed into the twenty-first-century version of the show.

Frick and her drama-department colleague John Braybon were asked to investigate the subject matter further in a second report itemising specific literary science-fiction titles the BBC could adapt. By July 1962, the pair had devised some rules for TV science fiction that might appeal to the BBC and had some definite suggestions of stories to be adapted. The 'rules' were simple: no bug-eyed monsters; no 'tin robot' central characters; no 'large and elaborate' settings, such as spaceship interiors or alien planets. They must feature 'genuine characterisation' and rely on the audience having to 'suspend disbelief on one fact only'. Frick and Braybon settled on stories dealing with telepaths or time travel as being most suited to adaptation to television on an inevitably limited BBC budget. They described the time-travel concept as 'particularly attractive as a series, since individual plots can easily be tackled by a variety of scriptwriters. It's the *Z-Cars* of science fiction'.

The stories listed in this second report that were considered suitable for adapting were time-travel adventure *Guardians of Time* by Poul Anderson, alien-invasion drama *Three to Conquer* by Eric Frank Russell, immortality tale *Eternity Lost* by Clifford Simak, trick story *Pictures Don't Lie* by Catherine McLean (aliens invade in tiny ships and drown in a puddle, later satirised by Douglas Adams in *The Hitchhiker's Guide to the Galaxy*), a Frankenstein-type tale *No Woman Born* by CL Moore, the humorous *The Cerebrative Psittacoid* by H Nearing Jr and a story of adventure and exploration, *The Ruum* by Arthur Forges.

Sydney Newman's own interest in science fiction, combined with the 1962 reports, which Baverstock and Donald Wilson brought to his attention, resulted in him issuing a brief to the drama department. He requested that they develop a full proposal for a science-fiction anthology series, consisting of a number of self-contained, short serials, to run for 52 weeks of the year, to fill the early-evening Saturday slot. The development of *Doctor Who* had begun.

Responding to Sydney Newman's directive, Baverstock and Wilson put together a committee to build upon the survey group's 1962 findings and develop a proposal for the Saturday-early-evening, science-fiction, family show. At the initial meeting on 26 March 1963 were Wilson, two of the authors of the 1962 report, Alice Frick and John Braybon, and script-department adapter Cecil Edwin Webber. According to Frick's notes of the meeting, Wilson suggested a series based around a time-travelling machine and those who used it. Crucially, Wilson maintained that the machine should not only travel forwards and backwards in time, but also into space and even 'sideways' into matter itself (suggesting other dimensions). Frick herself preferred the idea of a 'flying saucer' vehicle, very in vogue since the phrase was coined following US pilot Kenneth Arnold's sightings of 1947. She felt the saucer would be a better ship as it could contain a group of people, unlike (she assumed) a time machine that, in the style of HG Wells' time traveller in his novel *The Time Machine,* would only allow an individual to travel. Wilson wanted the new show to steer clear of anything computer-related, as this had featured quite heavily in the BBC's recent *Andromeda* serials. The telepathy idea from the original report was reconsidered, but not thought to be central to any possible series. Braybon suggested basing a future-set series around a group of scientific trouble-shooters who would investigate rogue science and scientists (this idea would later surface in slightly different form on the BBC in the 1970s as *Doomwatch* and in the twenty-first century as US TV show *Fringe*). Each individual serial within the overall series could be devoted to exploring the impact of a single scientific idea, suggested Braybon.

In developing a format for the proposed early-evening series, Wilson explained that the show must be built around a central group of continuing characters. Different members of the group could come to prominence in different serials, with others dropping into the background (a very modern drama structure now followed by soaps and TV drama).

He felt that, in order to ensure the younger audience tuned in, at least two of the characters should be teenagers, while Frick felt that the teen audience would prefer to watch characters slightly older than themselves, possibly in their 20s. Two key problems were identified: how would the group be exposed to 'wildly differing' adventures and how would they be transported to the different settings and environments that the serial nature of the show dictated? CE Webber was tasked with coming up with a cast of characters who could form the central group that would feature in the series.

Within the core of the subjects discussed at this meeting are the roots of *Doctor Who* as it would eventually come to the TV screen in November 1963, but the specifics were lacking. The committee approach, building on the previous work, came up with the idea of a group of characters travelling through time and space in a vehicle of some sort and enjoying/enduring a variety of different adventures each week. The task now would be to add the detail of the characters and pin down some of the specifics of the concept. Webber's subsequent character notes suggested a 'handsome young man hero', a 'well-dressed heroine aged about 30', and a 'maturer man with a character twist'. Webber's notes also went on to explore in more detail the scientific-trouble-shooters concept.

In April 1963, the notes from these meetings were given to Sydney Newman, who promptly annotated them in his regular brusque manner. He discounted the idea of a flying-saucer vehicle, and next to the trouble-shooters concept he simply scribbled a curt: 'No.' Next to Webber's character list he added: 'Need a kid to get into trouble, make mistakes.' Newman approved of Wilson's time-space machine idea and added that the show should be more like the exciting 1930s and 1940s cinema adventure serials than the old-fashioned and worthy traditional BBC children's dramas. Newman latched on to Webber's older man character, suggesting he should be older than the suggested 35–40, perhaps a frail, grumpy old man who has stolen the time-space machine from his own people. Perhaps he could come from an advanced civilisation on a faraway planet? This character would be called 'the Doctor'. In this synthesis of the survey group's ideas with his own off-the-cuff inspiration and his knowledge of socially relevant literary science fiction, Sydney Newman had devised the flexible and lasting concept of *Doctor Who*.

In May 1963, BBC staff director/producer Rex Tucker was appointed as a caretaker producer for the as-yet-unnamed new programme until Sydney Newman could find a permanent producer for his slowly gestating Saturday-series idea. Tucker brought a recently hired, young and enthusiastic TV director, Richard Martin, to the show, but he intended to direct the first episodes himself. In the summer of 1963, while the BBC bureaucracy prepared for the forthcoming show by allocating studio space at BBC Lime Grove and booking facilities personnel, the creative work in devising the series was still being done. Based on further meetings, Webber drafted a formal format document for the series, accepting Newman's cliff-hanger serial idea by describing each subsequent 25-minute episode as starting by 'repeating the closing sequence or final climax of the preceding episode'. A 'moderate' budget would be available, but the show should use 'repeatable sets' where possible and potential writers should not be afraid of calling for 'special effects to achieve the element of surprise essential in these stories'.

The characters who were to go on the adventures had been further refined and now had names and character traits. They were Biddy, a 'with it' 15-year-old; Miss Lola McGovern, a 24-year-old schoolmistress at Biddy's school; and Cliff, a 'strong and courageous' schoolmaster of 27 or 28. Newman's now central 'old man' character had become the Doctor, 'a frail old man lost in time and space'. His 'name' has been given to him by the others as they don't really know who he is. Webber's character description gave this draft Doctor a form of amnesia: 'He seems not to remember where he has come from; he is suspicious and capable of sudden malignancy; he seems to have some undefined enemy; he is searching for something as well as fleeing from something. He has a machine which enables them to travel together through time, through space, and through matter.'

Webber wanted writers of subsequent serials to explore the 'mystery' of who the Doctor was, with no one single explanation necessarily being definitive. He did, however, provide two 'secrets' that the series could reveal when the time was right. The Doctor had stolen the time-space machine when he fled from his own people, having 'opted out' as he objected to their ongoing scientific progress (later seen as reflecting the growing 1960s 'hippie' pop culture of 'tuning in and dropping out' from society). Casting the rebel Doctor as the ultimate conservative, though, Webber mentions his 'hatred of scientists, inventors, improvers. He malignantly tries to stop progress (the future) wherever he finds it, while searching for his ideal (the past)'. The second secret had the Doctor's own people in pursuit of him, out to stop him 'monkeying with time, because his secret intention is to destroy or nullify the future'. In drafting this document, Webber became *Doctor Who*'s second godfather, adding the essential mystery element (who is the Doctor?) and developing the backstory that he stole his time-space machine and is on the run from his own people.

As before, the document went to Sydney Newman for review. Accepting the parts he'd suggested, Newman violently objected to Webber's detailed characterisation of the Doctor, writing on the document that the Doctor should be 'a kind of father figure. I don't want him to be a reactionary!' While this Doctor's desire to fight the future and retreat into the past might have reflected Webber's political feelings, it certainly didn't chime with Newman, or his project of trying to drag the BBC – through its drama productions – into the soon-to-be-swinging, anti-reactionary, positively progressive 1960s. Against the paragraph outlining the Doctor's mission to 'nullify the future', Newman bluntly scribbled 'Nuts!' In nixing this character idea, Newman probably saved the nascent series from a short, ignominious run. The Doctor's accepting, tolerant and open character would be a large part of the series' ongoing success with subsequent generations, regardless of the actor playing the role at any given time. It would be the one core element of the character that remained unchanged.

Under Newman's direction the character of the Doctor was revised to become a scientist figure, albeit of the amateur, self-educated variety. He was old, maybe 650 according to one document, and occasionally forgetful, tetchy and selfish, but he was not to be evil. He was to be a positive force for good, an autodidact always open to learning something new, while being immensely knowledgeable. Although the other characters might be suspicious of him and his motives initially, they would all eventually become trusted friends and allies. This was, after all, intended as a Saturday early-evening TV serial aimed at a family audience: the central character couldn't be too much of an antihero, even in the 1960s. The character had now been dubbed 'Dr Who', reflecting his unknowable nature. There is an echo of Jules Verne's Captain Nemo in the naming of the character, with Nemo being Latin for 'no one'. There is some dispute as to whether Tucker or Newman came up with the new name, but it stuck, attached as it was to all the various revisions of the character description. Eventually, the central character's 'name' would become the title of the show, in the fuller form of *Doctor Who*.

As 1963 progressed, attention within the BBC drama department turned to the detailed nature of the Doctor's time-space machine. With a flying-saucer-type vehicle having been roundly rejected by Newman, Wilson and the team developing *Doctor Who* had to think of something else. Much of the basic time-travel concept of the series had come from a literary classic very familiar to post-war British readers: HG Wells' *The Time Machine*. The problem with the type of time machine featured in Wells' philosophical social satire was that, built as it was around an Edwardian saddle, it could only comfortably carry one passenger at a time. How would the Doctor and his several friends travel through time if only one of them could sit down and the others had to hang on? Something else had to be devised. The answer came from another British children's literary classic: CS Lewis's *Chronicles of Narnia: The Lion, the Witch and the Wardrobe*.

In his format document, Webber attempted to avoid giving the Doctor's time-space machine any form at all, as he simply couldn't devise a solution that the BBC could afford on a weekly TV budget. He didn't want a 'transparent plastic bubble' or the clichéd spaceship from 'low-grade space fiction [and] cartoon strip'. His solution was an absence of a ship, a 'shape of nothingness' into which the Doctor and his companions could pass to enter. In his notes in response to this, Newman criticised Webber's concept as 'not visual', feeling that a 'tangible symbol' was needed for the ship.

Webber had provided the answer in his document, but it took others to spot it. In his struggles to describe the ship while avoiding science-fictional clichés he suggested 'something humdrum… such as a night-watchman's shelter' through which the Doctor and the gang could pass to 'arrive inside a marvellous contrivance of quivering electronics'. Webber further suggested that the ship could adopt 'some contemporary disguise' wherever it went, and that 'many visual possibilities can be worked out'. He concluded that the ship could be 'a version of the dear old Magic Door'.

The 'magic-door' concept for the Doctor's time-space machine was a stroke of genius, one of the crucial elements that gives the show appeal, longevity and variety. This was CS Lewis's wardrobe – a doorway to a magical world – combined with HG Wells' time machine. Add in Newman's additional space-travel capability and Newman and

Webber's characters, especially the mysterious, fugitive Doctor and his human companions, and the basic concept of *Doctor Who* had finally been devised: a true group effort of popular creation.

There was much more detail to be added to the rather vague 'magic-door' concept, but each revision of the format document through the summer of 1963 brought the show that would debut in November closer into being. Webber suggested that the Doctor's ship should be unreliable and faulty, and that the Doctor would have trouble finding fuel and spare parts on his travels through space and time, a notion that Newman heartily approved of. Webber also suggested that, due to his memory loss, the Doctor didn't really know how to operate the machine properly. This lack of control would make the group's adventures unpredictable: just like the viewer, they wouldn't know where, in which time or on what planet they would land next.

Like the naming of the character as 'Doctor Who', the question of who devised the outward appearance of the time-space machine is lost in the mists of time itself. The notion is usually credited to Anthony Coburn, yet another BBC staff writer whom Donald Wilson had charged with developing ideas for the series. While on a stroll near his office, contemplating the nature of the Doctor's 'magic door' into his ship, Coburn supposedly passed a police box and suggested it to Webber as a replacement for his 'night watchman's shelter' idea. Police boxes were a familiar sight on the streets of 1960s Britain. Often located on street corners, they provided shelter for patrolling policemen and offered a telephone link back to police headquarters in the decades before widespread use of walkie-talkies or mobile phones. It was an inspired thought, as it served to ground the mysterious Doctor's 'impossible' vehicle in an everyday world that families could recognise from their own contemporary surroundings. It was also a curiously whimsical notion that would be one factor in *Doctor Who*'s unique sense of Britishness. The next draft of the format document, from mid-May 1963, described the time-space machine as having 'the appearance of a police box standing in the street'.

It's possible that those within the BBC concerned with the development of *Doctor Who* had at the backs of their minds (perhaps after an early-1960s TV transmission) the little-remembered Gainsborough comedy *Time Flies* from 1944. Writers Phil Norman and Chris Diamond suggested in *TV Cream's Anatomy of Cinema* that actor Felix Aylmer might count as the first incarnation of the Doctor, as in *Time Flies* he plays an old scientist who's invented a time-space machine that takes the form of a large silver sphere that seems to be bigger on the inside than it appears on the outside. The movie sees comedian Tommy Handley joining Aylmer, Evelyn Dall as showgirl Susie and George Moon as her husband Bill in a trip back in time to the Elizabethan era, where the gimmick of giving Shakespeare (John Salew) the ideas for his plays appears (as replayed in the *Doctor Who* adventure *The Shakespeare Code* in 2007). Aylmer's Professor even bears a more than passing resemblance to William Hartnell's TV and Peter Cushing's 1960s movie version of the Doctor in dress and mannerisms. There are other curiosities: the ship is launched by accident, the crew (a 'scientist' and his three companions) are rendered unconscious upon take-off and mention is made of possibly meeting primitive man at their new location – all strongly echoed in *Doctor Who*'s eventual first episode. The adventurers encounter Queen Elizabeth and Raleigh (the Queen appears in *Doctor Who* in a Hartnell-starring episode of *The Chase* entitled 'The Executioners' as well as in *The Shakespeare Code*), as well as Shakespeare (also in 'The Executioners' and, of course, *The Shakespeare Code*). The scientist's side-kicks are described as his 'companions', while Handley's antics could be compared to those of the Meddling Monk, a mischievous character met by Hartnell's Doctor in *The Time Meddler*. The film even climaxes with a hunt for a missing element (platinum) needed to make the ship work and effect their escape, a plot point repeated in Hartnell's second serial,

The Daleks, with mercury instead of platinum. The coincidences are certainly curious, to say the least.

The fact that the Doctor's human companions were to be two schoolteachers and a pupil was no accident. As well as being an exciting adventure serial, Newman wanted the new show to be broadly educational (living up to the promise of the BBC Charter to 'inform, educate and entertain'), to use the Doctor's travels through time and space to bring the facts of history and cosmology to an attentive audience, disguised as entertainment. For the young, radical, commercially driven newcomer to the Corporation, this was a very traditional, almost Reithian concept but he also saw it as a function of good, literary science fiction. In further revisions to the series' format document, teenager Biddy became Sue and was working class (seen as a 'good thing' in 1960s drama), while Cliff was a science teacher and Lola a history teacher, encompassing the two disciplines that might be useful in uncontrolled travels through time and space. Storylines were by now being devised for the character's adventures. An initial outline in which the travellers were to be reduced to miniature size and trapped in Cliff's school lab was rejected by Newman as 'thin on incident and character'. Writer Anthony Coburn was set to work by acting producer Rex Tucker on a second adventure that would take the central characters back to prehistoric times where they would meet a clan of cavemen, as alluded to in *Time Flies*.

In June 1963, *Doctor Who*'s first permanent producer arrived at BBC Television Centre to take up her post. Verity Lambert, then just 28 years old, had been selected by Sydney Newman for the still-vacant producer post. Newman's initial choice for the job had been Don Taylor, a BBC staff director associated with provocative single plays and the work of radical writer David Mercer. Taylor had been upset by the arrival of Newman at the BBC, believing Newman's commercial, populist approach to drama conflicted with his own conception of the BBC as the National Theatre of the airways. When Taylor passed on the new Saturday teatime series, Newman had suggested to Shaun Sutton, then best known for his children's drama serials (which Newman thought old-fashioned), that he take on *Doctor Who*. Sutton, too, passed. Newman then recalled Lambert, a production assistant who'd impressed him at *Armchair Theatre* on ABC.

'When Donald Wilson and I discussed who might take over the responsibility for producing the show I rejected the traditional drama types who did children's serials,' said Newman of his approach, 'and said that I wanted somebody who'd be prepared to break rules in doing the show. Somebody young with a sense of "today" – the early "Swinging London" days.'

Newman was essentially looking for someone in his own image, rather than someone trained in the 'old-fashioned' ways of the BBC. Although Lambert's experience was limited, Newman felt that enthusiasm and independence were more important to the task of running *Doctor Who* than familiarity with the inner workings of the BBC. 'She had never directed, produced, acted or written drama but, by God, she was a bright, highly intelligent, outspoken production secretary who took no nonsense and never gave any,' Newman stated. 'I introduced her to Donald Wilson and I don't think he quite liked her at first. She was too good looking, too smart alecky and too commercial-television minded. I knew they would hit it off when they got to know one another better. They did.'

Lambert had split her time at ABC with a year working on television in New York, an experience that had broadened her horizons and her experience. She arrived at the BBC to find there was little to the *Doctor Who* project other than the ever-evolving format document and a host of growing technical objections from the BBC facilities managers at the tiny and antiquated studios at Lime Grove. Lambert found she had to work closely with the series' associate producer Mervyn Pinfield, who'd been appointed to handle the technical side of what was proving to be an ambitious project. Lambert also met with director Waris Hussein, a young newcomer to the BBC like herself, who'd been attached to direct the planned second serial about the show's characters meeting ancient cavemen.

Most of the technical objections centred on the first storyline, which involved the main characters being shrunk to minuscule size, something those at Lime Grove believed was beyond the capability of the technical facilities available. Finally, the decision was taken to shelve the 'Giants' storyline and pull the caveman tale forward to form the first story of the series. Lambert and the team agreed that it would be sensible to postpone production by a few weeks to give them all time to get to grips with the complicated, technically challenging show. The core *Doctor Who* production team was completed with the arrival of script editor David Whitaker at the end of June 1963.

Scripts became the first priority, as without those basic blueprints no television drama could ever enter production. Anthony Coburn delivered his draft caveman adventure scripts, which contained some important changes. The male schoolteacher was now called Ian Chesterton, while the teen female character had become Susan Foreman. With two of the scripts for the first four-episode story delivered, scenic-design work could begin in earnest, a step especially necessary as the first episode introduced the Doctor's time-space machine, something that promised to be a major design challenge for BBC technicians more used to contemporary or period dramas.

Lambert and Whitaker were not entirely happy with Coburn's work on the opening adventure and, following the delivery of his third of four episodes, they requested that he embark on a major re-write. In the meantime, Lambert turned her attention to casting the ongoing central roles for the series. Her first task was to find the right actor to take on the leading role of the mysterious Doctor. Lambert may have been new to creative responsibility but she knew enough to be aware that the success or failure of a TV show often revolved around the leading actors. She had to find the right man to inhabit the role of the Doctor.

In conjunction with Waris Hussein, now set to direct the first story of the new series, based on Coburn's caveman scripts, Lambert drew up a shortlist of suitable stars. On the list were renowned thespian Cyril Cusack and Leslie French (who had apparently been the nude model for the statue of Ariel on the facade of the BBC's Broadcasting House in London and later appeared in a 1988 *Doctor Who* story, *Silver Nemesis*). Eventually, Lambert auditioned 55-year-old William Hartnell, based on a viewing of the Lindsay Anderson film *This Sporting Life* (1963), although he was best known to TV viewers for his role as the irascible military man in Granada's comedy series *The Army Game* (1957–61). Hartnell had often been typecast as tough guys or criminals, but *This Sporting Life* had allowed him to show a broader range, something he was intent on developing further. While his agent was reluctant to connect Hartnell with what was being perceived as a children's show, the actor himself was keen to break out of the typecasting that had been afflicting him and readily attended a meeting with Lambert and Hussein. Enthused by the project, he agreed to take on the lead role of the Doctor.

That major hurdle overcome, Lambert and Hussein quickly cast the remaining central roles. Science teacher Ian Chesterton was to be played by Russell Enoch, who performed under the stage name William Russell, and was well known to ITV viewers as the lead in *The Adventures of William Tell*. Jacqueline Hill became history teacher Barbara Wright following a meeting at a party attended by Lambert and her old friend, the director Alvin Rakoff, Hill's husband. The role of Susan, now the granddaughter of the mysterious Doctor, was a little harder to fill. Several actresses were auditioned (including Jackie Lane, later to play companion Dodo), but none were deemed suitable. According to longstanding legend, Hussein spotted a likely looking girl on a studio monitor at Television Centre, and soon 23-year-old Carole Ann Ford was signed as Susan Foreman.

With the cast in place, Coburn's revised scripts arrived in July 1963 and were much more to Lambert and Whitaker's liking, with characters having been strengthened, the cavemen given proper dialogue (the first drafts contained only grunts) and the backgrounds for the Doctor and Susan deftly sketched out in only a few lines of dialogue.

The first scripts for the show displayed the series' scientific and educational remit clearly. The two teachers would be the means by which the series could impart information or lessons in science and history and, while she now had an otherworldly background as the Doctor's granddaughter, Susan was clearly an audience-identification figure for younger viewers. She's even into then-contemporary early-1960s rock 'n' roll (fictional group John Smith and the Common Men, rapidly rising up the pop charts, play on her 'transistor' radio). These three characters would provide templates for the majority of the Doctor's travelling companions across the next 45 years, with their roles and functions within the drama evolving to reflect the times in which the programmes were made (spanning five different decades), but always staying the same at the most basic 'character function' level.

The new cast, along with the series' production crew, found themselves facing a series of technical challenges in getting the show made. The concerns initially raised by service departments (scenery, costume, make-up, lighting) about the limitations of shooting the new series at the antiquated Lime Grove studios continued to grow as preparations were made to record the first episode of *Doctor Who*. Those who ran the BBC technical departments that would have to provide set designs, build scenery, create costumes and produce special effects felt the proposed show was simply too ambitious given the budget of just over £2,000 per 25-minute episode. Sydney Newman probably saw their objections as symptomatic of the hidebound nature of the BBC, where embedded interests often didn't like to be challenged. Despite that, it was true that Studio D at Lime Grove, an old film studio bought by the BBC prior to the creation of Television Centre in Shepherd's Bush, was unlikely to make the production of *Doctor Who* easy. The huge technical challenges of mounting the series would be one of the next obstacles to face neophyte producer Verity Lambert.

Along with the technical problems came increasing doubts among the senior managers at the BBC about the wisdom of scheduling this seemingly unconventional new show to run for 52 weeks of the year (as was the plan at this early pre-transmission stage). With episodes recorded only three to four weeks prior to transmission, the launch date of the show had already been postponed several times, from July 1963 to an eventual November debut, by which time the per-episode budget had risen to nearer £4,000, due to the one-off costs of building the interior of the Doctor's time-space ship. BBC internal memos from the period reveal that Assistant Controller of Television Joanna Spicer had objected to the new series' apparent failure to go through the usual BBC approvals processes, while even Donald Baverstock was finding it difficult to justify the cost of the show in his overall annual planning. He instructed Donald Wilson and Lambert not to develop any material beyond four initial episodes, while a proposed *Radio Times* front cover promoting the first episode was abandoned, according to Newman due to 'lack of confidence in the programme at Controller level'.

In the middle of all this seeming chaos, Lambert was struggling to develop future scripts and ensure that the resources were available to support the show, as well as making sure that any technical challenges were overcome and that the cast were comfortable with their roles. It was a tall order and would have tested the most experienced television producer. Even in 1963, however, television was a young medium, one in which imaginative and motivated people could make a big splash. Something that allowed Lambert to chart her own course with *Doctor Who* was the fact that the BBC had never made anything like it before, so there was no 'right' way to do a weekly science-fiction-fantasy series in the UK.

It was 27 September 1963 before *Doctor Who*'s first episode went before the cameras (and it had to be re-shot on 18 October after Sydney Newman decided it was not technically polished enough for broadcast). By this time, Lambert had three additional storylines at various stages of preparation. *The Tribe of Gum* was Anthony Coburn's caveman adventure (with the first episode featuring much of CE Webber's series-setting material from his abandoned 'Giants' story-line), and this was to be followed by the same writer's *The Robots*, about a future world dominated by robotic life forms. Beyond this, John Lucarotti had been commissioned to write *A Journey to Cathay*, a historical adventure featuring Marco Polo, and former Tony Hancock comedy scriptwriter Terry Nation was working on *The Survivors*, about a race mutated due to a radiation war. Other writers had also been contacted and the TV industry was sufficiently aware of the upcoming series that agents and writers had started to submit unsolicited story-lines and sample scripts. By the end of October, the BBC hierarchy had only officially committed to 13 episodes of *Doctor Who*, consisting of an opening episode establishing the premise and the characters; three episodes of the caveman adventure; a seven-part serial; and a (possibly concluding) self-contained two-part serial. The future of the show beyond that point would be decided in the New Year based upon its success, or failure, to attract an audience for the early-Saturday-evening transmission slot between November 1963 and February 1964.

The recording of what is now regarded as the 'pilot' episode of *Doctor Who* was a fraught affair, with fluffed lines, problems with the complicated TARDIS set (the Doctor's time-space ship), wobbly camerawork and badly played-in music. When Newman viewed the episode the following week, he made a number of comments, covering everything from technical issues to characterisation. He didn't think the character of the Doctor was 'funny' enough, while he felt that Susan was 'too dour'. He also felt that the two teachers didn't react strongly enough to the situation of their pupil being seemingly locked up in a box. In technical terms alone, Newman deemed the episode not suitable for transmission. Revealing his personal commitment to the show, he gave Lambert and Hussein permission to remount the recording of the first episode, revising it accordingly. Lessons having been learnt, both felt that, second time around, they could improve on the first effort. In the second version, some of the original dialogue, which pinned down the Doctor and Susan's origins to 'the forty-ninth century', was rewritten to become the vaguer 'We are wanderers in the fourth dimensions of space and time, cut off from our own planet…' This simple act allowed for decades of fan speculation and production-team reinvention of the Doctor's mysterious origins. Hartnell's Doctor was also made less abrasive in the second version of the episode, following Newman's guidance that the serial's leading character had to be more sympathetic (or, at least, slightly less alien).

Although the show was off to a shaky start within the BBC, those involved in making it felt they were producing something unusual that would at least be interesting to a wide range of viewers. It was certainly unlike anything the TV audience had seen before. From the unusual, swirling title sequence and unearthly, 'whooshing' theme tune, *Doctor Who* was laying claim to territory the BBC had not previously explored. The show was verging on the avant-garde in its unique visual and aural effects, and must have been something of a shock to a 1963 TV audience unused to such weird images and sounds on regular television.

The innovative design of the *Doctor Who* titles, music, TARDIS exterior and interior and the Daleks played a huge part in the impact of the new science-fantasy show. The opening titles were devised by Lambert and associate producer Mervyn Pinfield, who was continuing to supervise the show's technical requirements. Drawing on the work of an experimental technical group within the BBC, led by Bernard Lodge, the *Doctor Who* team used electronic visual feedback to create the otherworldly, swirling clouds out of which came the words 'Doctor Who' and (later) the Doctor's face. 'I think it just looked so very strange and different from anything else,' Lambert said of the show's opening visuals. 'I just didn't want it to look like "time" – I wanted it to look familiar but odd, which is what the *Doctor Who* theme [tune] was.'

The series' theme tune had been developed by Delia Derbyshire from the BBC's Radiophonic Workshop, working from a composition by prolific TV-theme composer Ron Grainer. The rhythmic, pulsing theme seemed to match the abstract titles, while the weird bubbling and whooshing sounds set up the viewer to anticipate something unusual. Lambert and Derbyshire's inspiration was the French abstract *musique concrete* movement, which also influenced the selection of the series' early stock incidental episodic music. The scene-setting of the titles and music were just the curtain raiser to the drama about to unfold in front of an unsuspecting Saturday-teatime TV audience.

BBC staff designer Peter Brachacki designed the TARDIS interior (revised by Barry Newberry when the pilot episode was remounted), while Ray Cusick interpreted Terry Nation's description of the Daleks for the second story. Taking up half the floor space within the studio, the interior of the TARDIS was in dramatic contrast with the limited police-box exterior. The large recessed circles on the interior walls contrasted with the hard, straight lines of the police-box shape. In the middle of the all-white room was the ship's control console, a six-sided unit built around the (later-named) 'time rotor' central column, which would rise and fall to indicate the ship was in flight (combined with effective sounds). The hexagonal console reflected the staggered, almost hexagonal patterns made by the (fan-named) 'roundels' on the walls. At the end of the 2008 series, in the episode *Journey's End*, it is revealed that this six-sided console had been designed to accommodate the six pilots required to fly the TARDIS properly (a fan theory incorporated into the ongoing epic televisual narrative). Softening the alien effect of the ship's interior were the furniture and artefacts from various times that Brachacki chose to dress the set. This reinforced the Doctor's quasi-Victorian demeanour and suggested that the ship's original occupants had already travelled widely in history. All these design elements, absorbed by viewers in a near unconscious manner, went a long way to creating the initial impact of *Doctor Who*. The opening episode effectively bridged the narrative gap from the ordinary and everyday lives of a pair of London schoolteachers to the adventures in time and space that the series would pursue for the next 45 years and beyond.

According to BBC records, an audience of 4.4 million viewers were watching at 5.15pm on 23 November (the day following the assassination of President Kennedy) as the first episode of *Doctor Who*, entitled *An Unearthly Child*, was broadcast. The episode introduced the title character and his granddaughter Susan Foreman, a pupil at Coal Hill School who intrigues her science and history teachers, Ian Chesterton and Barbara Wright. As the teachers compare notes on their pupil, who is brilliant at some things and curiously ignorant of others, they follow her home to a junkyard in Totter's Lane. When the teachers enter the yard, Susan appears to have vanished, but there is a curious sight: a police box. Usually found on street corners, this police box is rather unusual: 'It's alive,' exclaims Ian as he discovers an electronic hum emanating from the strange blue box. The teachers hide as an older man, apparently Susan's grandfather, enters the yard and prepares to enter the mysterious box. Hearing Susan's voice coming from inside, the teachers engage the old man in debate and then force their way through the doors.

So far, so familiar, may have been most TV viewers' reaction to this pseudo-domestic drama that wasn't too different in style from a contemporary 1960s TV drama like *Z-Cars*. Apart from the strange music and swirling patterns in the title sequence, the first half of *Doctor Who*'s debut episode actually plays like a social-realist tale about a pupil and her concerned teachers. It's only when the action cuts, at the halfway mark, to inside the mysterious police box that *Doctor Who* really demonstrates its dramatic difference from anything else airing on British television in 1963.

The teachers spill into a vast white space, much bigger than the police box that seems to contain it. As they express astonishment at their new environment, the camera takes in the six-sided central control console, the circular indents on the walls and the computer banks and TV screen. As the Doctor taunts the confused and concerned teachers about their failure to understand what they see, and Susan pleads for her grandfather to free them, he sets the TARDIS in motion. As the ship rocks violently, knocking all the occupants unconscious, the series leads into its first ever cliff-hanger. Disappearing from contemporary London, the police box reappears in a desolate, primitive landscape, only for the shadow of a humanoid creature to fall across it. As the unfamiliar, eerie theme music returned, those initial 4.4 million viewers could have been left in no doubt that they were no longer watching a social-realist drama in the style of *Z-Cars*. There was nothing else on television the audience could compare *Doctor Who* to. All they could do was tune in again at the same time the following week to find out what would happen next.

Tune in they did, with viewing figures increasing by almost two million between the first two episodes. Concerned that the news of the assassination of John F Kennedy might have overshadowed the launch of the new series, the BBC repeated *An Unearthly Child* on Saturday 30 November, following it immediately with the serial's second episode, *The Cave of Skulls*. Around 6.4 million viewers were watching that night. The remaining three episodes of the first serial (collectively, the first four episodes are now widely known as *An Unearthly Child*) saw the time travellers getting to know each other as they fought to survive the conflict between the two would-be leaders of a primitive tribe of humans. Ian and Barbara are reluctant travellers, catapulted into a nightmare against their wills. For his part, the Doctor didn't invite them to enter his ship, so feels little responsibility for their subsequent troubles, even though only he and the TARDIS can get them back to 1963. Hartnell's Doctor, although softened through Sydney Newman's intervention, is still a selfish and potentially violent character. In the serial's third episode, *The Forest of Fear*, he is seen preparing to use a heavy stone to attack a wounded caveman in order that the group might escape. The story sees the travellers introduce fire to the caveman culture in the last episode, *The Firemaker*, and they escape to the TARDIS, pursued by the cavemen. As the ship dematerialises once more, any thoughts of safety are lost as they arrive at a new, even more alien destination and a radiation meter (unseen by the characters, but visible to the audience) lurches into the danger zone. This element, where one complete adventure would end with a cliff-hanger leading into the next, would soon be abandoned, but it served in the early months to blur the separation between one adventure and the next in the minds of the audience and would keep them viewing, one week to the next, one story to the next.

Amid the strangeness of the design, the incongruity of the police box and the oddness of the Doctor, there was arguably one thing that ensured the success of *Doctor Who* during those first few weeks on air: the arrival of the Daleks.

There is a certain irony to the fact that the very element which ensured the new show's future were the 'bug-eyed monsters' Sydney Newman and the committee that developed the show had hoped to avoid in their pursuit of literary science fiction for the screen. From the second serial's first-episode audience of 6.9 million (on a par with the preceding episodes), the audience would grow to in excess of 10 million by the end of the seven-part story entitled *The Daleks*. As 1963 ended, a delighted Donald Baverstock officially renewed the series, extending the run from the initial 13 episodes to 36 weeks. Thanks to the Daleks, who'd go on to become his perpetual, recurring enemy, *Doctor Who* was here to stay.

Scripted by Terry Nation, the Dalek serial featured situations and images that would have resonated greatly with an audience that had lived through the Second World War only 20 years before. In Nation's simplistic storyline, the hideously mutated Daleks are the fascist forces, while the pacifist, humanist Thals (in a neat inversion, they are blonde haired and seemingly blue-eyed – traditional Aryan traits) represented the various nations of the world forced to fight for their own survival.

Nation's script described the Daleks thus: 'Hideous, machine-like creatures [with] no human features. A lens of a flexible shaft that acts as an eye. Arms with mechanical grips for hands.' It's unclear exactly how Nation envisaged the Daleks should look: that was a detail he was willing to leave to the BBC designers, even though – as it turned out – he was to profit greatly from their iconic design. The main creative force behind the visual impact of the Dalek machine was BBC staff designer Raymond Cusick. It was Cusick, following Nation's blueprint, who tried to make the creatures as inhuman looking as possible, eliminating the human outline by removing arms, legs and any recognisable face. That the design was fundamentally unaltered when *Doctor Who* returned to television, over 40 years and several production teams later, is a testament to the vision of Nation and, particularly, Cusick.

Why did the Daleks capture the imagination of the UK's children, in particular? Their distinctive movements and grating, halting vocals were easy to imitate, a practice which quickly erupted in playgrounds up and down the land following Christmas 1963. They were easy for children to draw, with an instantly recognisable silhouette and simple shapes. More interestingly, within the serial itself, the Daleks had been mocked by the show's heroes: Ian showed children how to 'play' at being Daleks when he climbed into one of the casings and had fun altering his voice to be Dalek-like. The show itself undermined the implied horror of the creatures, allowing the children in the audience a way to accept the Daleks as monsters it was fun to be scared of.

The original impact of the Daleks is easy to underestimate, looking back now from the perspective of the twenty-first century, when they are so familiar to us. According to BBC information used to sell *Doctor Who* abroad in the mid-1960s, 'Eighty-five per cent of letters to the BBC's popular *Points of View* [a TV feedback programme] concerned the Daleks.' The document went on to itemise examples of viewers' Dalek-related activity, including one Birmingham girl who'd constructed a model Dalek from egg boxes and silver paper and a Scottish viewer who wanted to form a 'Society for the Prevention of Cruelty to Daleks'. There were many requests to purchase Daleks, either full-size props or toy models.

The back-story of a nuclear war between the Thals and the Dals (later Kaleds in the later revisionist history of *Genesis of the Daleks*) on the planet Skaro played right into 1960s Cold-War concerns, an issue that would have resonated with just about every one of the 10 million viewers of the serial (the Cuban missile crisis – during which Russia had deployed nuclear warheads to Cuba, just off the American coast, provoking an extreme political-military crisis – had taken place a mere 12 months earlier). The technology of body replacement (explored more chillingly later with the Cybermen) that had turned the Dals into the Daleks was also understandable to an audience familiar with the concepts of replacement limbs and then-theoretical heart transplants. Viewers could even have regarded the Daleks' tank-like, life-support 'travel machines' as giant iron lungs.

To make the first 13 episodes of the show self-contained (in case the series ended there, as was possible before the success of the Daleks ensured its continuation), Verity Lambert had commissioned a standalone two-part story to follow the Dalek adventure, utilising only the standing sets of the TARDIS and the regular cast.

The psychological drama that ensues when the TARDIS malfunctions in *The Edge of Destruction* allowed the characters to express and expunge their distrust of each other, clearing the air for them to return for future adventures as a more coherent team. It also allowed for the final clarification of the nature of the Doctor's character, which had evolved through the first 13 episodes from that of a self-interested but curious and reluctant traveller to an adventurer, willing to investigate situations and make moral judgements, taking sides in conflicts and energising the oppressed. This would be a format that would serve the series well for many years to come: the Doctor had become a crusader for freedom in all its forms.

Those first 13 weeks that *Doctor Who* was on air, and the many months of preparation that had preceded them, laid the foundations for an epic televisual myth which would grow and prosper over most of the next 26 years before being triumphantly reborn in the twenty-first century, where it once again captured the imagination and affection of the entire nation.

2. BLACK & WHITE HEAT

It is arguable that what are now popularly perceived as 'the 1960s' didn't really begin in the UK until 1964, the year of the Labour victory in the General Election following 13 years of continuous Conservative rule. Change was in the air in the run up to the October poll, and although the Labour victory was narrow (five seats), it reflected the huge political and social changes taking place in the whole country.

With the conclusion of the two-part, self-contained psychological thriller *The Edge of Destruction*, *Doctor Who* had successfully survived into 1964, despite the doubts of many within the BBC about the series' ongoing viability: the show now had a commitment that would see it last at least until the end of its second year. The challenge faced by producer Verity Lambert was how to broaden and deepen the adventures of the Doctor and his companions. Her solution was to split the Doctor's journeys into two broad categories: historical tales and science-fiction adventures, with the originally proposed 'sideways' adventures largely unexplored.

The earliest development work on *Doctor Who* had focused on ways of bringing literary science fiction to the small screen, but it was the barely developed educational remit that would drive the stories set in different periods of Earth's history. The mid-May 1963 format document, written by CE Webber and annotated by Head of Serials Donald Wilson, noted that 'each story will have a strong informational core based on fact'. During incoming Labour Prime Minister Harold Wilson's period in office there was a focus on educational opportunity for all, culminating in the establishment of the Open University, a government-backed distance-learning project. The growth of comprehensive schooling was another feature of the 1964–1970 Labour government, with *Doctor Who*'s historical tales loosely reflecting topics featured in history lessons in UK schools. The Newsom Report (*Half Our Future*, which led to the setting up of the Plowden Committee on primary and secondary education), published in October 1963, had promoted the development of a coherent national curriculum, including history alongside geography and social studies in a subject dubbed 'The Proper Study of Mankind'. It included a call for pupils to develop 'an ability to enter imaginatively into other men's minds' and added that 'people make history. It is an enlarging of the spirit for our boys and girls to meet great men...' The report's words are a clear mission statement for many of *Doctor Who*'s early historical adventures.

Sydney Newman's hope was that *Doctor Who* should be informative, as well as entertaining. Early episodes saw the past depicted as an exotic background for the characters' adventures, much the same as the early science-fiction stories. The fact that much of the historical subject matter (the French Revolution, the Romans and the Greeks would all be tackled) reflected the 1960s UK school history curriculum was a happy coincidence, rather than the result of any formal planning. Although Newman was clear about the show's educational remit – 'I was intent upon it containing basic factual information that could be described as educational, or at least mind-opening' – producer Verity Lambert was more focused on attracting an audience, especially in the wake of the reaction to the Daleks.

As we have seen, it was no accident that the two main human audience-identification figures were schoolteachers covering history and science. The characters of Barbara and Ian allowed the writers to fill in the background to an episode, whether historical or scientific, in a way that felt natural to the drama. Lambert saw Newman's loose educational remit bringing the show some prestige. 'We were going backwards and forwards in time,' Lambert told *Doctor Who Magazine* #234. 'Although our people could go back in time and observe, they could never change the course of history. It was a wonderful way of teaching, and certainly we had a lot of letters from teachers who said they'd asked their classes to watch those particular episodes.'

The history-themed stories following *The Edge of Destruction* were the epic travelogue *Marco Polo* and *The Aztecs*, the latter exploring in some depth the question of changing the past. These early episodes (alternating with the science-fiction adventures) continued to set down formats and story templates that would define the nature of the series. The majority of the historical adventures appeared during the first three seasons of *Doctor Who* and made up just over a third of the total stories. They helped give the series an educational respectability, within and outside the BBC, suggesting it had something worthwhile to offer viewers beyond mere entertainment.

John Lucarotti was the writer on both *Marco Polo* and *The Aztecs*, and he had a strong personal interest in both subjects. Lucarotti had avidly read the English edition of Polo's own account of his adventures and had adapted it once before for a 15-episode radio serial. He drew on these diaries to give his seven-week epic serial a sheen of authenticity. Similarly, the Aztecs were a personal favourite of Lucarotti, the writer having lived in Mexico. It didn't do any harm to Newman and Lambert's pseudo-educational project that both subjects were also taught in schools.

Marco Polo (the serial is now lost due to the BBC's short-sighted policy of recycling videotapes up to the late-1970s, thus erasing many irreplaceable recordings) had been designed as a travelogue, which saw the Doctor and his companions journey with Polo's caravan en route to the court of Kublai Khan. Political intrigue and stops along the way provide many opportunities for historical lessons to be imparted.

It was often believed later that the early historical *Doctor Who* serials suffered from low ratings and that's why they were eventually phased out. Given that the ratings for *Marco Polo* were on a par with those of *The Daleks*, ranging between 8.5 and 10 million viewers across the serial's run, that myth is easily discounted. Although recorded and transmitted in black and white, surviving colour photographs show the sets and costumes of *Marco Polo* to have been sumptuous, rivalling any equivalent theatre or movie production. Viewers would undoubtedly have learnt something about the historical period from this well-researched and constructed serial. Despite this and the high ratings, however, many children maintained they found the historical stories 'boring' in comparison to the more exciting space adventures.

It is no surprise that the *Doctor Who* stories that ventured into the past were more concerned with the central characters than with getting the historical details accurate. It is unlikely that any historian, then or now, would recognise the journey of Marco Polo as depicted by the BBC in the confines of Lime Grove Studio D, or agree with the programme's depiction of Aztec society.

An internal BBC memo from 1964 listed other possible historical settings and events that *Doctor Who* could explore, including Viking raids on Britain (*The Time Meddler*), Bonnie Prince Charlie (*The Highlanders*), Drake and the Armada, Raleigh and the colonisation of the Americas, the Globe Theatre (2007's *The Shakespeare Code*), Australian convict settlement, the Roman invasion of Britain, Richard I and the Crusades (*The Crusade*), Cornish smugglers (*The Smugglers*) and Boadicea. British television adventure series, especially those aimed at children or those made by Lew Grade's commercial independent production company ITC, were often based around historical, swashbuckling characters like Robin Hood, Sir Lancelot (William Russell, *Doctor Who*'s Ian Chesterton) or Sir Francis Drake (all the 'great men' of the Newsom Report), and this no doubt influenced *Doctor Who*'s depiction of history.

More important to the drama were the implications of the historical stories for the lost travellers. Following the epic tourist narrative of *Marco Polo*, in *The Aztecs* Lucarotti tackled one of the show's central concerns: the possibility, or otherwise, of changing history. Lucarotti had the Doctor's history-teacher companion directly address a key question which by now (this being the show's third historical adventure) must have been troubling alert viewers. Mistaken for the reincarnation of a Goddess in pre-*Conquistador* Mexico, Barbara decides to use her position to forbid a ritual sacrifice. Saving one life, however, is not enough for the newly empowered suburban teacher. 'If I could start the destruction of everything that is evil here, then everything that is good would survive when Cortés lands,' she says. The Doctor emphatically forbids any intervention: 'You can't rewrite history... Not one line! What you are trying to do is utterly impossible. I know, believe me, I know.' That's a clear statement of the inviolable nature of history. This rule was later adapted: some changes to history were allowable as they were minor or set things on the correct course. Later, when the show returned in the twenty-first century, the same discussion would recur when the Doctor (David Tennant) and companion Donna Noble (Catherine Tate) arrive in the city of Pompeii, prior to the volcanic eruption, in *The Fires of Pompeii*. Set on warning the citizens, Donna is told by the Doctor that history is unchangeable, although he is persuaded to save one family from the inferno, allowing that: 'Some things are fixed, some things are in a flux. Pompeii is fixed.'

There was a Mexican buzz in the mid-1960s. The South American-flavoured 1962 World Cup had taken place in Chile (who secured third place, with Brazil winning) and the 1968 Olympic Games were due to be hosted by Mexico, so *Doctor Who*'s foray into the country's turbulent history was part of a larger cultural focus. The decision to set a story during the Aztec period may have been influenced by the forthcoming debut of *The Royal Hunt of the Sun,* a new play by rising young playwright Peter Shaffer. As well as debating the ethics (or even the possibility) of altering history, *The Aztecs* was one of the few *Doctor Who* stories that gave the Doctor something approaching a romantic relationship (very much the norm for the twenty-first century series, but unusual previously). A delightful subplot has a bemused Doctor (Hartnell at his whimsical best) accidentally becoming engaged to an Aztec woman, Cameca (Margot van der Burgh), when sharing a cup of hot chocolate.

The straightforward historical tales continued to alternate with the science-fiction stories, but the effort to remain educationally relevant was relaxed somewhat after *The Reign of Terror*, the story that closed out the show's first season in September 1964. It shifted *Doctor Who*'s historical focus to the French Revolution and once again addressed the issue of altering history. The French Revolution was an obvious period for *Doctor Who* to visit, since it had appeared as the title of a history textbook in the debut episode, complete with Susan's comment, 'That's not right,' indicating she had some unusual knowledge of actual historical events. The Doctor clearly states that Napoleon cannot be assassinated, as it wouldn't be true to history. As history can be in flux and can be interfered with by powerful forces, it has to be protected, often by the Doctor and his companions. Making sure that the 'right' outcome happens (as it has *already* happened) is alright. The disengaged Doctor of *An Unearthly Child* has become the protector of time.

New series writer Dennis Spooner, who would be responsible for taking the historical serials in a new direction, played out the political machinations that followed the Revolution as an espionage thriller akin to the then-fresh James Bond films *Dr No* and *From Russia With*

Love. Additional inspiration seems to have come from Dickens' *A Tale of Two Cities* – probably the most populist account of the Revolution that people in the 1960s would have been familiar with (in the form of the movie, if not the original novel). Spooner saw the historical tales as narrative playgrounds in which he could exploit clichés and deploy humour, rather than as earnest, dry, educational texts. His black humour lightens the tone of *The Reign of Terror* (given the bloody subject matter) and makes it suitable for Saturday teatime. He's careful to hit all the correct historical markers, but this is closer to the twenty-first century style of 'celebrity historical' story in which the Doctor and friends interact with an important historical personage (*The Unquiet Dead*, *Tooth and Claw*, *The Shakespeare Code*, *The Unicorn and the Wasp*), or at least have to deal with the fallout from his activities (in this case, Robespierre, although Napoleon does make an appearance). *The Reign of Terror* was the beginning of a process that saw the historical stories adopt the same view of history as popular movies, rather than historically accurate (or educational) accounts.

Historical accuracy was all but abandoned altogether by Spooner for *The Romans*. Written and played as a West End farce, having more in common with the same year's *Carry on Cleo* in style and approach than with *Doctor Who*'s previous attempts at history, *The Romans* was a change of style and pace. When the hapless Ian and Barbara are kidnapped by slave traders, the Doctor finds himself caught up in events at Nero's court, even providing inspiration for the Emperor's plan to burn down Rome. The show was drifting further away from any intended educational purpose. *Doctor Who* had rapidly moved from recounting historical events for an educational reason to parodying history for simple entertainment.

Spooner set the template for *Doctor Who*'s future take on history when he mixed the two styles of stories – historical and science fiction – together. *The Time Meddler* was set in 1066, another of those obvious historical stopping-off points that 1960s viewers would be familiar with. Rather than exploring the historical period, however, Spooner introduced another of the Doctor's own mysterious (and so far unnamed) people: another time traveller named the 'Monk'. He's the time meddler of the title, setting out to equip King Harold with an atomic canon with which he can fight off the Viking hordes. The Monk is out to improve the past in the same way that Barbara hoped to. With his anachronistic technology (that must-have item of the 1960s, a record player!) and his own TARDIS (a Mark Four, evidently a better model than the Doctor's), the Monk is what the Doctor could become without the restraining influence of his human travelling companions.

The Doctor attempts to reiterate his doctrine of non-interference (it is unclear if this is his own invention or the policy of his people): 'You know as well as I do the golden rule about space and time travel,' he lectures the Monk. 'Never, never interfere with the course of history.' The younger audience, perhaps those bored with history at school, probably agreed with the Monk's rejoinder: 'And who says so, Doctor? It's more fun my way.'

With *The Time Meddler*, Spooner had accidentally signed the death warrant of *Doctor Who*'s purely historical adventures (with one or two notable exceptions) and simultaneously created a new type of story that would become core to the series' concept: the pseudo-historical. These stories (and while there'd be several of them, there are perhaps not as many as the popular conception of *Doctor Who* might suggest) would see the Doctor and his party arrive in a historical period, meet a historical celebrity, and become caught up in some kind of science-fiction plot. Perhaps someone is tampering with time (*The Talons of Weng-Chiang*, *Mawdryn Undead*) or aliens are manipulating historical events (*The Time Warrior*, *The Mark of the Rani*); either way, the historical background is simply a colourful setting for a science-fiction adventure.

While several more straightforward historical stories featured during William Hartnell's three-year run as the Doctor (including *The Massacre*, by which point viewing figures for the historical stories had taken a tumble; *The Gunfighters*, a pastiche of movie Westerns rather than the real West; and *The Smugglers*), none would have the ambition of those first attempts at making populist educational drama within an adventure-serial template (*Marco Polo*, *The Aztecs*). In fact, the history-as-backdrop approach became even more prominent in Donald Cotton's wittily scripted *The Myth Makers*, which abandoned any claim to historical accuracy, preferring the mythic version of events. From now on, *Doctor Who*'s historical tales would not be set in a researched historical milieu, but would instead take place in either a popular conception of the period (reinforced by movies and popular books) or within a widely accepted mythical version of the past.

Alternating with the historical stories were *Doctor Who*'s science-fiction adventure serials, which were rapidly becoming the heart of the show. During the 1963 Labour Party national conference, Harold Wilson made a well-remembered speech about the increasing speed and complexity of scientific and technological change in Britain in the early 1960s. He'd argued that this new Britain 'was going to be forged in the white heat of this revolution'. *Doctor Who* would capture this feeling of rapid technological change in its own televisual black-and-white heat.

Despite originating in a British cultural context, *Doctor Who* ultimately drew more on American cliff-hanger film serials from the 1930s and 1940s for its episodic format (including the 25-minute running time for each episode and regular narrative breaks in the form of end-of-episode cliff-hangers) than the initial research by the BBC into adapting literary science fiction for television.

An evening's entertainment at the American cinema in the early twentieth century would consist of a main feature (or features, if a double bill), accompanied by a cartoon, a newsreel and an episode from a serial or 'chapter play'. Serials would run for between 12 and 15 chapters, feature continuing characters, and each instalment would end with a cliff-hanger that put the heroes in some form of mortal jeopardy. Although many serials were Westerns or adventure tales (set in unexplored jungle regions and far-off exotic lands), there was a strong strand of science fiction, often featuring comic-strip characters such as Flash Gordon, Buck Rogers and superheroes like Captain Marvel. Each episode would run for between two and three reels, about 20 to 30 minutes, and the episodic format encouraged viewer loyalty, bringing audiences back to the same cinema week after week to see the next instalment. The coming of television saw the UK and the US adopt the serial format for ongoing drama, mostly for 'soap opera'-style shows, and American TV drama quickly settled on the 50-minute length (a full hour with advertisements) for weekly serial drama. The cinema serials themselves often appeared (right up until the end of the 1980s) on television on both sides of the Atlantic as holiday schedule fillers, so were familiar to generations of viewers.

A series built from discrete individual narrative serials, like *Doctor Who*, was relatively rare on television. Again, the format drew on the experience of soap operas, where narrative threads would weave in and out of individual episodes. The difference here was that (mostly) *Doctor Who* would wrap up an individual story within a set number of episodes (most often four), and repercussions or dramatic fallout rarely carried over from one serial to another (although there are exceptions). The science-fiction cinema serials of the 1930s and 1940s clearly influenced the structure and storytelling of the earliest *Doctor Who* science-fiction stories, with a dash of HG Wells fiction and space-age British comic-book and radio adventurer Dan Dare added for good measure.

Following the phenomenal success of *The Daleks*, Terry Nation had been asked to contribute a historical serial, but when that was abandoned the need for rapid replacement scripts saw him fall back on serial science-fiction adventures for inspiration. *The Keys of Marinus* was the show's second science-fiction tale (after *The Daleks*) and the one that most resembled the American cliff-hanger serials. Nation created a quest narrative for the six-episode 'chapter play' – the Doctor and his companions are tasked with retrieving the four missing 'keys' that control the all-powerful Conscience of Marinus (a computer) before the alien Voord can use it to dominate the planet's people. After the initial set-up, each episode took place in a distinctive environment on a different continent: among them Morphoton, a city of excessively contented people controlled by disembodied brains; a treacherous, living jungle (an environment that would become common in Nation's later Dalek scripts); frozen wastes and ice caves; and the futuristic city of Millennius (where bureaucrats rule and Ian is put on trial).

Finding the four keys (and a fake fifth one), the travellers return to their starting point – a pyramid on an island of glass surrounded by a sea of acid – only to discover that their contact (the Keeper of the Conscience) has been killed by Yartek, leader of the alien Voord. Switching the fake key with one of the real ones, Ian is able to trick Yartek into accidentally destroying the computer, freeing the people of Marinus. The conclusion allows Nation/the Doctor to outline one of the series' most basic tenets (one that would be revisited in a variety of stories): 'I don't believe that man was made to be controlled by machines,' says the Doctor. 'Machines can make laws but they cannot preserve justice. Only human beings can do that.' The episodes were broadcast just a few months before the technocrat Harold Wilson came to power in October 1964, and reflected the mood of the nation.

This theme related back to Nation's debut serial, *The Daleks*, and would recur in just about every script he would write for the show. The shadow of the Second World War loomed heavily over Nation's writing, resulting in the repetition of archetypes, themes and situations that Nation's audience would recognise: those over the age of

20 would easily relate the Daleks and the Voord to the real-world fascists of just two decades previously.

The serial nature of *Doctor Who*, and the almost-all-year-round transmission pattern of the 1960s, allowed the show to explore a large number of science-fiction ideas. *The Sensorites* (set in the same planetary system as the revived series' Ood stories) featured the perils of first contact between human explorers and alien life. The Sensorites are dying from a mysterious disease, which Ian also falls victim to. The origin of the poison in the water supply is traced to a trio of human expedition survivors who are now trying to destroy the aliens they fear. As in *The Aztecs*, humans sometimes make the worst monsters. In its design and realisation (such as the look of Sense-Sphere and the Sensorites) the story clearly draws on the Flash Gordon and Buck Rogers serials starring Buster Crabbe.

Other science-fiction staples explored included the long-mooted shrinking of the series regulars when they foil an attempted techno-logical blackmail in *Planet of the Giants*; an encounter with another bizarre, insect-like civilisation in *The Web Planet*; the experience of a time-slip in *The Space Museum* (one of the few 'sideways' stories), when the TARDIS 'jumps a time track' and shows the travellers a personal future they must avoid; the malevolent machinations of a matriarchal society in *Galaxy 4*; the near extinction and planetary relo-cation of mankind in *The Ark*; fantasy game-playing in *The Celestial Toymaker* (another rare 'sideways' story); and the Morlock/Eloi-like (from *The Time Machine*) degenerate future society of *The Savages*.

With *Doctor Who*'s science-fiction serials echoing serial chapter plays, as distinct from the classic literary and mythological sources for the series' historical tales, it is no surprise that the show's most popular villains would enjoy several subsequent adventures. Like cinema's returning serial villains, the success of *The Daleks* ensured that they would enjoy a quick encore. From the moment the first serial finished in February 1964, the BBC received numerous letters calling for the Daleks to return. The creative team quickly put plans in motion to bring the creatures back before the end of the year. Airing from virtually the show's first anniversary on 21 November 1964 through to Boxing Day, *The Dalek Invasion of Earth* was a very different Dalek tale that would have profound implications for the long-term future of the show.

A memo from the Head of Business for Television Enterprises to Sydney Newman, dated 20 February 1964, raised the possibility of commercial exploitation of *Doctor Who*. Specifically, the memo asked how long the series was intended to run and whether there were any plans for the return of the popular Daleks. Head of Serials Donald Wilson replied with the welcome news that the BBC was committed to at least 52 weeks of *Doctor Who* and said, 'We have in mind, of course, to try and resurrect the Daleks. I am asking Verity Lambert to keep you informed of any possible exploitation ideas, including the return of the Daleks.'

Just under one month later, series script editor David Whitaker commissioned writer Terry Nation to script a second Dalek adventure, under the working title *The Return of the Daleks*. The ratings and popular success of the Daleks was very clear to the BBC, so much so that, in April 1964, David Whitaker recommended that Terry Nation should become the senior writer on the show, contributing three serials for the show's second season. 'He has worked very well for us,' wrote Whitaker understatedly in an internal memo. 'His figures [ratings] are certainly the highest so far of all the writers.'

By mid-April the first stirrings of what would become known as 'Dalekmania' were beginning to be felt as products and merchandise proposals began to reach the BBC from interested manufacturers. First to be approved were novelisations of televised adventures, starting with the first Dalek story (under the unwieldy title *Doctor Who in an Exciting Adventure with the Daleks*) and the official *The Dalek Book*, an annual for Christmas 1964, nicely timed for the broadcast of the sequel serial.

Nation delivered his second Dalek adventure under the new title of *The Dalek Invasion of Earth*. The serial would be the first time that *Doctor Who* made an alien invasion of Earth central to a story, but it would be a format used with some regularity thereafter. Much of the serial was shot on location in and around a variety of London landmarks, another first for the show. Nation's conceit was to take his recent memories of France under occupation in wartime and use it for the background of a twenty-second-century-set tale of intergalactic conquest. When the Doctor and his friends arrive in this London of the future, it looks like the city during the Blitz (another fresh memory for many), as the Daleks have already arrived, conquered and destroyed. Nation's scripts reinforced the initial concept of the Daleks as space fascists by directly paralleling them with a British audience's image of the Nazis. The Daleks begin to use their 'exterminate' catchphrase (heard in school playgrounds across the nation). They even talk of implementing a 'final solution' and are seen (in location shots at London landmarks) to be making fascist salutes with their plungers! Their plan – to mine the planet's core and navigate it around the galaxy – involves the use of slave labour in camps. Terry Nation was never accused of subtlety.

Viewers of mid-1960s *Doctor Who* had likely been evacuated as children during the Second World War and returned to discover wrecked cities and devastated communities. Children being children, such destruction provided the greatest playgrounds they'd ever seen (see the Ealing film *Hue and Cry*, shot in 1947 on locations still showing the scars of wartime). Twenty years later, and perhaps with children of their own, they'd find Terry Nation's *Doctor Who* episodes evoking memories of their formative years. This wasn't the 'domestic catastrophe' of John Wyndham's fiction, in which alien threats (intelligent plants in *The Day of the Triffids*) are brought to bear on everyday locations. *The Dalek Invasion of Earth* presented a much broader canvas (the dialogue alludes to entire continents wiped out by the Daleks), although one brought to audiences in their own homes through the still relatively new domestic medium of television. This historical context helped to make the fantasy real to an audience who saw a city they recognised invaded by their new favourite television bogeymen. This is emphasised even more by the fact that, despite being set in 2167, this future Earth looks remarkably contemporary.

The popular myth of Britain in wartime was one of stoical resistance and D-Day-style bravery overcoming the evils of Nazism. *The Dalek Invasion of Earth* would be worrying to the audience as it took historical certainty and turned it on its head. What if Britain had come under Nazi rule (explored in another Ealing movie, *Went the Day Well* in 1942, in which disguised Nazis infiltrate an English village)? The result may have looked something like the scenes on *Doctor Who.*

Beyond using wartime iconography for an easy hit of recognition, Nation had also provided (whether he realised it or not) a handy metaphor in his second Dalek serial for the state of Britain in the mid-1960s. Post-colonial and post-Empire, the country was not perceived to be the same one that 'won the war' so successfully, especially following the 1956 Suez crisis that had culminated in the resignation of discredited Prime Minister Anthony Eden. Britain was economically and socially defeated by this time. Yet in the middle of the decade, with the election of the new Wilson government, there were the seeds of a new-found optimism, like that expressed by the characters when the Dalek threat is neutralised. The country may have been in a dreadful state, but the possibility of rebirth existed. It was, indeed, a time of 'white heat'. There was something in the air, and the viewers of *The Dalek Invasion of Earth* felt it too. Soon London would be swinging, and if they didn't take part in it, their children surely would. A new world was coming, it was being built all around them and, on screen, *Doctor Who* was showing exactly what it might be like.

The Dalek Invasion of Earth was the final story of 1964 and brought *Doctor Who* full circle, right back to HG Wells. This time the source novel wasn't *The Time Machine*, which had inspired the series' initial time-travel premise, but *The War of the Worlds*, which provided the aliens-invade-England template for so many of the *Doctor Who* adventures. Wells' conceit had been to look at things from the point of view of those countries that had been invaded and occupied by Britain during the forging of the Empire. As a result, his invaders devastate ordinary places like Weybridge and Shepperton, with calamitous events set in Woking, Putney and Chertsey, bringing the horror of war (long before the world wars of the twentieth century) home to readers.

The final episode of *The Dalek Invasion of Earth* attracted 12.4 million viewers. Many of them watched the episode clutching something Dalek-shaped received from Father Christmas the previous day. The return of the Daleks launched the era of 'Dalekmania'. Their original popularity had taken the BBC by surprise. Unlike today's franchise exploitation of *Doctor Who*, no one had thought of producing tie-in merchandise like toys and books until after the Daleks proved so popular.

Far from being the figures of fear intended by Terry Nation and the *Doctor Who* production team, the Daleks became favourites of 1960s children. Just in time for their return in the run up to Christmas 1964, shops in Britain were full to bursting with Dalek-related items, from badges to confectionery, from dressing-up costumes to ice-lolly cards, from comics to a variety of models and toys.

Naturally, all this interest meant that the Daleks would return to *Doctor Who* again and again, often overshadowing the series' title character. From 1965 to 1967, the Daleks returned roughly every six months (with a break in the summer of 1966), keeping children and toy manufacturers alike happy.

It could be argued that the runaway popularity of the Daleks had the effect of neutering them as serious adversaries. During their original appearance, Ian had clambered inside a Dalek casing as part of a narrative strategy to explain exactly what these creatures were and how they operated. Following *The Dalek Invasion of Earth*, the next time a Dalek appeared on screen it was played for laughs in the disposable adventure *The Space Museum* (April–May 1965). One of the exhibits in the museum is an empty Dalek casing, within which the Doctor hides, only to make fun of the Daleks by imitating one. He's acting exactly like the watching children, who'd been playing in upturned dustbins since early 1964, shouting 'Exterminate'. This neutering rather devalued the Daleks as a threat, a trend that was to continue in the next comic story, *The Chase* (May–June 1965).

For his third Dalek story, creator Terry Nation reverted to his serial style. Six months after the outbreak of 'Dalekmania', the Daleks were back, engaged in a chase through the cosmos after the Doctor. Nation gave the Daleks their own space-time ship (almost exactly, but not quite, like the Doctor's own TARDIS). Each individual episode of the six-part story saw the Daleks arrive at a different time and place in an attempt to catch up with the Doctor, including the desert planet of Aridius, a haunted-house theme park on a futuristic Earth, the top of the Empire State Building, the *Mary Celeste* in 1872 (the Daleks exterminate the crew, solving a long-standing, child-fascinating mystery) and the planet Mechanus where the Daleks engage in a battle for survival with robotic enemies, the Mechanoids. In an attempt to engineer another Dalek-like merchandising craze, the production team created the large, squat, hexagonal Mechanoids, echoing the Daleks with their mechanical voices and habit of zapping anyone who comes near. Despite the availability of some limited Mechanoid merchandise, they never caught on and did not return to the show (although they did have a rematch with the Daleks in the pages of the spin-off Dalek comic strip in *TV21* comic).

Much of *The Chase* is played for laughs, often at the expense of the Daleks. In a memo to director Richard Martin, producer Verity Lambert noted of the script: '...it is slightly tongue-in-cheek and obviously is purely an adventure story, but... there are lots of opportunities for imagination and excitement.' *The Chase* made the Daleks more child-friendly, but that's not what the children of Britain had responded to. They wanted the Daleks to be nasty, and their next serial would go some way to restoring that reputation.

The Chase also brought the most significant cast changes in the show's two-year history to date. Carole Ann Ford had left in *The Dalek Invasion of Earth*, with Susan replaced by Vicki (Maureen O'Brien), a space-age (though still very 1960s) teenager who was rescued by the Doctor. Now, Ian and Barbara are presented with the means (the captured Dalek time machine) to return home. A montage sequence sees them happily back on Earth, while the Doctor travels on with Vicki and astronaut Steven Taylor (Peter Purves), picked up after the defeat of the Daleks and the Mechanoids. However, the most significant cast change in *Doctor Who*'s history was just over a year away.

When the Daleks returned in *The Daleks' Master Plan* (November 1965–January 1966), they were taken more seriously, and were on air for a longer period than ever before. Originally planned as a six-episode serial, *The Daleks' Master Plan* was doubled to 12 episodes, supposedly at the suggestion of BBC Controller of Programmes (Television) Huw Weldon, on the grounds that his mother was a huge fan. The actual instruction came from Head of Serials Gerald Savory during the production of *The Chase* in July 1965 and was responded to favourably in a memo from Lambert, although she was concerned about keeping the cost of such an ambitious epic serial manageable.

The Daleks' Master Plan began as a magnificent space opera (distinct from the usual chapter-play serial hi-jinks), with the Daleks presiding over an uneasy alliance of various space powers out to conquer the galaxy. Set in AD 4000, the show sees Earth as part of a galactic federation, protected by the Space Security Service and represented by the Guardian of the Solar System, Mavic Chen (Kevin Stoney). Chen is secretly in league with the Daleks, and only the Doctor and his friends can disrupt their plans for galactic domination. This involves stealing a vital component of the Daleks' ultimate weapon, the Time Destructor. The rest of the 12 episodes play out as a more serious re-run of *The Chase*. The story features the death of not one, but two of the Doctor's newest travelling companions: Trojan slave girl Katarina (played by Adrienne Hill, who joined the TARDIS crew at the end of the previous tale, *The Myth Makers*) and Space Security agent Sara Kingdom (Jean Marsh), aged to death at the climax when the Time Destructor is activated. This was harrowing stuff for the Saturday tea-time audience, and reinstated the Daleks as a serious threat, responsible for death and destruction on a grand scale. The serial attracted an average of around 9.5 million viewers, many snared by a single-episode prelude story broadcast five weeks before and featuring the exploits of the Space Security Service, but none of the regular *Doctor Who* cast.

At the time *The Chase* was completing production in June 1965, a different side of the Daleks was about to be seen by the nation's children. The latest result of 'Dalekmania' was arriving: the malevolent pepper pots were about to be unleashed at the cinema, this time in glorious colour.

Two B-movies were produced by British-based film company Amicus and released under the Aaru banner of co-financier Joe Vegoda. Amicus, set up in the UK by Americans Max J Rosenberg and Milton Subotsky, were rivals to Hammer Films and were quick to jump on the Dalek bandwagon, adapting the debut TV story for *Doctor Who and the*

Daleks (1965). Streamlined from seven 25-minute episodes (175 minutes) to a more cinema-friendly 82 minutes, the film dynamically retold the Doctor's first encounter with the Daleks.

This, however, was a very different Doctor. For the first time, an actor other than William Hartnell played the character (not including doubles for Hartnell on the TV show). Amicus and Hammer stalwart Peter Cushing played 'Dr Who', an eccentric Earth scientist (the TV Doctor's origins were still shrouded in mystery) who appears to have constructed a multi-dimensional space-time machine in his backyard! With his granddaughter Susan (younger than on TV) and daughter Barbara and her boyfriend Ian, the Doctor is separated from the TARDIS on the mysterious planet Skaro. Aimed at a younger audience than the TV series, *Doctor Who and the Daleks* was a light and frothy adventure, fitting its colourful nature and the fact that it was released during the school summer holidays of 1965. The big draw was seeing the Daleks in action in colour, and seeing many more of them in one place than the TV series had yet shown.

More ambitious was the following year's sequel – *Daleks' Invasion Earth: 2150AD*. As the title suggests, the focus was clearly on the Daleks rather than the Doctor, and on spectacle over the more thoughtful content of the TV episodes. Again, the original serial, *The Dalek Invasion of Earth*, was condensed from six episodes to a sprightly 81 minutes by concentrating on the action and adventure elements of the story and dropping most of the philosophical content that Nation's original scripts contained.

Both movies succeeded with the audience they were aimed at: children. By 1966, however, the second film had fared less successfully at the box office, suggesting that the hankering after all-things-Dalek was beginning to wane. Plans for a third full-colour *Doctor Who* film, possibly adapting *The Keys of Marinus*, were abandoned. The Daleks had not been seen on television since early 1966, though they had appeared on the London stage in the play *The Curse of the Daleks* between December 1965 and January 1966. *Doctor Who* itself appeared to be evolving in a new direction, away from the cliff-hanger space fantasies of its first two years and towards a more down-to-Earth thriller format, as indicated by the late-Hartnell period serial *The War Machines*.

The most unusual episode of *The Daleks' Master Plan* was a comedy-driven Christmas Day run-around set behind the scenes of a silent-era film studio and featuring a spoof of fellow BBC TV show *Z-Cars*. In a development probably unnoticed by viewers, this episode brought the Doctor to Earth (1965) for the first time since the debut episode of the show, *An Unearthly Child* (although *Planet of the Giants* was set on contemporary Earth, the TARDIS crew were miniaturised).

The idea of rooting the Doctor's adventures in a more recognisable environment would take hold over the next few years, resulting in many periods of the show's history being heavily Earthbound or Earth-centric (much of Jon Pertwee's time, as well as the majority of the episodes of the revived show). The first time this was really tried properly was in *The War Machines*.

Doctor Who was clearly a significant part of the culture of swinging 1960s Britain, although the show itself had largely failed to acknowledge this significant cultural moment. *The War Machines* sets up much that would become central to *Doctor Who* (and perhaps, more importantly, central to the public image of *Doctor Who*). It is set in then-contemporary Britain (1966), and features an evil or a villain based around an easily recognisable landmark (the then-new Post Office Tower), a 'modern' development ripped from the day's headlines (computers) and media reports by genuine TV newsreaders (Kenneth Kendall), as well as building in a military response to an attempt to invade/takeover the Earth/Home Counties. The specifics here are that powerful new computer WOTAN has been established in the Post Office Tower. Linking up with other computers around the world,

WOTAN decides humankind is inferior and the machines should rule the Earth (a now-clichéd SF plot later echoed in films like *Colossus: The Forbin Project* [1970] and *The Terminator* [1984]). WOTAN organises the construction of robotic weapons, the 'war machines', and attempts to subjugate London. Out to stop the evil computer, the Doctor is joined by two new companions who are so 'swinging London' it hurts. Merchant seaman Ben (Michael Craze) and civil-service secretary Polly (Anneke Wills) provide the model for most subsequent Earth companions, from Jo Grant and Sarah Jane Smith in the 1970s to Ace and Rose Tyler in the 1980s and twenty-first century, reflecting much of the viewing audience in a way few companions prior to this ever did (with the notable exception of Ian and Barbara, neither of whom could be considered 'swinging').

The War Machines succeeded because it connected directly with the TV viewing audience. WOTAN uses telephone lines to communicate with and hypnotise those people it uses in its plan. With every home in the land installing a telephone, the threat had more reality than any battle with the Daleks in a far-off, futuristic, alien world. The action was taking place on streets and in environments that almost all those watching would recognise: it made the series relevant to viewers (a lesson that had been learned from *The Dalek Invasion of Earth*, nominally set in the future). Another important development instituted on *The War Machines,* and laying down groundwork for the immediate future of the series, was the involvement of a genuine 'scientific advisor'. New *Doctor Who* producer Innes Lloyd (who had succeeded Verity Lambert's short-lived successor John Wiles after *Galaxy 4*) and his script editor Gerry Davis drew on the services of Doctor Kit Pedler, a well-known TV pundit on scientific matters. Although consulted specifically to give some scientific accuracy to the serial's computers, Pedler would play a larger part in the coming Troughton era, contributing greatly to the establishment of the Cybermen. Similarly, the 1970s producer-and-script-editor team of Barry

Letts and Terrance Dicks would consult scientific magazines like *New Scientist* to find developments in science and technology upon which they could base exciting *Doctor Who* stories. *The War Machines* saw *Doctor Who* abandon the weird, far-out space fantasy of most William Hartnell episodes in favour of slick, often-contemporary or near-future SF thrillers dealing with the big scientific issues of the day. This change of approach was a harbinger of a bigger change coming for the programme, as William Hartnell neared the end of his time as the First Doctor.

There are many pop cultural icons that have been played, on film or on stage, by different actors who have brought their own unique interpretation to the roles. Several actors have played Sherlock Holmes, Superman and James Bond, and made their mark. Similarly, many see it as a challenge to deliver 'their' Hamlet, just as Tenth Doctor David Tennant did in the summer of 2008.

The recasting of the title character of *Doctor Who*, however, was a unique stroke of genius that, more than even the TARDIS, or the Daleks, or the show's wonderfully open-ended concept of exploration of time and space, allowed the series to prosper and change for over 45 years. The simple fact of being able to change the lead actor, introducing not only a new face but essentially a new character, and yet claim he's still the same person, is unique in television history. Each new Doctor can refer back to his predecessors as they are all part of an ongoing (albeit loose) continuity. There had been thoughts of replacing William Hartnell before 1966, and the idea of a different actor playing the character had been established when Peter Cushing provided a different interpretation in the big-screen Dalek remakes.

During *Doctor Who*'s third year on air, producers John Wiles and Innes Lloyd gave some thought to replacing Hartnell. Increasing health problems and a reputation for being difficult led each of the new producers to ponder how *Doctor Who* could continue without the lead actor. Broadcast in April 1966, the fantasy/'sideways' story *The Celestial Toymaker* saw the Doctor made invisible by the powerful, God-like Toymaker character (Michael Gough). One plan hatched by Wiles was to simply replace Hartnell by having the Toymaker restore the Doctor in a different body. The series could then continue with a new lead actor. Although not implemented, the thought of continuing the series without Hartnell had been mooted and it would be down to Lloyd, the then-current producer, to later enact the proposal.

Besides the change of lead actor, Hartnell's final adventure, *The Tenth Planet*, is also notable for introducing *Doctor Who*'s second-best-known monsters, the Cybermen. Following his work ensuring the scientific veracity of *The War Machines*, Kit Pedler was consulted by Lloyd on a variety of cutting-edge science concepts with a view to working them into other *Doctor Who* stories. The concept for the Cybermen developed from mid-1960s anxieties about organ replacement, then just beginning with successful heart transplants. The Cybermen were a race of humanoids from Earth's twin planet Mondas who had taken cybernetic replacement of failing limbs and organs to an extreme. Either as a deliberate policy or as a consequence of their conversion to a cyborg race, the Cybermen had removed, lost or inhibited their emotions. The warning was that Wilson's 'white heat' of technological process could have its downsides, as well as its benefits. Pedler extrapolated the Cybermen from trends in 1960s medicine – from a growth in cosmetic surgery and the use of technology to replace previously organic parts through to an increasing use of drugs to manage emotional or mental disturbance. At the same time, NASA were considering the survival of humanity in space. Several solutions were proposed, ranging from cybernetically augmented space suits to a blending of humans and spacecraft. Surgically or mechanically augmented humans were sometimes referred to as cyborgs, short for 'cybernetic organism'.

Combining these topics resulted in the Cybermen, presented in their first appearance as bandaged survivors, still clearly largely-organic. Lloyd was so taken by the creatures they quickly became a staple enemy, and were a returning monster for the rest of the decade. *The Tenth Planet* also established another format that would be ruthlessly exploited over the next few years: the base-under-siege story. The Cybermen begin their invasion of Earth at the South Pole in December 1986, assaulting an isolated space-tracking station. This set-up would recur in many of the stories made over the next three years, providing a ready-made template into which a variety of themes (and monsters) could be incorporated.

At the story's climax, as 7.5 million viewers watched, the Cybermen were defeated and their planet destroyed. A worn-out Doctor stumbled back to the TARDIS and, collapsing onto the floor, physically changed before his new companions' eyes. Signs had been building that all was not well with the Doctor – during *The Tenth Planet* he had commented that his body was 'wearing a bit thin', while his encounter with the Daleks' Time Destructor in *The Daleks' Master Plan* had adversely affected him, as had having his life force partially drained in *The Savages*. Although the concept of regeneration would become central to the series, at this point it was referred to as 'renewal': a change of bodily form, but not necessarily personality. Practically speaking, however, a different actor in the role meant a new personality.

Change had come not a moment too soon for *Doctor Who*. Ratings towards the end of Hartnell's time were falling after the highs of Dalekmania. It wasn't unusual during the first two seasons for serials to rate anywhere between nine million and 12.5 million viewers. However, while the third season started at a high of 9.9 million for the gender role-reversal space opera of *Galaxy 4*, viewing figures had tumbled to around five million for both *The Savages* and the format-freshening *The War Machines*. Changing the lead actor and the character of the Doctor in November 1966 (just seven months after Harold

Wilson had regenerated himself, securing a new lease of political life in a second election victory) proved to be a masterstroke. The novelty factor alone must have attracted a significant number of viewers, and audience figures for Patrick Troughton's three seasons in the title role consistently held at around the seven-million mark.

As the First Doctor himself said in *The Sensorites*: 'It all started out as a mild curiosity in a junkyard and now it's turned out to be quite a great spirit of adventure.' Now *Doctor Who* itself had a sense of rejuvenation, a fresh start with a new lead actor, and a whole new spirit of adventure awaited.

As a product of the BBC's unique institutional set-up, *Doctor Who* operated within a production process that changed little between the 1960s and the 1980s. From the start, *Doctor Who* faced technical challenges, and the show's ambition had been curtailed by the means of production available. In 1963, the producers had to work with the resources to hand. This served to limit what could be achieved on screen, while also (conversely) allowing the series to serve as a test subject for new technologies, from 'inlay' and Colour Separation Overlay (CSO, the BBC's 1970s version of blue- or green-screen production) to 'Scene-Sync' on 1980's *Meglos* and even 3D for 1993's *Children in Need* charity skit, *Dimensions in Time*.

While Verity Lambert and her production team were figuring out exactly what *Doctor Who* should be during the early months of 1963, the studio facilities allocated were causing much consternation and resulted in many caustic internal memos. Contrary to popular belief, *Doctor Who* was never transmitted live, but the early episodes were more or less recorded 'as live', with usually one recording break. This was due to the primitive videotape recording system used. Videotape editing was prohibitively expensive in 1963, so the only 'edit' allowed was to stop and start the recording in an emergency. Episodes were often shot using three cameras to cover the principal characters and any action. The cameras could not change lenses mid-shot, so close-ups of actors in dramatic moments were only possible by 'dollying' (moving in on the subject on tracks or wheels) the camera into the scene itself. These – and a whole host of other limitations arising from shooting the series in Lime Grove Studio D – account for the unique look and feel of *Doctor Who* for most of its first years on air.

This production process explains the distinctive way in which early *Doctor Who* recreated history or imagined far-off alien civilisations. Sometimes the show would try to work within these restrictions, and writers and producers would be realistic about what could be achieved on a budget of somewhere around £2,300 per episode. At other times, attempts would be made to produce something more ambitious, like the truly alien environment and insectoid eco-system of *The Web Planet*.

Lime Grove Studios had been built in 1915 in Shepherd's Bush as a film studio by the Gaumont Film Company and purchased by the BBC in 1949 as a 'temporary measure' while the purpose-built Television Centre was constructed in nearby White City. While Lime Grove had been a state-of-the-art studio following a refurbishment by Gaumont-British in 1932, it was something of a technological relic in 1963. Despite that, the studio continued to be used by the BBC. Verity Lambert was not happy about trying to make an innovative new science-fiction show in such circumstances. The studios were small and difficult to light, given the out-of-date equipment available. Memos from the time reveal that, just like the BBC's original purchase of the studio, use of Lime Grove Studio D for recording *Doctor Who* was intended to be a temporary situation, with the use of studios at Television Centre or Riverside (another small BBC studio) planned. For one thing, the police-box prop being designed for use as the exterior of the TARDIS had to be slightly scaled down from the real thing (then still widely seen on the streets of London), as it would have been too large to fit into the lifts at Lime Grove.

As noted, with video editing unavailable, each 25-minute episode of *Doctor Who* was recorded more or less 'as live' on a Friday evening across about 75 minutes, anywhere between two to four weeks in advance of transmission. Anything more complicated than dialogue scenes (like a dynamic fight sequence or a complicated model shot) was captured on film the previous week, usually at the BBC-owned Ealing Studios. Everything else was shot, usually in chronological order, on the Friday evening following a week of script read-throughs, rehearsals and an in-studio dress rehearsal earlier on the same day. Mistakes were to be avoided, although the £100 videotape used could be rewound to the beginning of a fluffed scene and recorded over if a retake was required. These tapes could later be recycled, accounting for the loss of over 100 original recordings of black-and-white episodes of *Doctor Who*.

These primitive production conditions explain why vast alien vistas (the Dalek city on Skaro in *The Daleks*) and historical cultures (*The Aztecs*) were all rather more limited than the imagination of the writers intended. Thankfully, the imagination of the audience could usually be relied upon to fill in the illusion, creating in the mind's eye the kind of amazing worlds that black-and-white 405-line television trans-missions could only suggest.

The result was that *Doctor Who* had to be a dialogue-heavy series, in which the fantasy situation was often conveyed in spoken conver-sations rather than shown. The drama was mostly framed theatre-style, square on from the audience point of view, with the camera and the characters moving left to right (and vice versa) across frame rather than backwards and forwards into the depth of field (as Studio D at Lime Grove allowed for very little in the way of depth in set building). This was one reason why attempts to realise fully-formed alien worlds, like that in *The Web Planet*, were abandoned, while later episodes featuring the 'base-under-siege' situation succeed. These adventures were built around one large, significant set that could be accommodated in Lime Grove Studio D, but could be shot from a diversity of angles to convey the drama and generate novelty from episode to episode. It also allowed the show to stay within its limited budget.

Post-production work on these early *Doctor Who* episodes was minimal. With two or three sections of videotape (with minor line fluffs and clumsy movements left in, as retakes were not economical) recorded in order to make up each 25-minute episode, all that had to be added was music (and sometimes even this was played in 'as live' during the studio recording) and sound effects, with very limited special-effects or (primitive) electronic-effects work being done. If additional post-production work or editing was required, the finished episode could be transferred to 35mm film through a process called 'telerecording' (which basically consisted of pointing a film camera at a video screen and recording the video image). This allowed for the option of more extensive editing on the less expensive film copy if necessary, but, more often than not, was done so the costly video-tape could be reused to record a future episode. The film recordings were also useful to create duplicate copies for sales to foreign tele-vision stations, as transmission from film was much more common in the 1960s than from videotape. This process, though, would prove to be significant in saving many episodes of *Doctor Who* that were otherwise deleted by the BBC in the late-1970s.

By 1967, *Doctor Who* had changed dramatically. The Doctor had a new face and personality, as character actor Patrick Troughton took over from William Hartnell. Troughton had played Robin Hood in a 1950s TV series and appeared several times in *Dr Finlay's Casebook* on the BBC. In 1963, he'd featured in the fantasy film *Jason and the Argonauts*. Cast to bring new life to the series, Troughton's take on the Doctor was dubbed a 'cosmic hobo' by Sydney Newman. His arrival was little remarked upon, and certainly did not provoke the press frenzy that would later be attached to the series' regular change of lead actor. *The Daily Sketch* was one of the few newspapers to pay much attention to the curious change, referring to 'the strange affair of The Changing Face of Doctor Who. The time travelling Doctor is back as usual on BBC1 this afternoon – and advance reports say that his return will be an explosive event to woo the kids away from Guy Fawkes bonfires. But something is very much out of the ordinary – instead of being played by William Hartnell, the Doctor is spooky character actor Patrick Troughton. When veteran Bill Hartnell decided to drop out it could have meant the end for *Doctor Who*. Scriptwriters have been turning mental somersaults to explain why a new hero is appearing, without warning, to young fans. Full details of his debut are being kept a secret, until today.'

There was no suggestion that Patrick Troughton should play the same character as William Hartnell, even though they were both portraying the same Doctor. The critically acclaimed Troughton took the path of playing up the Doctor's whimsical nature in response to Hartnell's perceived severity. His 'cosmic hobo' version of the Doctor was someone whose clowning meant he'd be underestimated by his adversaries. He connected much more with his human companions, too, as he was somewhat less alien and a lot less threatening than Hartnell's incarnation had been.

Producer Innes Lloyd, who'd been running the show since *The Celestial Toymaker* and had been instrumental in removing Hartnell, was now firmly in charge. The budget-busting experimental shows of the past, like *The Web Planet*, were dumped in favour of a handful of more manageable and affordable formulaic story templates. The main format for the remainder of the decade was the 'base-under-siege' story, in which an isolated community (often the staff of a scientific outpost or institution) is attacked by an alien menace, with only the Doctor and his friends to help. A lot of these outposts were either on Earth, nearby on the Moon, or else in orbiting space stations (locations also featured regularly in the revived twenty-first-century series, for many of the same reasons). This allowed for economy in set building and in the creation of environments. Lloyd appeared to have been heavily influenced by the Hollywood movie *The Thing from Another World* (1951) that showed a scientific and military community under attack from a revived alien creature.

Similarly, the series moved on from creating alien cultures, as in the Hartnell era, and relied instead on the shock value of various 'monsters'. Troughton's time in the TARDIS is remembered as one in which the series ruthlessly exploited old and new monsters, with return engagements commanding viewer loyalty, shown by the reliably consistent viewing figures of seven million. Lloyd relied less on the Daleks to draw viewers, featuring them in Troughton's debut story *The Power of the Daleks* to bridge the change of lead actor, and then only once more in *The Evil of the Daleks*, a story that narratively set up the Daleks' 'final end' by wiping them out. This was due to Dalek creator Terry Nation's hopes of spinning off a separate Dalek TV series, and his pursuit of this would keep the Daleks off screen until 1972.

Troughton's time on the series is defined by its reliance on formula and sequels: the Doctor encounters the Cybermen four times in just three years (1966–69), with return appearances for the armoured Martians known as Ice Warriors and the robotic Yeti helping to build up a feeling of expectation and excitement in viewers. Many one-off creatures were also featured, including the Macra (giant crabs who made a brief return in the David Tennant adventure *Gridlock*), killer robots called Quarks in *The Dominators* and the Krotons, crystalline entities feeding off human intelligence. This approach gave the show a distinctly different identity from previous years, beyond the change of lead actor. However, it was a restrictive format that could not last too long. Regular change – in front of and behind the cameras – would become part of *Doctor Who*'s unique signature.

One very noticeable effect of this revised approach to the series was the end of the purely historical adventures. *Doctor Who* had abandoned long ago any pretence at fulfilling its original educational remit. Shortly after the Daleks arrived, the bug-eyed monsters took over. A rapid progression of Dalek wannabes (Mechanoids, war machines) and ever more fanciful alien creatures (Voord, Sensorites, Zarbi and Menoptra) continued into the Troughton period with a parade of menacing monsters. Innes Lloyd disliked the history tales, as did many of the viewers. After Troughton's second story, *The Highlanders*, the purely historical story (with no science-fiction elements apart from the Doctor, his companions and the TARDIS) lay dormant for 15 years, only returning briefly when Peter Davison took on the leading role.

The Highlanders was notable for one other significant reason: the arrival of Jamie McCrimmon (Frazer Hines), one of the Doctor's longest-lasting companions. The role of the companion had changed during the three years the series had been on air, moving from the audience-identification figures of Susan and her teachers to an alternative team of three, each of whom served a key narrative purpose. While Hartnell's era worked through a variety of unsuccessful Susan replacements (Vicki, Dodo, Polly), the removal of Ian and Barbara allowed for a more fundamental change. The mid-1960s line-up comprising the Doctor, lost astronaut Steven Taylor (Peter Purves) and rescued space orphan Vicki (Maureen O'Brien) would serve as a template for some of the series' most successful character combinations over the years.

These three symbolised the brains (the Doctor), the brawn (Steven/Jamie) and the emotions (Vicki/Victoria/Zoe), the acceptable gender stereotypes of the period. Thus the Doctor could solve the problem in an intellectual way, the young male companion would function as a strong-arm physical resource, while the female companion could humanise the alien Doctor and (more often) scream at the monster or be captured to await rescue. It was a formula settled on in the Troughton period following the departure of Ben and Polly in

The Faceless Ones, leaving the Doctor, Jamie and Victoria Waterfield (Deborah Watling) – and later Zoe Heriot (Wendy Padbury) – to see out the 1960s.

Later years would see this line-up recreated many times, with Jon Pertwee's Doctor teamed up with UNIT soldiers or the Brigadier, and with Liz Shaw (Caroline John), Jo Grant (Katy Manning) and Sarah Jane Smith (Elisabeth Sladen). The early Tom Baker era saw him teamed with Sarah Jane and Harry Sullivan (Ian Marter), a throwback to the Ian- or Steven-type character, and, later, with Leela (Louise Jameson), a primitive warrior, who took on the physical role. Later still, the Doctor's robot dog K-9 was often used as the mindless muscle, a weapon as a pet. Even in the twenty-first century, the formula still proved useful when Christopher Eccleston's Doctor, shell-shocked from the Time War, came to rely on Captain Jack Harkness (John Barrowman) for the strong-arm stuff, while moulding young shop girl Rose Tyler (Billie Piper) into an intergalactic warrior.

Frazer Hines proved to be an effective partner for Troughton's Doctor, sticking with him right up to the end of the 1960s (Troughton would reappear in the series, alongside Hartnell and his own successor, Jon Pertwee, in 1973's tenth-anniversary story, *The Three Doctors*, while both Troughton and Hines returned separately in 1983 for the anniversary adventure *The Five Doctors*, and again – this time together – in 1985 for *The Two Doctors*, indicating their ongoing popularity with the public and fans).

The Troughton era of the show presented an attempt to build a coherent universe, although there's no explicit sense of continuity. It would have been possible for casual viewers to have built a sense of a future Earth 'history' from the Doctor's various late-1960s adventures. This future history consisted of moon bases and wheels in space, with mankind slowly spreading out among the stars, bringing their own problems with them, like space 'pirates', and encountering new threats, like the Cybermen or the Ice Warriors. The technological achievements of humanity depicted in *Doctor Who* in the 1960s could be seen as the ultimate results of Labour Prime Minister Harold Wilson's technological 'white heat' writ large across the solar system.

The threats encountered from space were representative of genuine issues perceived to be threatening Britain in the late-1960s. The 'base-under-siege' strand of storytelling in *Doctor Who* might be seen as a reaction to immigration issues facing the nation. Those invaders from space (Cybermen, Ice Warriors, Yeti) could easily be the newest post-war wave of foreign immigrants coming to take up residence in the UK. The island of Britain was, at least according to political mavericks like right-wing Conservative MP Enoch Powell, a 'base-under-siege' itself.

Just before *Doctor Who* debuted on TV, the Commonwealth Immigrants Act 1962 was passed, changing the nature of immigration to Britain. In the years after the Second World War, immigrants had come from former British colonies or newer Commonwealth countries to set up residence in the UK. There were few restrictions. Following the 1962 law, however, immigration controls were applied requiring those without directly issued UK passports to hold work permits or else have relatives already resident in the UK. Since Indian independence in 1947, more than 60,000 Indian immigrants had arrived in the UK, many working in the service sector, especially in small retail shops and post offices. In the post-war years, many displaced Eastern Europeans would also make their way to the UK to live.

This arrival in large numbers to major metropolitan centres like London, Birmingham and Glasgow of peoples from other cultures had made the UK urban population aware of the 'alien other' among them. It often became the aim of new immigrants to assimilate, to become just like those born in the UK. English language and customs would be learned and would be passed on to children, often in preference to the family's original native language or culture. This assimilation of immigrant communities would, in part, be responded to by second-generation immigrants, many of whom would show greater interest in their 'roots' or the cultures from which their parents or grandparents came. There is an echo in the Cybermen's threat to humanity that 'you will become like us' through cybernetic conversion.

The political and social issues surrounding immigration came to a head in the UK in April 1968, just as the Cybermen were invading *The Wheel in Space*. On 20 April 1968 (just a week before *The Wheel in Space* began), MP Enoch Powell made a controversial speech in Birmingham, in which he warned his audience of what he believed would be the consequences of continued unchecked immigration from the Commonwealth to Britain. It became dubbed the 'rivers of blood' speech, after his use of a quote from Roman poet Virgil. The speech, responding to unrestricted immigration and the implementation of the Race Relations Act of 1968, cost Powell his shadow-cabinet post, but it brought the simmering issues of immigration and race relations to the forefront of the political agenda in Britain.

The repeated invasion narratives used in *Doctor Who* in the late-1960s reflected the real fear of 'the other' or the unknown that British people may have been feeling in their real lives as they adapted to their new friends and neighbours. Although never referred to directly in the series, as they would be in cutting-edge comedy shows like *Till Death Do Us Part* and even *Steptoe and Son*, issues of foreign/alien invasion, assimilation and domination thread themselves through the *Doctor Who* of the 1960s in a way that makes the stories told inseparable from the politics and culture of Britain at the time. This engagement with real-world issues in the guise of space fantasy goes a long way to explaining the inherent popularity of the show and the connection it was able to build with British television viewers, a connection it would eventually carelessly abdicate in the 1980s.

There are other echoes of the political realities of the 1960s in the stories and iconography of Troughton's *Doctor Who*. The alternative story to the 'base-under-siege' tale was the alien invasion of Earth, drawn from the experiment of *The War Machines*. Instead of an isolated outpost, the invaders would be seen in recognisable contemporary settings, often marching past national landmarks in the way the Daleks had in *The Dalek Invasion of Earth* in 1964. After battling his signature monsters, the Cybermen, on *The Moonbase* (where they attempt to destroy the Earth by commandeering the Moon's weather-control system), uncovering their tombs in the far future (in a pastiche of the classic Universal 'Mummy' movies, remade by Britain's Hammer Films in 1959, with sequels running through the 1960s into the 1970s) and fighting them on *The Wheel in Space*, the Doctor faced the Cybermen on Earth in *The Invasion*.

Prior to this, the soldiers-versus-invaders formula of *The War Machines* had been repeated in *The Web of Fear*, the London-set sequel to *The Abominable Snowmen*, which had introduced the robotic Yeti. Repeating the trick pulled off previously with the Daleks, the alien creatures were brought from their remote location (Skaro/the Himalayas) directly to the centre of British political and social power (contemporary 1960s London). Yeti battling British soldiers in the London Underground was an image retained by viewers for many years to come (and became the basis for a famous Jon Pertwee quote about bringing the strange and unusual into conflict with the everyday, which he characterised as 'finding a Yeti on the loo in Tooting Bec').

Soldiers in action on British streets had not been seen since the Second World War, but it would become a very familiar sight for BBC viewers based in Northern Ireland. The 'Troubles', stretching from the 1960s to the 1990s, were the latest manifestation of a conflict between Republican and Loyalist forces dating back to the 1600s and the partition of Ireland early in the twentieth century. British television audiences would become used to seeing British troops in recognisable urban environments, from Aden to Belfast. The final episodes of *The Invasion* revealed the mysterious invaders to be Cybermen, and the involvement of UNIT (looking pretty much like the British Army) presaged the real-world deployment in Northern Ireland.

The United Nations Intelligence Taskforce (UNIT, reconfigured by the twenty-first-century version of the series into the Unified Intelligence Taskforce to avoid any association with the UN itself) had its roots in *The Web of Fear*, but would continue to feature in the programme right through until the last regular Russell T Davies scripted episode, *Journey's End*, in 2008. The appearance of Colonel Lethbridge-Stewart (Nicholas Courtney, previously Space Security Agent Brett Vyon in *The Daleks' Master Plan*) commanding troops against the Yeti invasion led to his reappearance (this time as a Brigadier) as the commander of UNIT in *The Invasion*.

UNIT supposedly operated under the auspices of the United Nations, and was tasked with the job of battling and resisting alien invasions of Earth wherever they were found (oddly enough, usually within day-trip travelling distance of BBC Television Centre). This military force would prove very useful to the Doctor (especially in the 1970s, following his regeneration into Jon Pertwee and exile to Earth, when it seemed as though the planet was being invaded every few weeks). The use of the military wasn't restricted to being a solution to conflict (who else could repel these alien invaders en masse?): they were often useful authority figures that the Doctor could come into conflict with, thus playing out the series' often opposing ideologies.

Another worldwide political-military threat of the late-1960s reflected in *Doctor Who*'s storytelling was that of nuclear annihilation. The ending of the Second World War with the deployment of two nuclear weapons by the USA against Japan haunted post-war politics and popular culture, and *Doctor Who* was no exception. Ultimate weapons had been and would be referenced many times: in *The Tenth Planet*, mankind threatened to unleash the Z-bomb on the invading Cybermen.

The fear of atomic destruction (or of the misuse of nuclear power) was represented in *Doctor Who* – in a way that echoed the Japanese

Godzilla/Gojira movies – in a series of threats from the deep: *The Underwater Menace*, *The Macra Terror* and *Fury from the Deep*. *Godzilla* (1954) is largely seen as a metaphor for the effect of the atomic bombs on Nagasaki and Hiroshima in Japan. In the movie, atomic testing awakens the slumbering lizard-like creature that then wreaks havoc on Odo Island and Tokyo. While *The Underwater Menace* is a 'destruction of Atlantis' story (the first of three alternative non-compatible versions of that myth presented in *Doctor Who* TV adventures), drawing on the cliff-hanger serial *Undersea Kingdom*, it also features mad professor Zaroff (Joseph Furst), who has a crazy plan. In an era when the discovery of North Sea oil was big news (and would fuel increasing Scottish nationalism as ownership of the resources was disputed), undersea drilling was an accepted form of exploration. Nutty Professor Zaroff, however, plans to use a nuclear reactor to crack the Earth's crust and drain the oceans. In the way of many stock comic-book villains, he never really explains his motivations.

This story was soon followed by *The Macra Terror*, featuring giant, gas-guzzling, crab-like creatures who secretly dominate a totalitarian pleasure camp (a kind of ersatz Butlins, a popular holiday destination in 1950s and 1960s Britain). The exploitation of mineral wealth (the gas needed by the Macra to survive) vies with the fears of brainwashing and totalitarianism. Finally, *Fury from the Deep* more explicitly tackles the off-shore oil and gas industry, with the pipes carrying the gas also home to a form of parasitic, intelligent seaweed. The fear that North Sea oil mining might uncover something unknown, in the way that atomic testing had awakened Godzilla, was not entirely unreasonable. In the 1960s, the undersea world was as much an alien environment as outer space, one being brought to television regularly in all its weird wonder by Jacques Cousteau. In the 1960s, Cousteau had fought against the dumping of nuclear waste at sea, for fear of its impact on living organisms and the environment. While it was highly unlikely that nuclear-mutated creatures, like Atlantean fish people, giant crab monsters or intelligent seaweed might emerge from the depths, the health of the undersea environment was becoming a genuine popular concern.

These examples show how, through the late 1960s, *Doctor Who* repeatedly exploited political, social and scientific fears that were prevalent in British society for the purposes of entertaining an actively engaged television audience. It may have looked like a science-fiction adventure show in which an oddball, eccentric but well-meaning alien tackled creatures from outer space, but *Doctor Who* was taking note of the audience's real-world fears and reflecting them back, often with fantastic solutions attached.

The emphasis on formulaic 'base-under-siege' tales left little room for the creation of fully-realised weird alien cultures that had been a hallmark of the Hartnell years, or indeed for fantasy-based 'sideways' adventures like *The Celestial Toyroom*. The singular exception came towards the end of Troughton's run in *The Mind Robber*, a meta-text about the creation of stories themselves. Written (mostly) by Peter Ling (who co-created soap opera *Crossroads*), *The Mind Robber* sees the Doctor and friends deposited in the 'Land of Fiction' where they encounter a series of literary characters brought to life. Those encountered include Rapunzel, Lancelot, Gulliver, Medusa and futuristic super-hero Karkus, from a comic strip (from the far-future year 2000) known to Zoe. After several fantastic, threatening and confusing adventures, it is revealed that the imaginary story-world is controlled by a 'Master of Fiction'. He's a human, kidnapped from his magazine-adventure-serial-writing duties on Earth in 1926 and plugged into the computer that generates this 'Land of Fiction'. Battling with this Master (not the same character later created as an adversary for the Doctor in the 1970s, despite fan attempts to reconcile the two), the Doctor attempts to take control of the telling of the story himself, by dictating alternative outcomes to the computer. The entire adventure is a satire of *Doctor Who*'s own serialised storytelling, even down to the production-line nature of telling an ongoing story. The previous adventure's troubled production process resulted in a standalone opening instalment (which Ling did not write), using the basic studio and some second-hand robot costumes to create a 25-minute prelude set in a featureless white void.

The struggle that the show's writers had in the 1960s to keep up with the pace of production was evident as Troughton's time came to a close with the ten-episode epic adventure *The War Games*. Emerging as a solution to behind-the-scenes production problems, writers Malcolm 'Mac' Hulke and Terrance Dicks started *The War Games* as a serial-style story that saw the Doctor and his friends encountering soldiers from different historical eras in each episode, before coming to the realisation that they've been kidnapped by interfering aliens and placed together in a fight to the death. By the end of episode nine, the Doctor realises he can't solve the problem himself (the villainous 'War Chief' is a member of his own species gone bad, like the time-meddling 'Monk'). He calls in the Time Lords – this is the first serial to name the Doctor's own people – to help, knowing that it will likely result in his own capture. The final episode sees the situation with the War Chief resolved, and climaxes with the Doctor put on trial for breaking the Time Lords' non-interference policy. The Doctor argues his case passionately, having developed from his initial non-involvement with the struggle of the cavemen in *An Unearthly Child* and disengagement with the need to defeat the Daleks in *The Daleks* to declaring, at his trial, that, 'There is evil in the universe that must be fought.' Accepting his justification, the Time Lords decide that the Doctor could be useful, agreeing he 'may have a part to play' in the defeat of galactic evils. They exile him to Earth at a time in its history (the end of the twentieth century) when it is considered to be under particular threat. As part of his sentence, the Time Lords impose another change of appearance on the Doctor, resulting in his regeneration. His companions, Zoe and Jamie, are returned to their respective times, their minds wiped of all memory of their adventures with the Doctor except for their first encounter.

This conclusion to Patrick Troughton's time as the Doctor brought to a close six years of epic fantasy adventures and marked the end of the black-and-white era of *Doctor Who*. In doing so, writers Hulke and Dicks created a back-story for the Doctor, answering some of the questions posed by the show's own enigmatic and unexplained title. This was a brave move, but the production team had determined that the mystery couldn't stand forever. While concerned about burdening a new, incoming production team with a rigidly established mythology, there was also a strong possibility that the series might have ended entirely in 1969, so they felt under some obligation to provide a conclusion to the show's past six years with some answers to the big question of the Doctor's identity. The material they produced would form a strong part of the series' foundation myth, right through its run. Even though Russell T Davies would kill off the Time Lords with his 'Time War' back-story, the fact that the Doctor was the last of his kind became central to the new conception of the revived series.

When the show returned, post-Troughton, in 1970, it would be in colour and the entire production process would change along with the creative team behind the scenes. But *Doctor Who*'s continued reflection of social, political and technological changes in Britain would become even bolder.

3. COLOUR SEPARATION OVERLAY

Where William Hartnell's time on *Doctor Who* had been one of innovation in storytelling and technology, Patrick Troughton's three-year
run had been one of consolidation, in narrative, budgetary and structural terms. As the series entered the 1970s, with colour television
and ever-greater technological development ahead, it faced its biggest
challenges to date.

As the Conservatives returned to power in 1970 under Prime
Minister Edward Heath, Britain was in crisis. Industrial strife was
rampant, with a series of crippling strikes affecting transport and
power. The global oil crisis was having an effect, while a growing
environmental movement was enjoying its first popular successes.
The new government's desire to join the forerunner of the European
Union, the European Economic Community (EEC), was beginning to
play a part in British life and politics.

Doctor Who was also facing a crisis as the 1960s drew to a close.
Ratings had fallen off once more, with the potentially series-concluding
epic *The War Games* averaging just under five million viewers, half
the number who'd witnessed the arrival of the Daleks back in 1963.
It wouldn't be the last time that the show faced cancellation due to
apparent dwindling popularity with viewers. At this point, the BBC

considered a six-year run to have been a success and there was some internal debate about whether to end the show. Troughton's Doctor had been shown starting the process of regeneration, a change forced upon him by the Time Lords, but, with no new actor cast, the decision to either cancel the show or launch a new actor as the Doctor was still open.

Upper management at the BBC always had an uneasy relationship with *Doctor Who*. For some of the 'old guard' the show was too populist, 'low brow' even, and had abandoned its original educational remit in favour of ratings-grabbing creations like the Daleks. This view put the late-1960s version of the show in opposition to the *raison d'être* of the BBC: a publicly funded corporation with ambitions to educate and enlighten the masses. Although originally developed within this ethos, by 1969 *Doctor Who* clearly no longer fulfilled it. However, the BBC itself had been changing throughout the 1960s, starting with the arrival of Director General Hugh Carleton Greene. *Doctor Who* itself had been part of that process. The programme could be cited as both an example of the BBC's conservatism and part of its radical agenda, reflecting a changing nation back to itself via the medium of popular entertainment.

With the departure of *Doctor Who* champion Sydney Newman from the BBC in 1967, the prospects for the series' continuation had taken a downward turn. The renewal of the show that producer Innes Lloyd and star Patrick Troughton brought about was enough to win it another few years on air, during which time it continued to develop and change. As the end of Troughton's time in the TARDIS drew near, however, there were rumblings that *Doctor Who* no longer deserved a place on primetime BBC1 Saturday evenings.

Terrance Dicks – a figure who would become very important to *Doctor Who*'s narrative development during the 1970s – joined the show as Assistant Script Editor in Spring 1968. The first thing he heard when joining was that the BBC was considering cancelling the show. 'I thought, "That's a great start to my career; three months and that will be the end of it!"' recalled Dicks. 'For a while they did actually consider ending it, because even then it had been going for a pretty long time in television terms. The viewing figures were OK, but they weren't marvellous any more. I was actually involved in looking around for something else to replace the show.'

Several *Doctor Who*-type shows were being considered as the 1960s drew to a close, but it is unclear if these were ever intended as direct replacements. Returning to the science fiction literary origins of *Doctor Who* itself, the BBC considered producing a series of dramas drawing on the adventure stories of Jules Verne, whose Captain Nemo may have been a source for *Doctor Who*'s title character. Another possibility was an updated remake of Nigel Kneale's 1950s Quatermass dramas. These groundbreaking serials had seen an Earthbound professor battle alien incursions amid official scepticism.

When the BBC decided that none of these shows, or several others mooted for production, was a suitable replacement for *Doctor Who*, a decision was taken to continue with the series. However, when it returned to screens in January 1970, *Doctor Who* would be a very different show. The lead character would have a different face, there would be a new production team behind the scenes, there would only be 26 episodes per year (rather than the 1960s average of 43), and, most noticeably of all, it would be in colour.

Outgoing producer Peter Bryant was tasked with setting up the first story of the 1970s (*Spearhead from Space*, filmed in 1969) before handing over to the team of producer Barry Letts and script editor Terrance Dicks, who would remain with the series for the next five years, as long as new Doctor Jon Pertwee.

Several actors had been considered as Patrick Troughton's replacement in mid-1969, when it became clear the show would be continuing. Among them were Ron Moody (then best known as Fagin in

Oliver Twist, 1968), and ex-Goon Michael Bentine, before Letts settled on Pertwee, better known as a radio comedian, master of silly voices and star of the long-running radio comedy *The Navy Lark*.

As well as changing the lead actor, the way the show was made had to change radically, too. In line with every other BBC-produced show, *Doctor Who* would enter the 1970s in full colour. This development was echoed at the end of 2008, when the producers of the revived and phenomenally successful twenty-first-century *Doctor Who* faced a similar challenge. Just as the BBC wanted all programmes and live output to be in colour in 1970, by 2010 all content would be transmitted in High Definition (HD). By 2008, the teams at BBC Wales, after a shaky technical start, had already notched up a couple of years' experience of HD television production with *Doctor Who* spin-off *Torchwood*. Starting with *Planet of the Dead*, at Easter 2009, the BBC's flagship show was finally using the new process.

Faced with similar upheaval in the 1970s, the new *Doctor Who* production team discovered there'd be no additional budget available to cover the expense of making the switch. Colour television was broadcast on a higher-definition 625-line system, meaning clearer, crisper pictures (even more so in HD by 2008). As a result, the design detail of costumes, sets and make-up all had to be upgraded to a new level. This was expensive. Amid a general move to shorter seasons for TV drama, reducing *Doctor Who* from over 40 episodes per year to the mid-20s therefore made a lot of sense. It allowed the budget to go further and addressed complaints from the series' previous two leading actors about the gruelling workload that their almost all-year-round schedule entailed. Shooting on location would also make for a more intensive production process, as had been discovered in making serials like *The War Machines* and *The Invasion*.

As well as these superficial, though important, changes, there was also to be a major change to the format of the show, as set up in the final episode of *The War Games*. No longer a wanderer in time and space, Jon Pertwee's Third Doctor would be an exile on Earth, battling aliens trying to invade the planet. This clearly echoed the Quatermass serials of the 1950s (to such an extent that author Nigel Kneale felt aggrieved) and may have been a hangover from the BBC's vague thoughts about remaking the series. This way, the corporation had the best of both worlds: a new series of *Doctor Who* that was not entirely unlike the previously popular Quatermass. Terrance Dicks, script editor during much of the 1970s, felt the comparison was inevitable: 'If you're doing a science-fiction serial set on Earth, you're going to echo Quatermass whether you like it or not,' he said on *What Lies Beneath*, a DVD documentary. In the same programme, Barry Letts called the new Doctor 'a cross between Quatermass and James Bond'. Jon Pertwee was tasked with playing the Doctor as a new, dynamic, Earthbound action hero.

Another long-fought battle was won as the *Doctor Who* base of operations was finally moved to Television Centre (with model work and additional film work based at Ealing Studios, as always), away from the limiting facilities of Lime Grove and Riverside, with production offices based in the BBC facility at Union House in Shepherd's Bush. Stories could be recorded in blocks now, as more time was available, and could even be produced out of broadcast order (a luxury not afforded the black-and-white era). Location and studio shooting could be maximised to best use the available budget and resources. Broadly, this production set-up would remain in place for the rest of the show's original 26-year run, until 1989.

All these changes were seen by incoming producer Barry Letts as opportunities to be exploited. He had a new vision for the series, with a new leading man and a whole new electronic box of tricks to bring special effects to colour television drama. As 1970 began, *Doctor Who* had not so much regenerated as become an entirely different show.

Despite all the superficial changes, the opening adventure of 1970 was as traditional as they come. *Spearhead from Space* had been shot entirely on film at the BBC facilities at Evesham as a strike made Television Centre initially unavailable to the production. This gave the opening story a distinctive look, building on the gritty, contemporary feel of *The Invasion*, but one that would not be repeated as the show settled into its regular production pattern.

This first story continued the established format of the Troughton years, with an alien invasion of Earth thwarted by the Doctor with the help of UNIT, now co-opted as a regular part of the series' format. With the new Doctor exiled to Earth and unable to escape (and he tries quite hard to do so, even while there's an ongoing alien invasion), he reluctantly allies himself to UNIT as a base of operations. New companion Liz Shaw (Caroline John) is introduced as an intelligent UNIT recruit who is almost as smart as the Doctor himself. The role built on that of her immediate predecessor, the equally smart Zoe Heriot, and both had been created in reaction to the mostly more dependent female companions of the 1960s.

Letts and Dicks approached the show under the assumption that a large part of the audience had grown up with it. Those kids from seven years before who witnessed the arrival of the Daleks were now teenagers, so the show was retooled to be more 'grown up', more in line with filmed adventure shows from ITV like *The Avengers*. 'By the time we were doing it,' said Letts on the DVD documentary *What Lies Beneath*, 'it was definitely a grown-up programme, as well as a children's programme. [We felt] the stories should be about something of deep interest to the adults.' Additionally, Terrance Dicks had a strong dislike of the 'sideways' fantasy-based shows, such as *The Celestial Toymaker* and *The Mind Robber*. These were banished in favour of Letts' realism: *Doctor Who* in the style of the procedural cop or doc shows increasingly popular in the 1960s, like *Z-Cars* or *Emergency Ward 10*.

The new Doctor would be debonair, an adventurer in the style of John Steed from *The Avengers* or Adam Adamant (the character Verity Lambert had launched after *Doctor Who*). He would dress in Victorian garb with a dash of 1970s élan, and he'd have a fascination for fast cars and gadgets. A lot of this reflected Jon Pertwee's own personal style and interests (as part of his first costume, Pertwee wore his own grandfather's cloak) as much as it drew on any characterisation developed by Letts and Dicks.

The newly re-tooled *Doctor Who* debuted to eight million viewers, a significant leap upwards from the five million who saw Patrick Troughton's exit in *The War Games* the year before. That success had been aided considerably by plenty of press coverage, something Troughton had avoided, and a *Radio Times* cover. Now Letts and Dicks knew they'd have a decent chance to develop the series over a longer term than they feared when they took up their jobs.

Jon Pertwee's first season consisted of only four adventures, spread across 25 episodes. Following the four-episode introduction, *Spearhead from Space*, each of the remaining stories was seven episodes long, and some of them outstayed their welcome. However, this was a budgetary consideration, in that sets and locations could be stretched further if the stories ran for more episodes. It was an approach that was deemed not to be successful, despite an average audience for the season in excess of seven million viewers, and it was largely abandoned in future years.

The three stories that make up the remainder of season seven have much in common, in theme and approach. *Doctor Who and the Silurians* (the only time the show's title was used in a story title) sees a revived race of lizard men lay claim to Earth. While the Doctor engages in détente (echoing the real-world Cold War conflict between the West and the Soviet Union), the Brigadier prepares to use force and blow the 'monsters' back to prehistoric times. Despite the Doctor's moral outrage, the Brigadier (representing the military establishment) ultimately wins.

The serial's writer Malcolm Hulke, a committed left-wing dramatist, had told Terrance Dicks that the new *Doctor Who* format only allowed for two stories: the alien invasion and the mad scientist. The outline for the Silurian story was an attempt to breach these limitations by having the 'aliens' as the original natural possessors of the Earth: they're already here. This allowed the story to deal with issues of Britain's colonial past: newly-evolved mankind has colonised the Silurians' home (while they slept), but the Silurians now plan to do the same to mankind in retaliation.

Hulke also explored some topics that would recur throughout the Pertwee episodes, and which became hallmarks of the era. The Doctor, throughout these five years, is played as a very moral hero, outraged by injustice and willing to stand up against authority, even those who nominally 'employ' him. The end of deference (destroyed in the 1960s through the rise of the new youth culture and television satire like *That Was The Week That Was*, as well as political scandals like Profumo) was heavily reflected in the series' depiction of politicians and civil servants as bumbling no-hopers at best and open-to-corruption, self-serving bureaucrats at worst. The military were to come off no better, depicted in the Silurian tale and many thereafter as 'shoot first, ask questions later' types, while UNIT appears to be staffed by buffoons, such as recurring characters Yates and Benton.

Hulke was also an uncredited rewrite man on the next story, *The Ambassadors of Death*, originally drafted by one-time series' script editor David Whitaker in the late-1960s but adapted for the show's new 1970s format. This plays like a remix of themes from the previous story: humans are terrified of radioactive alien ambassadors from outer space (more intergalactic immigrants) and a scientific institution is undergoing a crisis (as with the Wenley Moor facility in the Silurian story). The overlay this time is the iconography of a late-1960s, early-

1970s British spy thriller, like the early James Bond movies, or Michael Caine's Harry Palmer series, especially *The Ipcress File* (1965). This was another sign of the growing maturity of *Doctor Who*, moving away from material aimed exclusively at children and including genres and references that teenagers and adults could equally appreciate.

Finally, wrapping up the show's first colour season was *Inferno*. Again, the story features a scientific institution in crisis (the Inferno project, drilling to Earth's core in search of a new source of energy). The Doctor lives through the events of this story twice, once in a parallel universe where his friends from UNIT are all evil fascists and the planet is destroyed by the Inferno project's drilling (but only after primordial ooze escapes from the planet's core and turns a few people into hairy throwbacks to our primitive ancestors called 'primords'). A recurring theme of this season – distrust of science and scientists – features prominently in this story, written by Don Houghton. By 1970, the North Sea oil discoveries of the 1960s were being actively exploited with the construction of active drilling platforms that would begin delivering oil and gas to the mainland via pipeline in 1971. The drilling project in *Inferno* tapped directly into the era's news headlines, while unleashing the primords brought the season back full circle to the ancient lizard men of the Silurian episodes.

These long stories, at seven weeks duration each, may have been a money-saving gambit, but in storytelling terms they suited neither Barry Letts nor Terrance Dicks. By the final episode of *Inferno*, viewing figures were right back where they'd been with the last episode of *The War Games*, at just 5.5 million. Additionally, each new story's first episode proved to be the highest rated, encouraging the producers to believe that more 'first nights' would help the series. An increase in the number of stories per season would therefore be required.

The following year would see *Doctor Who* adopt a style that was much more representative of the way Letts and Dicks wanted to run the show. The season kicked off with the introduction of an adversary for the Doctor who would prove to be the most important addition to the series' mythology since the creation of the Time Lords. Feeling the Doctor was akin to Sherlock Holmes, Letts decided he needed a Moriarty, resulting in the creation of the Master (Roger Delgado). A renegade Time Lord, he was the Doctor's evil mirror image. The presence of the Master in each of the eighth season's five stories gave some justification for the repeated invasions of Earth as he teamed up with the invaders to pursue his own agenda. *Terror of the Autons* opened the season, and was almost a direct remake of *Spearhead from Space*, with the addition of the Master and the storytelling tweaked to suit Letts' and Dicks' growing social and political agenda. Alongside the first appearance of the Master, the story standardised the UNIT set-up that would be a recurring element.

Additionally, Jo Grant (Katy Manning) was introduced as a dizzy UNIT operative who becomes attached to the Doctor. She was in total opposition to the knowledgeable, more mature Liz Shaw, who had proven difficult to write for and was unceremoniously written out. As a scientist, she had been expected to understand what the Doctor was talking about, thus robbing the audience of an identification figure whose major function was to ask questions clarifying the sometimes complicated plots or concepts. Jo Grant fulfilled this role admirably.

Keeping faith with Sydney Newman's initial impetus, Letts and Dicks were determined to continue to develop the political content of the series, reflecting British society in the guise of science-fiction adventure drama, as had been the case in the late-1960s. '*Doctor Who* always tended to deal with fairly serious matters,' confirmed Terrance Dicks, 'very often not in a didactic, pre-planned way. I've always said that what a writer thinks and feels, what his opinions are and the general climate of the time, they're going to creep into the show by osmosis.'

This resulted in Pertwee-era *Doctor Who* becoming a more politically committed drama hugely resonant with the times, while still being entertaining and emotionally engaging. This resonance also attracted big audiences: *Doctor Who* was not simply entertainment, but fantasy drama that related to viewers' experience of the real world. During season eight the show tackled issues like prison policy (*The Mind of Evil*), nuclear power (*The Claws of Axos*), the fall-out from decades of British colonialism (*The Colony in Space*) and the rise of alternative religion (*The Daemons*), all in the guise of disposable, episodic, action-adventure television.

Both *Spearhead from Space* and its sequel/remake *Terror of the Autons* tackled the consumer society that was in full bloom in the early 1970s. They take the sudden ubiquitous availability of plastic (due to the new products being developed from oil) and show how newly mass-produced goods may not be good for the population after all. In *Spearhead*, a small, family-run plastics company is taken over and turned into a more efficient automated outfit (a metaphor for the collapse and rebuilding of British industry), but it's all a front for an alien invasion. *Terror of the Autons* retold the same story, with the addition of the Master, but upped the ante as writer Robert Holmes terrified the nation's children with a series of plastic products (including much-loved toys) that turn on people, killing them.

Colony in Space, in addition to the obvious colonial theme, introduced a concern for the environment that would become central to *Doctor Who* in the 1970s. Environmentalism had risen up the political agenda, so the show reflected the interests of its audience and key writers. Later adventures like *Frontier in Space*, *The Green Death* and *Invasion of the Dinosaurs* continued to interrogate environmentalism from a variety of points of view, exploring one of the hot-button political topics of the times. *Colony in Space* sees human beings of the future leaving a ruined, over-populated planet to start fresh elsewhere. Colonising other planets is not an easy task, and the inhabitants of Uxarieus find themselves enduring a harsh existence, caught between Interplanetary Mining Corporation, the exploitative company that funds and supplies the expedition, and those being colonised. Although, superficially, *Colony in Space* resembles a land-grab Western, Hulke's script starts off as a political parable that is thrown off track by the need to service the arrival, in the final two episodes, of the season's recurring villain, the Master.

Regarded as a classic by fans of the show, *The Daemons* tackled the 1970s social phenomenon of alternative 'new-age' beliefs, wrapping them up in an alien invasion straight out of Arthur C Clarke's *Childhood's End.* The 1960s had seen the dawning of the Age of Aquarius (largely thanks to the hippie musical, 1967's *Hair*), but things had taken a sour turn with a series of political assassinations and the Charles Manson killings in 1969. It was a time of changing values, and the so-called 'New Age Movement' came to symbolise a switch from materialism to spirituality. In *Doctor Who*, Satanic magic in *The Daemons* turns out to be no more than very advanced science (Arthur C Clarke had once posited that 'any sufficiently advanced technology is indistinguishable from magic', while his novel *Childhood's End* revealed the arriving aliens to have an uncanny resemblance to Satan). *The Daemons*' idea that powerful aliens had visited Earth in ancient times and left their technology behind unearthed a strand of Erich Von Daniken-style thinking in *Doctor Who* that recurred in several stories, and was also a very prominent concern of 1970s pop culture. In a series of best-selling books, starting with *Chariots of the Gods?* in 1968, controversial Swiss author Von Daniken had suggested that humankind had been the beneficiary in ancient times of visitations from advanced alien civilisations. In coming years, *Death to the Daleks* and the Tom Baker serial *Pyramids of Mars* would feature elements of Von Daniken's ideas.

By the end of *Doctor Who*'s eighth year, Letts and Dicks had manoeuvred the show away from the gritty 'realism' of the Doctor's exile to Earth. Costs had been held under control by utilising the formula of Earth-centric adventures and by featuring the regular UNIT 'family' as a springboard for stories. However, Letts was not prepared to be so limited, and in *Colony in Space* gave the Doctor his first off-Earth adventure for two years. It was the shape of things to come as *Doctor Who* continued to adapt, thrive and reflect the political and social concerns of its almost eight million regular viewers.

Doctor Who had always been an outlet for experimentation in the way television was produced. The technical demands of the show had proven to be a major factor in the delay in getting the series on air in 1963. Since then, the very nature of the Doctor's adventures had called for a wide range of innovation in special visual-effects techniques. The black-and-white era allowed for electronic 'in-lay' effects to be achieved in the studio, giving the Doctor and his companions the chance to gaze out over a (model) Dalek city through an in-studio composite shot in *The Daleks*. This combined the output of two separate cameras, looking at two distinct scenes, one a model, one live action. The merged scene provided the visual 'wow' factor that the series increasingly relied upon in creating each new alien environment. This was by no means new, being an old film technique prominently used in 1933's *King Kong* and many other movies.

With the arrival of colour in the 1970s, *Doctor Who* had access to a new BBC technology: colour separation overlay (CSO), the television equivalent of modern cinema's blue-screen or green-screen special effects. A colour version of the electronic 'in-lay' technique, CSO would be fervently (some would say recklessly) embraced by producer Barry Letts as a way of both stretching *Doctor Who*'s shrinking budget (in the deflationary economic climate of the 1970s) and of realising the otherwise unrealisable on the television screen. Letts even appeared in a BBC training film enthusiastically demonstrating the uses of CSO in drama. The indiscriminate way in which CSO was used was largely responsible for the distinctive, colourful 'look' of 1970s *Doctor Who*.

Doctor Who found itself being used as a test bed for many new televisual techniques, and only after CSO had proved its worth on the show was it adapted for use on others like *Top of the Pops* or even the nightly news. Later stories were also used to test out new technologies. In 1979, *Destiny of the Daleks* saw the production loaned a cut-rate Steadicam (used extensively on Stanley Kubrick's *The Shining*, 1980) in order to provide proof of its efficacy on television, while 1980's *Meglos* would see extensive use of a development of CSO called Scene-Sync, in which the cameras could move in relation to the model backdrops and live action.

Letts' enthusiasm for CSO resulted in a series of experiments in *Terror of the Autons*, in which CSO replaced simple sets. Several scenes saw the actors appear in front of flat photographs, having originally performed in front of a green screen. It may have saved money, but it wasn't particularly convincing, especially as the CSO process had a tendency to result in blue lines or fringes appearing around actors. Similarly, instead of using a puppet to represent a killer doll, Letts used CSO to drop an actor in a rubber suit, electronically shrunk down, into the scene. Even views outside car windows were faked using CSO. While this sense of experimentation was admirable, and paid many dividends, so much CSO usage in one story gave it a very strange look. CSO would become a standard tool during the 1970s, until further advances in electronic television effects made the results more convincing and more commonplace. However, as in so many things, *Doctor Who* was there first, pioneering the technique.

As his seasons progressed, Barry Letts became convinced of the power of a strong 'first-night' start to each new series, and began to develop the idea of always ending each run on a high with an important 'season-finale' story. Such overall structural planning is second nature in television now (as can be seen by the heavily US-influenced revival of *Doctor Who*), but it was not as common in the early 1970s. Letts' seasons had already enjoyed a boost from the debut of a new Doctor (although he'd not produced that particular story himself), as well as by the creation of a new recurring foe in the Master for season eight. As his third season loomed, Letts found himself considering the return of old enemies as his hook, so summoned the Daleks.

For a series featuring time travel, *Doctor Who* very rarely tackled the consequences of altering history, but it was a topic season nine's opening story *Day of the Daleks* would approach head-on. The Daleks returned to *Doctor Who* in 1972 for the first time in five years. Although grafted on to a pre-existing storyline, their presence gave the adventure's grim future more of a focus. Aping the real-world vogue for summit-conference diplomacy in the ongoing Cold War between the US and the USSR, the story sees a gathering of world leaders come under attack by armed terrorists from the future. In attacking the conference, the freedom-fighter guerrillas set off the very chain of events the diplomats are endeavouring to avoid. The storyline echoed two Harlan Ellison-written episodes of the American 1960s TV series *The Outer Limits* (*Demon With a Glass Hand* and *Soldier*) that went on to inspire James Cameron's film *The Terminator* (1984). In *Day of the Daleks*, the Doctor reworks history (in contradiction to earlier precepts laid down by the series, notably in *The Aztecs*), avoiding a future dominated by the Daleks.

This kind of fascinating time paradox works well in this story, but it is clear why the series avoided such storylines in general. If any action can be changed or undone, it makes all the Doctor's adventures rather pointless, as he can just zap back in time repeatedly until he fixes things to his satisfaction (a key problem with the 1996 Paul McGann-starring TV movie, which has the Doctor's companions restored to life as the TARDIS travels back in time). Of all the show's writers, the one most associated with time-related quirks is the revived, twenty-first-century series' lead writer Steven Moffat, all of whose stories have included some time-twisting element.

Dalek creator Terry Nation had withheld his permission for their use since *Evil of the Daleks* in 1967 (apart from a brief appearance during the Doctor's trial in *The War Games* in 1969). Part of Nation's reason for withholding the Daleks was his long held, but repeatedly thwarted, hope of launching them on American television. After effectively concluding the history of the Daleks with their 'final end' in *Evil of the Daleks*, Nation had approached the BBC about featuring his creations in their own spin-off. This would have focused on the Space Security Service and its agents, as featured in Nation's *The Daleks' Master Plan*. Nation drafted a pilot script, entitled *The Destroyers*, but when his proposal was rejected he turned to the American market, while the BBC opted to remove the Daleks from *Doctor Who*. Having tried without success to interest various US broadcasters, including NBC, by 1972 Nation was ready to allow the return of the Daleks to *Doctor Who*. Disappointed by the script from Louis Marks (who'd written the troubled *Planet of Giants* in the 1960s) for the four episodes of *Day of the Daleks*, Nation insisted he write any future Dalek scripts himself.

Following *The Day of the Daleks*, *Doctor Who* reflected the political reality of 1972 very effectively in *The Curse of Peladon*. The none-too-subtle subtext in a tale about a backward planet's attempt to join a Galactic Federation would have been plain to UK residents watching the TV news debates about the pros and cons of Britain's proposed membership of the EEC, known more informally as the 'common market'. With the Second World War still a recent event to anyone in their early-40s, the idea of seceding political or economic control to a European body proved to be politically controversial. The case for and against membership had long been debated in newspapers and on television. Anyone with a passing interest in the news would have seen the gathering of delegates and backroom machinations of *The Curse of Peladon* as curiously familiar.

Letts again fell back on the gambit of featuring a returning monster, the Ice Warriors (last seen in 1969's *The Seeds of Death*), but with the spin that they would not (as viewers probably expected) be the villains (as Germany had been). The new ambiguity attached to the Ice Warriors reflected the complexity of the European issue: in real life, there were no bad guys or good guys, just differing points of views and ultimate aims.

Having brought back the Daleks and the Ice Warriors from the 1960s version of the series, Letts and Dicks then turned to a setting last exploited in that decade (in *The Underwater Menace* and *Fury from the Deep*): the deep sea. As *Terror of the Autons* had been a remake/sequel to *Spearhead from Space*, so *The Sea Devils* was a companion piece to 1970's *Doctor Who and the Silurians*. Naturally, the Silurians couldn't return, having been blown up by the Brigadier, so returning writer Malcolm Hulke was charged with developing a similar aquatic nemesis and adding the return of the Doctor's newest enemy, the Master.

Having secured the RAF's co-operation in the making of *The Mind of Evil* the previous year (making use of a real-life missile convoy in an action sequence), Letts now turned to the Navy for support on *The Sea Devils*. This resulted in the serial being shot in and around some significant naval assets, heavily boosting the production values. The story is recalled by many thanks to the episode-four cliff-hanger: an army of Sea Devils emerges from the water to menace the Doctor and Jo.

While *The Sea Devils* went for spectacle, exploiting the visual iconography of Britain's newly operating oil rigs, the next story got back to directly reflecting contemporary political concerns in a heavy-handed way. *The Mutants* was a post-colonial parable of the situation in South Africa in the mid-1970s. Far in the future, the Earth Empire is collapsing, but the bureaucrats are still resisting moves towards independence by formerly dependant planets. The racial divide between humans and aliens is played as a form of apartheid, which was at that time the ideology of social control in South Africa. Equally, the story of oppressive colonialism could be seen as applying to British history in India. Overlaid onto this is the emergence of transcendental life on the planet, as the 'mutants' transform from 'mutts' into enlightened super-beings, an ascension the forces of Empire wish to suppress. This aspect of the story was picked up by Salman Rushdie and included in a portion of *The Satanic Verses* dealing with human transformation: 'It seemed to him, as he idled across the channels, that the box was full of freaks: there were mutants – "Mutts" – on *Dr Who*, bizarre creatures who appeared to have been crossbred with different types of industrial machinery… children's television appeared to be extremely populated by humanoid robots and creatures with metamorphic bodies.'

The closing story of season nine was the epic adventure *The Time Monster*, a climax to the ongoing UNIT and Master storylines. Greek mythology is plundered as a backdrop for a battle between the series' two great egos: the Doctor and the Master. *The Time Monster* was able to tap into cheap package holidays taking families to Greece, growing 'new-age' mysticism and a vogue for popular history on TV that had brought the myths of the audience's long-forgotten classical education back to life.

Oddly, the over-the-top nature of this adventure seems more like the over-wrought season finales of the modern version of *Doctor Who* than anything previously attempted. There is an epic scope and ambition to this tale of the Master using experimental technology to raise an ancient God-like monster. UNIT battles menaces from different times, and everyone finds themselves back in ancient, mythological Atlantis, caught up in the legendary city's final days. The climax sees the Doctor and the Master crashing their respective TARDISes in a 'time ram'. As ancient mythological stories often do, *The Time Monster* depends partly on *Doctor Who*'s own mythical narrative past. The story reveals more of the Doctor's own personal history, and something of how the TARDIS works (including hints that it might be organic, even sentient), and functions as a concluding battle between arch enemies (as the planned 'final confrontation' story was not made due to Roger Delgado's untimely death in a car accident in 1973). The celebratory nature of this story, and the show's willingness to invoke its own history, would be developed further in the opening story of the tenth season, *The Three Doctors*.

With an average of over eight million viewers consistently tuning in, Barry Letts had reason to be happy with the direction his *Doctor Who* was heading. The show still suffered from stories that – for broadly economic reasons – were simply too long, running for a total of six weeks. Letts would persevere with the six-episode (and occasional four-episode) story formats for another two years, until his successor Philip Hinchcliffe imposed a 'standard' story length of four 25-minute episodes that would last until the show's lengthy hiatus from 1989.

Faced with launching their fourth season in charge, producer Barry Letts and script editor Terrance Dicks felt they had to come up with a hook to rival the arrival of the new Doctor in *Spearhead from Space*, the Master in *Terror of the Autons* and the long-awaited return of the Daleks in *Day of the Daleks*. 'We always used to try to think of a gimmick to launch each of our seasons,' admitted Dicks. For the first time in *Doctor Who* – apart from the disguised critique of television storytelling in *The Mind Robber* – the programme itself was to become the focus of a televised adventure. Dicks' idea was to bring together the three actors who had played the Doctor, in celebration of the series' own tenth-anniversary year. The justification for this comic-book-style team-up would be a danger that no single Doctor could handle. 'The Time Lords feel the Doctor will be unable to cope, so they bend the rules of time and allow the Doctor to meet and ally with his other selves, thus tripling his powers,' wrote Dicks in a memo to *The Three Doctors*' scriptwriters Bob Baker and Dave Martin.

Both Hartnell and Troughton had quickly agreed to their one-off return, although Hartnell concealed his deteriorating health. The writers suggested that the three Doctors should be brought together to battle a dark figure from the Time Lords' own past: Ohm, a legendary Time Lord lost in an anti-matter world at the heart of a black hole. Ohm was renamed Omega, a founder of Time Lord society, whose stellar manipulations had gained them the power of time travel, but at great cost to himself. Abandoned by the Time Lords, Omega has been trapped for eternity in the black hole and has gone slowly mad. Omega's plan is to trick the Doctor into switching places with him (just like the Master of the Land of Fiction in *The Mind Robber*) so he can escape to the real universe. At the climax, just before he is defeated by the united Doctors, it is revealed that all that remains of the masked and cloaked Omega is his will to survive: his physical being has long since evaporated, leaving nothing but his ego.

Rewrites were necessary to accommodate Hartnell's relatively restricted mobility (he mostly appears on the TARDIS scanner screen) and the action sequences central to the story were redrafted for Troughton and Pertwee alone. The return of Hartnell and Troughton to the series provided a massive publicity boost (and won the programme another *Radio Times* cover, a regular event for each of Letts' season openers). The nostalgia effect, the resultant publicity and the almost 12 million viewers for the final episode were all noted by an occasional floor manager and production unit manager named John Nathan Turner, who would return to the series in a more significant capacity in 1980.

Several key things were changed for the tenth season. The TARDIS console room was redesigned, falling more in line with the original Peter Brachacki design; an attempt at revamping the theme music was tried and abandoned prior to broadcast; and (in story terms) the

Doctor's exile to Earth was officially lifted, freeing the series to return to the classic 'wanderer in time and space' format.

The Three Doctors is full of fantasy physics and scientific buzz-words like black holes, singularity, supernova and anti-matter, torn from the pages of *New Scientist*. None of them is used in any recognisably proper scientific way, despite the production team's claim to have been scouring the pages of science magazines to keep up with the latest developments. Later dubbed 'technobabble' by fans of *Star Trek: The Next Generation*, this meaningless scientific talk is used simply to move the drama forward, introduce Hitchcock-style 'MacGuffins' or to make dialogue sound portentous, dramatic and meaningful.

Following *The Three Doctors*' celebration of the show's own history, Letts and Dicks continued to plough a limited, cleverly self-reflexive furrow with the Robert Holmes-scripted adventure *Carnival of Monsters*. On the surface, this is a comedy that sees the Doctor and Jo caught up in events when the owners of a travelling show come up against a planet's petty bureaucracy. Alien showman Vorg and his assistant Shirna are stopped upon arrival on the planet Inter Minor, as head bureaucrat Pletrac is not satisfied with the safety of their entertainment device, the Miniscope. This device – a banned peepshow that contains miniaturised life forms from many worlds – allows Holmes to satirise television, and specifically *Doctor Who*. Vorg comments that the 'monsters' contained in the scope are 'great favourites with the children' and that the machine is there 'simply to amuse. Nothing serious, nothing political.' Both could be seen as comments on the role of *Doctor Who*, with Letts and Dicks proving the most successful at concealing the 'political' within stories told 'simply to amuse'. Vorg is portrayed as the producer of a show like *Doctor Who*, marshalling his resources to put together the best entertainment he can within political, social, institutional and technological constraints.

The first episode plays as an accomplished BBC period drama, with the Doctor and Jo finding themselves on the ship SS *Bernice* in 1926, only for the second instalment to reveal that they are actually trapped within the Miniscope itself. The next producer of the show, Philip Hinchcliffe, came to realise that utilising the expertise of the BBC design departments to produce what they were good at – period drama sets and costumes – within a *Doctor Who* fantasy story would immeasurably improve his production values. The BBC design departments always had an easier time with a 1926 ship, or Victorian times, than they ever did with the far future, vast space ships or alien cultures.

The satire of television and popular entertainment in *Carnival of Monsters* is wrapped up in the by now standard drama of alien immigrants (literally so, as the Inter Minor bureaucracy blames the violence that erupts on the relaxation of the immigration rules) and a plot to overthrow the government. This is in the background, though, and comes secondary to the Doctor's attempts to have Vorg stop using the 'Scope and release its captives (this story's eco-concern: captive animals). Perhaps it is significant that Letts directed this story himself, as it is a template for the kind of clever writing and issue-raising-in-the-guise-of-entertainment that he and Dicks excelled at.

Originally intended to lead up to the climax of the Doctor/Master relationship/rivalry, the space-opera double bill of *Frontier in Space* and *Planet of the Daleks* proved to be a narrative whose ambitions exceeded the reach of the production's resources. This was a return to the epic storytelling of the mid-1960s, exemplified by *The Daleks' Master Plan*, but Letts and Dicks ensured the script was prepared in advance (necessary thanks to the new production system in operation during the 1970s) rather than being worked out on a week-to-week basis, as was occasionally the case in the 1960s (and certainly with *The Daleks' Master Plan*).

The ambition for *Frontier in Space* was to introduce a new galaxy-spanning setting in each episode, thus giving the entire story a sense of scale and movement that the series rarely attempted (and rarely achieved). Among the individual episodic settings are an Earth space-ship under attack, Earth in the twenty-sixth century, a lunar prison colony, a prison ship operated by the Master, the power base of the Draconian Empire and the planet of the Ogrons (last seen as supporting shock troops in *Day of the Daleks*). Scripted by Malcolm Hulke, the Earth-Draconian conflict is the US-USSR Cold War of the post-Second World War era dressed up as science fiction. Hulke paints the Master as a manipulator who uses the spectre of fear (rather than any real threat) to provoke both declining empires into conflict. Who benefits from such a conflict? The Master's allies are revealed in the final episode of *Frontier in Space* to be none other than the Daleks, an early 1960s-style cliff-hanger continuing directly into the next adventure, *Planet of the Daleks*.

One reason why *Frontier in Space* is so well regarded by *Doctor Who* fans is the design and execution of the Draconians. Make-up designer John Friedlander pioneered a form of mask-making that included the performer's own eyes and mouth that has since become standard. At the time, it was a radical development that allowed the alien, lizard-like, slightly Japanese (culturally, at least) Draconians to come across to viewers as real characters, rather than 'the monster'. Unfortunately, a dispute between the director (Paul Bernard) and the producer about the quality of the Ogron god-monster prop (it resembled a giant testicle!) meant that the ending of the story was fluffed, resulting in a very poor send-off for Delgado's Master. His death in a car crash while on location for a film shoot in Turkey resulted in the abandonment of a final face-off between him and Pertwee's Doctor and was one of the factors that contributed towards Pertwee's eventual decision to leave the show in 1974.

The following story completed the narrative and saw Terry Nation's first return to *Doctor Who* since *The Daleks' Master Plan* in 1966. Unfortunately, Nation ignored any attempts by other writers to progress or develop the Daleks and reverted to a number of themes (not to mention clichés) that he was familiar with. *Planet of the Daleks* features a jungle world called Spiridon upon which a division of militant Thals have arrived, set on wiping out a hidden Dalek army. Nation is still stuck in the *Flash Gordon* serial-style scripting that served *Doctor Who* so well in the 1960s but had been largely abandoned in the 1970s in favour of more political and social depth. Nation's favourite elements featured in the serial, besides the jungle setting, included killer plants (*Mission to the Unknown/The Daleks' Master Plan*), invisible monsters, heroes hiding inside Dalek casings, bacterial weapons, and the standby of all lazy dramatists: a countdown. Nation's scripting deficiencies meant that *Planet of the Daleks* was a throwback to the basic *Boy's Own* adventure-serial style, and that Letts' and Dicks' trademark political and social commentary was missing. They'd more than make up for that lack in the next story, however: the conclusion of *Doctor Who*'s tenth-anniversary year.

For the third year in a row, producer Barry Letts brought writer Robert Sloman in to craft a season finale to Letts' own brief. Aware of the political and social commentary running through the series, Letts decided to finish the year with a full-on eco-parable. Environmental concerns had featured in a variety of *Doctor Who* stories, but *The Green Death* would be the first to put them front and centre. Sloman was charged with writing out companion Jo Grant after three years, as Katy Manning wanted to leave. This was yet another factor in Pertwee's developing resolve to depart at the end of the following year (his fifth, making him the longest-running Doctor up to that time).

Growing awareness of environmental issues, especially among the young, could not be ignored by the media, especially after the formation of Friends of the Earth in 1969 and Greenpeace in 1971. These campaigning groups were beginning to win airtime and the expression of pro-environmental, anti-business views was becoming commonplace. Rachel Carson's book *Silent Spring* (1962) tackled the overuse of pesticides in agriculture (and may have influenced *Planet of Giants*) and explored issues of environmental poisons, topics echoed in *The Green Death*. The book was controversial, but led to the banning of DDT and other pesticides and a growing public awareness of environmental issues.

A mysterious death in a disused mine in South Wales sees the Doctor and UNIT called in. Toxic waste products have been pumped into the mine by Global Chemicals, rather than being disposed of properly. The resulting green goo is the cause of death, but it has had a wider environmental impact, mutating local insects to produce giant, man-eating maggots and super-sized flies. The villains are the men-in-suits who run Global Chemicals, who are in turn being led astray by their mad computer called BOSS. The heroes (besides the Doctor, Jo and UNIT) are the inhabitants of the 'Nut Hutch', a local environmental group seemingly staffed by hippie drop-outs and led by Professor Cliff Jones (Stewart Bevan), a love-interest figure for the departing Jo Grant (Bevan was Manning's real-life, off-screen boyfriend at the time).

It may have been a fairly simple depiction of some big issues, but for popular television (the first episode attracted 9.2 million viewers, while an omnibus Christmas repeat saw 10.4 million tune in) aimed at a young audience in 1973, this was radical political and social drama disguised (barely) as adventure fiction. It was a big step forward from the disposable space adventure serials of a decade before, like Terry Nation's *The Keys of Marinus*.

Letts had no regrets about the overtly serious content he was building into *Doctor Who*. He wrote in *Dreamwatch* magazine in 2004: 'One of the first things I did when I took over as producer was to ask Audience Research for a breakdown of the *Doctor Who* audience – and I discovered that 58 per cent of it was over the age of 15. In other words, the majority of our viewers were adults. Yet that also meant that 42 per cent were children of all ages, the children that the programme was aimed at from the start, and we certainly couldn't let them down.' This audience breakdown showed Letts that, while he had to make the series attractive to younger viewers, the majority of the audience had grown up with *Doctor Who*, having been five years old or above when it had begun a decade before in 1963.

'We tried to offer stories on several different levels,' Letts wrote. 'First and foremost, we wanted good drama, solidly based on character; secondly, a fascinating science fiction idea and/or a theme with relevance to a real issue (such as the mining corporation versus the settlers in *Colony in Space*, or the ecological background of *The Green Death*); thirdly, a cracking action adventure; and lastly, scary bug-eyed monsters for the younger children. Maybe we went too far sometimes, but this is one of the core features of *Doctor Who*.'

The Green Death was perhaps the pinnacle of *Doctor Who*'s political and social commentary in the 1970s. Many more stories would contain a similar subtext, but never again would it be so overt, so persuasive and so dramatically entertaining. Even though it is six episodes long, in terms of successfully melding a contemporary issue or concern with engaging character-driven drama and monstrous scares, few *Doctor Who* stories do it as well and as accessibly as *The Green Death*.

While *Doctor Who*'s eleventh season consolidated much of the work done by Letts and Dicks during the early 1970s, it also featured many superficial changes that would be carried over into the Tom Baker period. Prime among the changes was the arrival of a new companion: feminist journalist Sarah Jane Smith (Elisabeth Sladen). The character was devised as a more savvy version of Jo Grant, smarter and more inquisitive and independent, but not as intelligent as Liz Shaw, so no threat to the Doctor. The stories still required an audience-viewpoint character to ask the questions that would allow the Doctor to deliver the story's exposition. Another very visible change was a new, dramatic title sequence and logo, the first since the series' debut in colour in 1970. A similar 'time tunnel' sequence, with a change of the lead character's face, would survive until 1980.

Opening the season was *The Time Warrior*, in which Linx – a Sontaran warrior trapped when he crash lands in the Middle Ages – uses his technology to kidnap contemporary scientists to help repair his ship and hasten his escape. This story revived the idea of tales set in the past and featuring aliens and their technology (last seen in 1967's *The Abominable Snowman*). Pioneered in *The Time Meddler* back in 1965, this would now become a standard storytelling component of the show. This technique addressed one of the BBC's design weaknesses by putting the (usually) well-designed alien creature in the kind of period setting the BBC excelled at. The story also allowed the Doctor to deliver a classic line that summed up the approach of the series. Asked by Sarah if he's 'serious' about being a Time Lord with a time-travelling police box, the Doctor replies: 'About what I do, yes. Not necessarily the way that I do it.' Pertwee's debut tale, *Spearhead from Space*, had introduced the idea that the alien Doctor had two hearts. Similarly, the first story of Pertwee's final season introduced another important mythological innovation by naming the Doctor's home planet: Gallifrey.

In *The Time Warrior*, the position Linx finds himself in parallels that of the Doctor: he's an alien scientific advisor to a 'military' group. The application of advanced technology in a historical setting drew on the real-life situation early in the Vietnam war where the superpowers would help one side or the other with weaponry and advice, without becoming directly involved (already depicted in the 1968 *Star Trek* episode *A Private Little War* – *Star Trek* having begun its initial run on UK television in between Troughton's final story and Jon Pertwee's debut.)

The political commentary in the following story, *Invasion of the Dinosaurs*, was a lot more substantial than that of *The Time Warrior*.

Following the eco-environmental message of *The Green Death*, Malcolm Hulke once again flexed his agit-prop muscles under the guise of a teatime adventure. The Doctor and Sarah return to the present, only to discover London deserted. The city has been evacuated (as ever, *Doctor Who* draws on Second World War iconography) due to the appearance of prehistoric dinosaurs! The villains are radical environmentalists intending to use a time machine to return Earth to its unspoilt state, as it was before the effects of technology and pollution. Only a select few will survive Operation Golden Age.

Rather than an alien invasion, the story presents a group of driven idealists as the 'threat of the week', while still delivering the requisite serial thrills with the arrival of various (unfortunately unconvincing) dinosaurs on the streets of London. *Doctor Who* had featured scientific-conspiracy storylines before (notably in *The Ambassadors of Death*). This conspiracy tale stretched all the way to the government (through the minister, Grover) and involved the army (a dramatic conflict personalised as UNIT's own Mike Yates – series semi-regular Richard Franklin – is revealed to be in on the conspiracy following his experiences during *The Green Death*). Fear of an armed takeover of Britain was a political reality in the UK in the 1970s, reflecting concerns about the possible actions of Labour in government. Labour were returned to power in February 1974, just as the last episodes of *Invasion of the Dinosaurs* were being transmitted. The involvement of Mike Yates on the 'wrong' side of the conspiracy demonstrated the show's new interest in longer-term character development (anticipating the way that much television drama is now made). Rarely in *Doctor Who* had characterisation of minor supporting characters been consistent (the Brigadier having suffered some odd character swings through the years). Very few were dealt with in anything more than a perfunctory manner, even when the series was as grounded in an ensemble group as it was in the first half of the 1970s.

Hulke concluded *Invasion of the Dinosaurs* by allowing the Doctor to deliver a speech backing the aims of Operation Golden Age, while condemning their methods. It was an environmental plea made directly to viewers, via a comment to the Brigadier, and one that appears years ahead of its time: 'At least [they] realised the dangers this planet of yours is in, Brigadier. The danger of it becoming one vast garbage dump, inhabited only by rats... It's not the oil and the filth and the poisonous chemicals that are the real cause of pollution, Brigadier. It's simply greed.' It was an unusually bald, uncompromising statement for the show to make, and one that probably struck a chord with younger viewers. *Invasion of the Dinosaurs* simultaneously appealed to the 1960s idealists who'd seen their hoped-for advancements dissipate in the 1970s and to children (of all ages) who think dinosaurs are 'cool'.

The boldness of *Doctor Who* in foregrounding such obvious political content at this time may have been a result of the end-of-an-era feel. During the broadcast of *Invasion of the Dinosaurs* in February 1974, Jon Pertwee announced he'd be hanging up his frilly shirts and velvet capes and handing the keys to the TARDIS to a new occupant. Three reasons were eventually cited for his departure: he'd allegedly been refused a requested raise in his fee by the BBC; he wanted to move on to new acting challenges; and he felt that, with the death of Roger Delgado and the departure of Katy Manning, his *Doctor Who* team was disintegrating around him. Both Barry Letts and Terrance Dicks then announced their intention to also move on to pastures new with the end of the eleventh season. They had tried to leave two years previously, after *The Time Monster*, but the BBC had persuaded them to continue, afraid that breaking up the team would harm the success of the show (a situation later echoed in the behind-the-scenes story of the latest revival of *Doctor Who*). Terrance Dicks wittily commented that '*Doctor Who* is the only prison where time gets added on for good behaviour!'

The third annual outing for the Daleks (following *Day of the Daleks* and *Planet of the Daleks*) arrived in Pertwee's final season in the form of Terry Nation's *Death to the Daleks* and plunged the programme back once again from the relative sophistication of its 1970s scripts to its 1960s *Flash Gordon*-style serial origins, the only mode of scripting *Doctor Who* that Nation seemed comfortable with. The Doctor arrives on the planet Exxilon where a sentient city is draining power from everything (including the TARDIS and a Dalek expeditionary force). While the opening TARDIS power-cut scene might have mirrored the genuine power cuts caused in the UK by the mid-1970s energy crisis, Nation's script quickly descends into sub-Eric Von Daniken code breaking as the Doctor and local 'primitive' Bellal make their way to the centre of the city.

By this stage, it was clear that the Daleks had been mishandled in their 1970s appearances, largely due to the show's reliance on creator Terry Nation to script for them following *Day of the Daleks*. His repeated reuse of old ideas was painfully obvious, as was the lack of imagination brought to the Dalek serials by their respective directors. It wouldn't be until the 1980s and the arrival of director Graeme Harper that the Daleks would get the kind of inventive visual direction they'd long deserved.

Barry Letts and Terrance Dicks had always been open to writers using allegory (some subtle, some not) in *Doctor Who* to tackle contemporary social and political issues. It gave the series some heft, above and beyond its status as Saturday entertainment and, no doubt, made it more interesting to work on. Having dealt with topics such as environmentalism (*Doctor Who and the Silurians*, *The Sea Devils*, *The Green Death*, *Invasion of the Dinosaurs*), the end of colonialism (*The Colony in Space*, *The Mutants*), the nature of television itself and specifically *Doctor Who*'s own history and function (*Carnival of Monsters*, *The Three Doctors*), the duo were running out of topics as their time on the show drew to a close.

Where *The Curse of Peladon* had featured an allegory for the UK's entry into the EEC, the sequel story *The Monster of Peladon* dealt directly with UK industrial relations, particularly the miners' strikes of 1972 and 1974. Set 50 years later, the Doctor returns to Peladon with Sarah to find the planet in turmoil. The Federation, of which Peladon is a part, is at war with Galaxy 5 and is dependent on Peladon's reserves of trisilicate. Those who mine it, however, are refusing to adopt 'modern' technological working practices, while protesting that they are not earning enough 'to feed our families'. The roles of the moderates and radicals within the planet's various factions mirror those of the principals involved in the bitter real-life mining dispute of 1972, as astute viewers would have recognised.

This political content was (lightly) disguised under the same cod-medieval fantasy trappings as seen in *The Curse of Peladon*. The castle settings and faux-*Lord of the Rings*-style court served as the setting for a space opera, featuring a similar menagerie of glam-rock alien delegates and a mining class who uniformly sport badger hair-styles. It may not have featured the most convincing alien society ever created, but *The Monster of Peladon* reflected the culture of the mid-1970s as much in its mise-en-scène as in its politics. The big boots, the even bigger hair and the out-of-control glitter make-up reflected a typical night out in a 1970s disco.

This mining melodrama led into Pertwee's final story, *Planet of the Spiders*. Barry Letts – himself a Buddhist – took the opportunity to explore a subject little touched upon in his five years in charge of the show: religion. Conceived by Letts (and written, as was traditional now for the final story in a season, by Robert Sloman), *Planet of the Spiders* was a Buddhist parable that tackled the Doctor's repeatedly displayed thirst for knowledge. The upcoming regeneration offered Letts the chance to have the Doctor learn a hard lesson in the process of, essentially, losing one of his lives.

Following *The Green Death* and *Invasion of the Dinosaurs*, *Planet of the Spiders* builds on the character development of Mike Yates.

Sarah is drawn by Yates into investigating a rural meditation centre where he has been recuperating. The residents have made contact with an alien force that manifests on Earth as over-sized spiders that can possess humans by leaping on their backs (a fate that befalls Sarah). After helping the humanoid inhabitants to try and overthrow their spider masters, the Doctor returns to the planet Metebelis 3 from where he'd previously stolen a powerful crystal (representing his quest for knowledge). He confronts the Great One (the spider god) and loses his life due to excessive radiation. The Doctor has to sacrifice his ego (his third persona) to make up for past mistakes and to secure the future (his fourth persona). 'It is wrong to have a greed for knowledge,' said Letts. 'Greed presupposes a preoccupation with the self, the ego. We know that in the beginning the Doctor stole a TARDIS to satisfy his greed for knowledge, and in *The Green Death* he steals one of the [Metebelis 3] blue crystals for precisely the same reason. He is willing to allow himself to be destroyed, the false ego being destroyed to find the real Self. He knows he will be destroyed, but knows also that he will be regenerated.'

The *Doctor Who* concept of regeneration was filtered through Letts' Buddhist philosophy in *Planet of the Spiders*. The meditation retreat is run by Abbot K'anpo Rinpoche and his deputy Cho-Je. K'anpo is revealed to be a Time Lord mentor of the Doctor. He is killed while protecting Yates from attack by the spider-controlled residents. In death, K'anpo is reborn as Cho-Je, his own future self. At the climax, K'anpo reappears to aid the Doctor's regeneration. 'The old man is destroyed and the new man is regenerated,' explained Letts. 'Yes, it was all a quite deliberate parallel.' As if to emphasise his attachment to the tale, Letts not only devised the storyline, he also directed the six-episode serial.

It is surprising that *Doctor Who* had not tackled religion in any serious way (while *Star Trek* seemed to deal with some alien pretending to be one god or another every other week). It is fitting, though, that the Pertwee era should have come to an end in a celebration of that most 1970s of all religious philosophies, Buddhism, which had grown in prominence (or, at least, in media coverage) in the West since the late-1960s. It seems appropriate, after half a decade spent helping UNIT defend the Earth from threats coming from 'out there', that the Third Doctor should end his time looking inward.

Layered on top of the Buddhist parable is an examination of psychic powers, another 1970s social topic. The opening episode sees the Doctor investigating psychic powers and referring obliquely to notorious 1970s spoon bender Uri Geller. This leads into the adventure with the mind-controlling spiders, whose modus operandi is through mental domination of already wicked or weak people.

Planet of the Spiders was Barry Letts' attempt to sum up his approach to *Doctor Who*. Reflecting his leading man's interest in fast-moving vehicles, he indulges Pertwee with a 12-minute chase scene in episode two featuring a variety of vehicles on land, at sea and in the air. Each of the long-running team of characters has significant character moments, as if to draw a line under their participation (although some would return, notably Sarah and the Brigadier). The wrapping up of the character of the Third Doctor secured the concept of regeneration as central to the series, and is given a name for the first time. The first change of actor was narratively mysterious, referred to simply as a 'renewal'. Troughton's Second Doctor doesn't go to any great lengths to explain the change, except to connect the process to the TARDIS. The then script editor Gerry Davis even believed the change to be akin to that featured in Robert Louis Stevenson's *The Strange Tale of Dr Jekyll and Mr Hyde*. The next change is similarly provoked by a crisis, brought on by the Time Lords who punish the Doctor (yet still finding his existence in the universe to be of use to themselves). The change of physical appearance is part of this punishment.

Although mention of the Time Lords had been a common factor

throughout the early-to-mid-1970s (especially with the involvement of the Master), little mention had been made of regeneration until *Planet of the Spiders* required another real-world change of actor. It was only then, as a fourth leading actor was sought for *Doctor Who*, that the concept of regeneration really took hold, both in the programme and with the public at large. The use of the term 'regeneration' to describe the process of change that the Doctor undergoes is in keeping with Letts' religious/philosophical take on the series. He felt it necessary to not only explain to viewers afresh about the Doctor's ability to change (it had been five years since the last such occurrence), but also the need to codify the process, give it a name and normalise it for future producers (who'd be free to follow his template or not).

During the early-to-mid-1970s, under producer Barry Letts and script editor Terrance Dicks, and with Jon Pertwee as the title character, *Doctor Who* had undergone significant change and consolidation. It had shown itself capable of flexible narrative strategies that could deliver compelling action-adventure storylines aimed at a young, Saturday-early-evening audience, while still offering up complex takes on contemporary political and social issues. The technology of television production had changed and progressed in this time, and *Doctor Who* had proven itself to be (if not always successfully) at the forefront of such technological exploration, partly due to Letts' own enthusiasm and willingness to experiment. As always with *Doctor Who*, the only constant was change and the changes coming in the mid-to-late-1970s would be some of the most significant in the series' history.

4. GOTHIC THRILLS

The mid-1970s saw Doctor Who regenerate in more ways than one. Starting in December 1974, the Doctor had a new face in the shape of little-known Tom Baker, but the changes went deeper than that. Incoming producer Philip Hinchcliffe (previously not associated with the programme) and script editor Robert Holmes (a writer on the show since 1968's *The Krotons*) developed new storytelling strategies in a concerted effort to distance their *Doctor Who* from the (largely) Earthbound action-adventure template the series had adopted most recently. Their partnership was to be as strong as that of Letts and Dicks, and would move the show in new creative directions.

'I had the good sense to realise that I needed to do a lot of research and listen to a lot of people who knew what they were talking about,' admitted Hinchcliffe, then a young producer coming to his first job, having previously been a writer (on *Crossroads*, amongst other shows) and script editor, knowing little about *Doctor Who*. 'I think I brought a fresh outlook and new ideas to it, but I tried to soak up the required technical knowledge.'

Doctor Who had been a consistent ratings success throughout the early 1970s, increasing the audience from an average of seven million in 1970 to almost nine million by the time Letts, Dicks and Pertwee departed. Their politically and socially engaged fantasy-drama version of *Doctor Who* struck a chord with the viewing public. Despite pressure to maintain this level of success, it was in the nature of Hinchcliffe's job that he should reformat the series with the arrival of a new Doctor. After five years, the UNIT 'family' and the largely Earthbound settings would be abandoned, with a move away from engagement with real-world events in favour of a lively strand of drama drawn from classic gothic tales.

Letts and Dicks oversaw the first Tom Baker story, with Hinchcliffe shadowing them. *Robot* was a remake of *King Kong*, written by Dicks almost as a 'greatest hits' compilation of 'best *Doctor Who* bits', as a new lead actor had not been found when it was written. Ian Marter had been brought in to play the 'strong-arm' companion (a role fulfilled previously by teacher Ian Chesterton and astronaut Steven Taylor), in case an older actor was cast (as Letts favoured). The casting of a fit, 40-year-old Tom Baker as the Fourth Doctor made Marter's role superfluous, although his Dr Harry Sullivan character remained for the next year or so.

As Letts had believed five years previously, Hinchcliffe felt that the audience for the now 12-year-old show had grown up and were now teenagers through to students. 'The audience was evolving,' Hinchcliffe explained. 'I began to get letters from university students. I thought, there's something going on with the audience. They're not just the intelligent 12-year-old and the little six-year-old hiding behind the sofa: everybody else is watching. Here was an opportunity to take the show into a more adult area without losing its identity as a family show. We wanted it to work for the four- or five-year-old, for the 12-year-old, for the older member of the audience, not just the mums and dads. Clearly, students were beginning to tune in to it.'

Season 12 saw a period of renewal on the show. While *Robot* was a *Doctor-Who*-by-numbers adventure, it still found some space for a little political allegory in the midst of the giant-robot-as-King-Kong spectacle. The villains represented the rise of the technocracy, a political philosophy gaining currency in the 1970s. Faced with rising pollution and power cuts caused by an energy crisis, one strand of political thought (espoused by Miss Winters and her Scientific Reform Society) suggested that society and individual lifestyles should be managed along logical lines, a form of social control that amounted to fascism by another name (the Daleks would approve). Sarah Jane Smith was written as a combination of fearless reporter Lois Lane (her investigations uncover the plot) and Fay Wray (as the object of the Robot's attentions at the climax). Dicks' script also played with cinematic robot iconography. The title robot looks back to giant, out-of-control movie robots of the past, like the (semi-organic) *Colossus of New York* (1958), Tobor in *Tobor the Great* (1954) and space sentinel Gort from *The Day the Earth Stood Still* (1951). It also anticipates a host of late-1970s popular-culture androids, from *Star Wars*' C-3PO to UK sitcom star Metal Mickey, and Twiki in *Buck Rogers in the 25th Century*, ITV's much-vaunted, bought-in 1980s rival to *Doctor Who*, and even *Doctor Who*'s own K-9.

It was only with Baker's second story that Hinchcliffe's blueprint for a radical new approach to the series became clear. Hinchcliffe had a distinctive approach to storytelling. 'I thought there was a way we could take the "naffness" out. Early on, we took some very basic decisions about taking these stories seriously. We were going to tell stories really tightly, make them as compelling as we could, ramp up the suspense and cliff-hangers and generally make it work in terms of good adventurous storytelling.'

Hinchcliffe's period on the show is described as 'gothic', an appropriate label given the period's reliance on both the 'horror' side of gothic entertainment, as well as the literary aspect of the genre's origins. 'It evolved naturally. I don't think we ever used the term "gothic",' noted Hinchcliffe. 'There were about three shows in early draft script form that [script editor] Bob Holmes had. I had the most influence on *The Ark in Space*. If you look at *The Ark in Space*, it is exactly the same concept as the movie *Alien* (1979). Robert [Holmes] had a leaning towards that kind of gothic thing [and] so did I, up to a point. I don't think we consciously put seasons together that would add up to that. We looked at every story idea on its merits.'

The Ark in Space featured the eruption of 'body horror' into *Doctor Who*, capturing the 'Me' generation's inward-looking self-absorption and obsession with body image and disease, especially uncontrollable diseases like cancer. Thirty years after the Second World War, an entire generation had grown to adulthood in relative peace and prosperity. With little in the way of outward threat (the Cold War was constantly looming, but rather abstract and certainly not personal), affluent societies (like that in California) turned inwards. Plastic surgery and modern dentistry 'improved' appearance, but, despite high-tech health care, some diseases could not be conquered, like various cancers. The body could still turn against someone, no matter how rich they were. The fear of disease and transformation is even more basic than that, but the mid-1970s context of *The Ark in Space* gave the story an additional resonance. Movies at the time were dealing with similar fears of loss of control over the body, whether through demonic pregnancy in *Rosemary's Baby* (1968), or loss of identity in *The Stepford Wives* (1975) and *Invasion of the Body Snatchers* (1978). More pertinently, the SF thrills of *The Fly* (1958), with its transformation of a scientist into an insect, were also directly echoed.

Finding themselves adrift on a space station in the far future, the Doctor, Sarah and Harry have to save the remnants of mankind (who've been hibernating to escape a ravaged Earth) from infestation by the Wirrn. The space-borne, wasp-like Wirrn reproduce by laying eggs in other species (hence Hinchcliffe's feeling that Ridley Scott's 1979 movie *Alien* bears a passing resemblance), but they can also transform other species into Wirrn hybrids (as happens to Noah, leader of the station) and absorb their knowledge. It's a fantastic premise for an alien species, mostly well realised by the designers, and supported by the cast taking the threat seriously, in line with Hinchcliffe's 'new seriousness' approach. The audience clearly liked this less-jokey approach to the show, with 13.6 million switching on for episode two, surpassing the series' previous highest-rated episode (episode one of the imaginative Hartnell adventure *The Web Planet*, where 13.5 million viewers tuned in for an adventure that coincidentally featured several complex alien life-cycles!).

Outgoing producer Barry Letts had developed the remaining stories of season 12, so Hinchcliffe worked with the material he inherited. Although none of the other adventures would feature his 'gothic' take to the same extent as *The Ark in Space*, he was able to have some input into the feel of *Genesis of the Daleks*, the story that revived the much-maligned Daleks and introduced the character of Davros, their mad-scientist creator. Returning monsters were very much part of Letts' plan for the new Doctor's first season, so *The Ark in Space* was followed by a two-part rematch between the Doctor and the Sontarans, *The Sontaran Experiment*. Slight though this tale was, it still managed to pack in commentary on the ethics of torture, as Sontaran commander Styre experiments on captured humans in a post-apocalyptic landscape. The setting – although shot on location on Dartmoor – was supposed to be a futuristic London reclaimed by nature, a riff on the disaster fiction of JG Ballard.

However, it was the Daleks who were to make the biggest impact in the 1975 series. After years of low-rent appearances in poor scripts written by their creator Terry Nation in the style of 1960s cliff-hanger serials, they were in serious need of reinvention. Nation's inspiration was to explore their origins, something only hinted at in 1963. Audiences had supposedly seen their 'final end' in 1967's *The Evil of the Daleks*, but had never been privy to their creation. In pursuit of this, Nation again fell back on the tried-and-tested allegories he was comfortable with. *Genesis of the Daleks* presents two armed camps

– the Thals and the Kaleds – fighting a war of attrition across the wastelands of the planet Skaro. Most of the story explores the Kaled struggle for survival, and the environment presented is akin to that of Hitler's bunker in the final days of the Second World War. Nation presents a science-fiction take on Hitler's Nazi fantasies of genetic purity, as Kaled chief scientist Davros struggles to find a way of preserving his people, aware that time is running out for the whole planet. Davros is a scarred humanoid figure locked into a mobile survival unit whose bottom half resembles a classic Dalek chassis. He has created a 'travel machine', modelled after his own high-tech wheelchair, to contain the genetically re-engineered form he sees his own people eventually becoming. These future Kaleds are already being engineered by Davros himself, in anticipation of nature.

The Time Lords send the Doctor and his companions, Sarah and Harry, to Skaro, with instructions to destroy the Daleks at their creation. Their aim is to avert the death and destruction the Daleks will cause, or to at least affect their genetic development, resulting in less aggressive creatures. With no choice but to get involved, the Doctor is soon engaged in a variety of riveting ethical debates with Davros. It's unclear how much of the finished script was Nation's and how much was due to extensive rewriting by script editor Robert Holmes, but *Genesis of the Daleks* was a huge improvement over Nation's scripts for the Pertwee-period Dalek adventures. Holmes and Hinchcliffe rehabilitated the Daleks, lifting them to a new metaphorical level at a time in Britain when the pseudo-fascist National Front was on the rise. To present debates about eugenics, genetic engineering, racial purity and race survival to peak BBC1 audiences in the mid-1970s was brave, but it succeeded admirably with the public. *Genesis of the Daleks* has become one of the most clearly recalled and oft repeated (the two may not be unrelated) of all *Doctor Who* serials.

Although there are elements of the *Frankenstein* story (Davros creates the Daleks in his own image, only to have them turn on him as their programming refuses to allow them to recognise any other being as superior to them), the story tackles other deep-seated issues. Faced with the opportunity of destroying the Daleks outright – all he has to do is touch two wires together to detonate explosives in the Dalek embryo chamber – the Doctor hesitates. 'Have I the right?' he asks himself, fearing that destroying the Daleks in this way makes him just the same as them, a perpetrator of genocide ('If I kill... wipe out a whole intelligent life form, then I become like them. I'd be no better than the Daleks.') This is a distillation of the philosophical question of the 'problem of evil': how can the existence of God be reconciled with the existence of evil and suffering in the world? For a popular drama, primarily aimed at children and reaching over 13 million viewers, to tackle such a weighty topic was unusual.

In the news at almost the exact time of *Genesis of the Daleks*' first broadcast, the tragedy of Cambodia and the Pol Pot Khmer Rouge regime of the mid-1970s showed that such fascism wasn't a thing of the past. Mass extermination of perceived enemies was a key Khmer Rouge tool, a policy echoed in the Daleks' ultimate practices. The Doctor, however, sees a bigger picture: 'Many enemies will become allies because of the Daleks.' In the end, he adopts a liberal compromise, setting Dalek development back by a thousand years.

When *Doctor Who* returned to television in 2005, an early episode, entitled *Dalek*, saw the Daleks recreated once more as a threat to be feared by the Doctor and the audience. Showrunner Russell T Davies referred back to *Genesis of the Daleks* as the first move in the 'Time War', an off-screen conflict primarily between the Time Lords and the Daleks that forms the back-story to the new series. This retrospective continuity (known in fan circles as 'retcon', see chapter six), makes *Genesis of the Daleks* an even more important story to the series' narrative history.

The season concluded with *Revenge of the Cybermen*, another returning old monster with a script written by their co-creator Gerry

Davis (heavily reworked by script editor Holmes). This, however, lacked the dramatic reinvention accorded the Daleks, simply presenting the Cybermen as an almost generic robotic threat, attempting to wipe out Voga, a planet rich in gold content, as gold is deadly to the Cybermen. In a Letts-inspired, cost-cutting exercise, *Revenge of the Cybermen* was filmed immediately after, and on the same space-station sets as *The Ark in Space*, with the narrative set on the same station at a different point in time. This was a cleverly economical use of resources, one not often repeated (but used by the new series producers, both on the 2005 series, with the space-station setting of *The Long Game* and *Bad Wolf*, and in the 2006 series, again in episodes featuring the Cybermen, where mid-season two-parter *The Age of Steel/Rise of the Cybermen* was shot back-to-back with season finale *Army of Ghosts/Doomsday*).

This first season overseen by Philip Hinchcliffe and Robert Holmes provided clear signposts of the direction the show would be taking. Although much of the material and approach had, of necessity, been inherited, the new team had put enough of their individual stamp on *Doctor Who* to make it distinct from the preceding Jon Pertwee period. *The Ark in Space* was a clear marker of the gothic direction in which Hinchcliffe and Holmes would take the show, while *Genesis of the Daleks* showed how their 'serious' approach to the drama, and the themes it could contain, would pay off in terms of audience popularity. The average audience for the season was 11.5 million, a definite step forward from the first five years of the 1970s.

It was with the following season, the show's thirteenth, that Hinchcliffe and Holmes' modus operandi became clear: literary pastiche wrapped in B-movie homage. This was a new spin on the *Doctor Who* formula and gave fresh life to a show that was heading towards a decade and a half on air. 'We were led sometimes to revisit some of the motifs that had worked in the past [in literature], but we wanted to reinterpret them through the format of *Doctor Who*,' explained Hinchcliffe.

The season 13 opener had been intended to close-out the previous season, but was held over as the debut of the series was moved to August from its traditional New Year slot. *Terror of the Zygons* saw the final appearance of the true UNIT 'family', with both the Brigadier and Harry Sullivan making their final appearances as regulars (Harry briefly returns, after a fashion, in the mid-season *The Android Invasion*). The 'Doctor-travelling-with-single-female-companion' model, as used by Letts, returns here, cementing Elisabeth Sladen's Sarah Jane Smith as one of the series' most fondly remembered companions (and the only one to make multiple comebacks outside of anniversary celebration stories).

With its Scottish setting and guest appearance by the Loch Ness monster (a rather poorly realised puppet standing in for a supposedly remote-controlled alien robot), *Terror of the Zygons* relates directly to the 1970s outbreak of Nessie monster sightings, a perennial happening since the first twentieth-century sighting in 1933. Although oil rigs feature in the opening of the story, the then-ongoing nationalist political battles over 'Scotland's oil' only feature in passing in early dialogue. Holmes and Hinchcliffe were inspired by loss-of-identity Hollywood B-movies from the 1950s like *Invasion of the Body Snatchers* (1956) and *I Married a Monster from Outer Space* (1958). The invading Zygons (giant, orange, embryo-like creatures who made a huge visual impact, but have yet to recur onscreen) are shape-shifters, able to impersonate anyone. Relocating this body-snatching theme to the Scottish Highlands allowed writer Robert Banks Stewart to ally the theme to Scottish myths and legends like that of the Selkie (supernatural creatures able to transform from seals to humans).

There was another Scottish connection in the second story of the season. Robert Louis Stevenson's *The Strange Tale of Dr Jekyll and Mr Hyde* and the 1956 film *Forbidden Planet* (by way of Shakespeare's

The Tempest) provided the literary and pop-culture inspirations for *Planet of Evil*. Writer Louis Marks (who'd previously scripted environmental-thriller story *Planet of Giants* in 1964) adapted Professor Jim Lovelock's Gaia hypothesis (that sees the Earth as a self-regulating organic system) to create a planet that is fundamentally evil. However, this intention is lost in the realisation of the story, which focuses more on Professor Sorenson's split personality and the were-wolf-horror aspects of the plot than on any abstract notion. An expedition to the planet Zeta Minor finds a mysterious black pool: a gateway to an anti-matter universe. Attempting to harness the power of the anti-matter (a critique of the damage done by mineral exploitation to Earth), the expedition members are either killed or transformed. The monsters, supposedly protecting the planet from the invaders, are invisible and are only seen when struck by weapons fire. The realisation of the creature is like that in *Forbidden Planet*, while the Shakespearean connection comes from *The Tempest*.

The literary source in the case of *Pyramids of Mars* was Bram Stoker's 1903 novel *The Jewel of the Seven Stars* – about an archaeologist's attempt to revive an ancient mummy – mixed with a heavy dose of Von Daniken. Just as relevant, and perhaps fresh in the audience's mind, was the 1972 UK 'Treasures of Tutankhamun' exhibition that revived memories of the 'cursed' Howard Carter expedition of 1922. Over 1.5 million people visited the British Museum and the display of artefacts was a cultural sensation in the press. In addition, Robert Holmes (who scripted this serial under a pseudonym) was a fan of Hammer movies from 20 years previously (and would have been aware of the Universal mummy movies of the 1930s featuring Boris Karloff). 'Bob liked to rework some of the old themes of Sax Rohmer [Fu Manchu]-type stuff and some of the more gothic pool of material that provided action-adventure stuff,' admitted Hinchcliffe.

Pyramids of Mars drew on the myths of the Egyptian gods and provided a scientific-seeming overlay to make the whole thing science fiction, a regular gambit during the Hinchcliffe period. Set in 1911, the story sees trapped alien God Sutekh manipulate (from his prison on Mars) Egyptologist Marcus Scarman. He instructs Scarman to construct a missile (with his robotic, mummy-like helpers) that can destroy the beacon on Mars that his fellow Osirans used to entrap him centuries ago. The setting allowed the BBC design teams to excel once again with the period-drama trappings of the locations, while the actual pyramid is a rather bland corridors-and-puzzles set-up, as last seen in *Death to the Daleks*.

Hinchcliffe said of *Pyramids of Mars*: 'It's a historical show, but imaginative in the way that it combines the science-fictional element with the historical situation. There's some very nice characterisation and some very nice acting, and a bit of humour in it. It did seem to combine everything that Bob and I were trying to do. It's a typical 'good one' from us. I think [our stories have] got the qualities of a costume drama because people are very good at doing that at the BBC, but I think the stories were very different. We weren't trying to be educational in any way!'

Despite an atmospheric opening set in a seemingly deserted English village, Terry Nation's script for the next story, *The Android Invasion*, is a muddled affair that reverts to standard Earth invasion and body snatching doubles before the end. The initial set-up is intriguing, however, even if its main cultural source appears to be Nation's own post-apocalypse series, *Survivors* (1975–77). The 'duplicate village' idea was one from spy fiction (or real-life myths about foreign spies), where they were used for training purposes to familiarise agents with environments they'd be invading. The same training function is served by the village the Doctor and Sarah land in. The android part of the invasion came from popular 1970s movies like *Westworld* (1973) and *The Stepford Wives* (1975, based on the 1972 novel), which director Barry Letts directly references visually more than once. Notable is the cliff-hanger to episode two in which the duplicate Sarah's face falls off, revealing her robotic innards. It's a minor, confused tale that serves simply as a breather before the gothic double bill that closed out the thirteenth season of *Doctor Who*.

Mary Shelley's Frankenstein, or The Modern Prometheus is the most obvious gothic literary source for *The Brain of Morbius*, in which the brain of an executed Time Lord war criminal (and their former leader) is being prepared by mad scientist Solon (Philip Madoc, an actor who'd appeared in several guest roles over the years) for transplant into a body constructed from the parts of various alien species. A second strong influence is HG Wells' novel *The Island of Dr Moreau*, which deals with cross-species pollination, an underlying theme in *The Brain of Morbius* (some of Solon's dialogue even appears to be quoting from Wells' book). Also present on the planet Karn, along with Solon and the remains of Morbius, are an un-ageing, mysterious Sisterhood who are the guardians of the 'sacred flame' that produces a life-giving elixir which aids Time Lord regeneration. They have kept an eye on Solon's activities (while being unaware that Morbius has survived). The Sisterhood appears to have been inspired by Victorian adventure novelist H Rider-Haggard's *She* (the 1965 film version would have been familiar to Holmes, who again contributed the bulk of the writing, reworking a script by Terrance Dicks). Hinchcliffe admitted that the Hammer movies 'influenced Bob a little, but they never influenced me', claiming Rider-Haggard or John Buchan were more his style. 'Both Bob and myself were probably in that tradition.'

As so often with *Doctor Who*, the ideas and the writing are let down by the realisation. The 'castle' and 'laboratory' interiors are well done (Solon has adapted an old fuel refinery), and the lair of the Sisterhood of Karn features some great set decoration, but the exterior scenes take place on a planetary surface constructed in the studio. The cliffs over which the characters clamber on their journeys between locations sound exactly like wooden flats painted to look like rock. 'The big challenge was that we didn't have any post-production,' admitted Hinchcliffe, explaining why the visuals of the show sometimes didn't match up to the ambition of the scripts. 'Everything had to be completed in the studio or during the bit of filming that you had. When you were being very ambitious with some of the effects, you were never quite sure whether they were going to work out, and neither were the special-effects guys! They were limited by time and money. You can't say they were no good: most of them were excellent. But even the really good stories have some effects that worked well and others that didn't. It's the time element.'

The all-studio *Brain of Morbius* gave way to a six-episode, location-shot season finale, *The Seeds of Doom*, which drew heavily on the Christian Nyby/Howard Hawks 1951 film *The Thing from Another World* (later remade in 1982 by John Carpenter as *The Thing*). Opening in the Antarctic as a research team are taken over by an alien-pod-from-outer-space, the story climaxes in a pastiche of *The Avengers*. Mad botanist Harrison Chase wants to secure the pod for himself, but instead unleashes a giant Krynoid monster that proceeds to eat his house. Hard edged and fairly violent, *The Seeds of Doom* is a combination thriller and horror film, with the Doctor and Sarah thrown into the mix. One entire episode sees them trapped in a cottage under siege. The monster plant's plot origins may have been obvious, but *Doctor Who* put a new spin on it. The first two episodes are a pretty shameless remake of *The Thing from Another World*, but soon the action switches to the British countryside and the threat mutates into another retelling of *King Kong*, the giant Krynoid monster rampaging across the countryside.

Costume-drama techniques were to the fore in the opening tale of the following season, *The Masque of Mandragora*. After accidentally picking up some malevolent 'Mandragora energy', the TARDIS takes the Doctor and Sarah to Renaissance Italy (filmed on location in Portmeirion, Wales, where much of the 1960s espionage show *The*

Prisoner was filmed) where they try to prevent a cult from realising their (alien-assisted) plan of plunging the world back into the Dark Ages. 'For the following seasons we wanted to try and bring in some more interesting settings,' noted Hinchcliffe, 'where the stories would go in time and space, whether historically or out into space.'

The Masque of Mandragora certainly achieved that, with a successful raid on the BBC's period-costume holdings and location filming that makes the most of Portmeirion, but with a director who seems to have gone out of his way to avoid many of the recognisable shots or locations viewers may have remembered from *The Prisoner*. Writer Louis Marks had been a lecturer in Renaissance history, so was able to turn to his passion for his final script for the series. The story explicitly plays out the battle between science and religion (albeit under the guise of a fictional cult worshipping an alien entity), or knowledge and ignorance, using the dawning Renaissance period as a thematically suitable and colourful backdrop. It came at a time when there was growing interest in creationism and the beginnings of a new attack on the scientific method, especially in the US. The story lacks a physical monster (the helix energy is an abstract threat) and instead is played out as a battle of ideas between superstition and reason. The Doctor is on the side of reason and science, but he can at least understand the importance of obviously 'wrong' supernatural ideas to the functioning of a certain type of society. These were big conceptual issues for *Doctor Who* to be tackling and showed that, as they entered what would turn out to be their final year in charge, Hinchcliffe and Holmes had lost none of their ambition.

Remembered mainly as the story that saw the departure of Sarah Jane Smith, *The Hand of Fear* returns to several themes that the series had dealt with in the recent past, with influences including mummy movies (again) and the social-political side being concerned with energy production (again). The 'energy' part of the story, however, is so muddled that it has little impact, beyond simply revealing that the writers (Bob Baker and Dave Martin, later to invent K-9) seem to have little understanding of nuclear power. Landing in a quarry (narratively a real quarry, not one standing in for an alien world), the Doctor and Sarah are caught up in a crisis at the Nunton nuclear power plant when the fossilised hand of alien exile Eldrad is re-energised by radiation. A possessed Sarah helps revive Eldrad, who sets out to return and conquer its home world (Eldrad's gender is fluid, depending on what life form inspires its revival). Twelve million viewers tuned in to see Eldrad defeated and the Doctor drop Sarah off back in Croydon (or, as later revealed in the David Tennant episode *School Reunion*, Aberdeen). The slate was now cleared for the next tale, one that would have a dramatic impact on *Doctor Who*'s future internal narrative history.

Tom Baker had long wanted to see the Doctor feature in a story without a companion at his side, and he got his wish in *The Deadly Assassin*. Robert Holmes took the opportunity to return the Doctor to his home planet of Gallifrey (named by Holmes in *The Time Warrior*). This did more to demystify the series' central character than even *The War Games* at the climax of the Troughton period or the anniversary adventure *The Three Doctors* (which had featured brief scenes on the Doctor's then-unnamed homeland).

The Time Lords are revealed to be a bureaucratic, stuffy, desiccated society, and the story makes plain the Doctor's reasons for wanting to escape and explore the universe. Drawing on the recent history of political assassinations in the US (particularly that of John F Kennedy the day before *Doctor Who*'s first episode aired) and films like *The Manchurian Candidate* (1962) and the more recent *The Parallax View* (1974), the opening of the story sees the Doctor apparently brainwashed into assassinating the President of the Time Lords. Later developments reveal this to be a plot orchestrated by the Master to discredit the Doctor. Holmes returns the Master to *Doctor Who* three years after Roger Delgado's death, but has him appear as little more than a skeletal creature in a dark cloak. The ridiculing of politicians, through the buffoonery of the Time Lords, was a reaction to the fall of the political classes in Britain (as a result of the Profumo affair and the Jeremy Thorpe scandals) and the US (the fall of Richard Nixon and Watergate). The growing *Doctor Who* fan base (see chapter six) reacted badly to Holmes' depiction of the Time Lords, although the story is now seen as something of a classic.

Apart from the political pastiche, *The Deadly Assassin* is notable for its third episode, set almost entirely within a computer-generated fantasy world called 'the Matrix' (this was 1976, long before the film series of the same name). Filmed on location, the episode sees the Doctor and his unknown adversary (later revealed to be Chancellor Goth) fighting it out using the power of their minds to warp 'reality'. It made for innovative television and was years ahead of its time in depicting alternative interactive realities on screen. It would also lead directly to the end of Hinchcliffe's time on the programme...

The companion-less *The Deadly Assassin* was a one-off experiment, falling directly mid-season. The remaining three stories of the year would introduce and develop a new companion, the savage Leela (Louise Jameson), a wild warrior woman dressed in animal skins and descended from the crew of a crashed spaceship from a time far in humanity's future. *The Face of Evil*, along with *The Masque of Mandragora* and *The Deadly Assassin*, is a story that would not have happened without the Doctor's previous involvement: he brought the Mandragora Helix to Earth and he's the subject of the plot in *The Deadly Assassin*. Baker's Fourth Doctor apparently had an unscreened adventure prior to *The Face of Evil,* where he'd thought he was solving a problem for the survivors of a crashed spaceship by fixing their semi-sentient computer. Instead, however, he'd driven it mad by inadvertently downloading his own personality. Returning to the planet, he discovers a primitive society split in two (the Sevateem, descended from the ship's 'survey team', and the Tesh, once the 'technicians') and dominated by Xoanon, a computer suffering from multiple-personality disorder. The Doctor's previous involvement is confirmed by a giant, Mount Rushmore-like carving of his head on a mountainside after the locals recognise him as the (jelly) baby-eating 'Evil One'.

The society-secretly-run-by-computer is another mild (and not particularly hidden) attack on religion, as both the Sevateem and the Tesh accept their place in Xoanon's world without question. The one exception is Leela, who quickly comes under the Doctor's wing. The Doctor sees potential in Leela and over the next few episodes develops a kind of Henry Higgins educator role where he attempts to broaden her horizons and mould her into someone better able to fit into the universe at large. The moral of the story was clear – and fitted nicely with growing political disenchantment in the 1970s: question your leaders; question everything.

The theme is continued through into *The Robots of Death*, in which the decadent crew of a giant 'sandminer' vehicle are shaken out of their passive reliance on servant robots by the arrival of the Doctor and the revenge plot of disgraced robotics genius Taren Capel. Heavily reliant on Frank Herbert's *Dune* for its planetary setting and the industry of (spice) mining, *The Robots of Death* is just as indebted to Isaac Asimov's rules of robotics, which posit that a robot must never harm a human being. The most interesting thing here is a visual conceit: rather than trust the BBC's designers to come up with suitable futuristic fashions for the sandminer crew, Hinchcliffe had them model everything from sets to costumes on the art deco designs of the robots themselves. This results in an outlandish, though entirely consistent and thematically coherent vision of a society that the viewer can extrapolate from a handful of characters and one enclosed setting. It was a lesson that future producers of *Doctor Who* might have learned, though not all of them seem to have paid attention – or when they did look into the show's past, they took inspiration from the wrong things (as in the 1980s). Modelled after a 1920s 'whodunit' plot, *The*

Robots of Death is a critique of a society grown decadent off the back of mineral wealth with a reliance on an 'under class' used to produce that wealth. In that way, it's a critique of 1970s oil-driven Capitalism in the UK, and the design and make-up anticipates the cultural change on its way as Punk played itself out and gave way to the New Romantics.

With Philip Hinchcliffe's time as producer of *Doctor Who* coming to a forced end (see later for details), he clearly decided to go out all guns blazing. His final story, *The Talons of Weng-Chiang*, is a glorious summation of his pulp-literature-driven storytelling style and period-drama art design, all in one near faultless six-episode adventure. Hinchcliffe recognised the importance of his key BBC collaborators to the success of his episodes, and he intended to allow them to end his time on the show on a high, regardless of budgetary impact.

The Talons of Weng-Chiang is a brilliant fusion of Victorian pulp fiction conventions, warped to fit the *Doctor Who* format. Tom Baker is essentially playing a version of Sherlock Holmes (complete with cape and deerstalker), while the script gives him three Watsons (Leela, Professor Litefoot, and theatre impresario Henry Jago). The villains – Weng-Chiang/Magnus Greel, misled magician Li H'sen Chang and Mr Sin – are all drawn from the writings of Sax Rohmer and the movie and serial versions of cod-Chinese villains like Fu Manchu. Design-wise, the story draws on the (by then 20-year-old) traditions of Hammer horror, while the character of Weng-Chiang, who spends much of the story skulking about in the sewers under a theatre, allowed for a design riff on *The Phantom of the Opera* (complete with dramatic unmasking at the cliff-hanger climax of episode five).

The Talons of Weng-Chiang was the apotheosis of Hinchcliffe and Holmes' time on the show, putting aside any but the most cursory social or political commentary for the more abstract purpose of decon-structing English literary archetypes. Spoofing Sherlock Holmes was nothing new after a series of mid-1970s movies deconstructed the 'great detective' (*The Private Life of Sherlock Holmes* [1970], *Sherlock Holmes' Smarter Brother* [1975], *The Seven-Per-Cent Solution* [1976]) but *The Talons of Weng-Chiang* extended its targets to cover many of the great heroes and villains of Victorian pulp (and classic) literature. It was the culmination of Holmes and Hinchcliffe's habit of dropping the Doctor into the middle of other genres of fiction (rather than SF), causing the programme to reform itself around him. His era encompassed horror (*The Ark in Space*, *Terror of the Zygons*, *The Seeds of Doom*), politics (*Genesis of the Daleks*, *The Deadly Assassin*), new ageism/Von Daniken-ism (*Pyramids of Mars*) and the nature of belief (*The Masque of Mandragora*, *The Face of Evil*). Not a bad achievement for an entertainment show primarily aimed at a family audience.

Philip Hinchcliffe was forcibly removed from his position as producer on *Doctor Who* after three years of critical and ratings success as a direct result of the activities of 'clean-up-TV' campaigner Mary Whitehouse. It wasn't the first time that Whitehouse's group had targeted *Doctor Who* (and it wouldn't be the last), but the mid-1970s was when she was most effective.

On 13 November 1976, the third episode of *The Deadly Assassin* ended (as with so many of the series' cliff-hangers) with the Doctor in mortal peril. Battling Chancellor Goth within the fantasy world of the Matrix, the climax of the episode saw the pair fighting at the edge of an expanse of water. As Goth got the upper hand in the struggle, the Doctor was held under water, with the episode ending on a close-up freeze frame of his submerged, anguished face. While the majority of viewers would have reacted to this particular cliff-hanger as they had to so many others – the Doctor couldn't be dead; the show was back on again next week – there was one particular viewer who took it upon herself to write a letter of complaint to the Director General of the BBC, Charles Curran: Mary Whitehouse.

Since the early 1960s, Whitehouse had been the figurehead of a small but vocal campaign group that had set out to 'clean up TV' by reining in what they saw as the corrupting influence of many television shows on the nation's youth. With the 1960s being a period of significant social and political change, Whitehouse had decided to ignore the wider causes of moral and social unrest and lay the blame solely on the media. It was as if, in order to fight against the mass changes in society that she disapproved of, she'd had to narrow her focus to a target she felt she might have some chance of affecting. Her main obsession would be the publicly funded BBC.

Driven by her Christian values and the (in her eyes) lack of values shown by her pupils when she was a schoolteacher, Whitehouse had engaged in a battle of wits with the former BBC Director General Hugh Greene, declaring that the BBC was 'more than anybody else responsible for the moral collapse in this country'. Greene ignored her concerns and blocked her from participating in BBC programming. Through petitions, letter-writing campaigns and public meetings, Whitehouse developed a higher profile. She successfully had the BBC ban the video for Alice Cooper's 'School's Out' in 1972 and had complained about the release of Stanley Kubrick's *A Clockwork Orange* the previous year. The formation of the National Viewers and Listeners Association (NVALA) gave her a platform, and she used her base to hit out at programmes such as *Till Death Us Do Part* and violence in *Tom and Jerry* cartoons.

Part of the remit of *Doctor Who* was to scare the nation's children. Perhaps that hadn't been the original intention of Sydney Newman and Verity Lambert when they devised and launched the series back in 1963, but by the mid-1970s it was a strong, widely appreciated facet of the show. Whitehouse first complained about this fundamental aspect of the series in relation to Jon Pertwee's final story, *Planet of the Spiders*. A psychiatrist from the Church of England's Children's Society complained to the medical magazine *General*

Practitioner that the story 'was probably responsible for an epidemic of spider phobia among young children'. This was enough for the *Daily Mail* to contact Whitehouse and solicit a quote attacking the show. 'This underlines the warnings we have been giving about the effect of *Doctor Who* on the very small child,' said Whitehouse, before going on to declare war on the programme. 'We intend to ask the BBC, as a matter of urgency, to finance independent research into the effect of *Doctor Who* on the under-fives, and in the meantime ask it to switch the programme to 6.30pm.'

In response to further *Doctor Who* serials like *Genesis of the Daleks* and *The Seeds of Doom*, Mary Whitehouse and the NVALA described the show as being full of 'obscene violence and horror'. In one public speech, Whitehouse complained specifically with regard to *The Seeds of Doom* that 'strangulation – by hand, by claw, by obscene vegetable matter – is the latest [*Doctor Who*] gimmick, sufficiently close up so that they get the point. And just for a little variety, show the children how to make a Molotov Cocktail.'

Looking back on his run-in with Mary Whitehouse, Philip Hinchcliffe was sanguine, even though her actions had essentially cost him his job. 'She was very vocal at the time on a lot of programmes and she homed in on us,' he recalled. 'I think she confused violence with thrills. Our aim was to be thrilling, but I don't think there was a huge amount of violence. At the time, television boundaries of taste were evolving very quickly. I was a young producer, and I think probably I was pushing the envelope for that type of programme in that tea-time Saturday slot. I don't think we ever got it massively wrong. We were bumping up against the limits of what we could do at that time with that audience, but I don't think we got it grotesquely wrong at all.'

However, it was the now-notorious, 'drowning' cliff-hanger at the climax of episode three of *The Deadly Assassin* that saw Whitehouse finally find a target that the BBC could not ignore. Whitehouse's complaints were a mix of the nonsensical and the appreciable. She was worried that children would not comprehend the nature of the cliff-hanger and so would believe that the Doctor would be held under water for a whole week. 'At a time when little children are watching, you showed violence of a quite unacceptable kind,' she wrote to Curran. Violence, she asserted, 'permeated the programme', and the cliff-hanger itself 'could only be described as sadistic'. In addition, Whitehouse delivered anecdotal evidence that a neighbour's son had threatened to hold his brother's head under the bath water the next time he annoyed him 'like the man did with Doctor Who'.

The problem for the BBC was that, although it had already been trimmed, against Hinchcliffe's wishes, by Head of Serials Bill Slater, the sequence as broadcast was actually in contravention of the BBC's own 1972 guidelines on the depiction of violent material. The guidelines warned about taking care with material where a large proportion of the audience would be children, urging 'caution' in relation to episodic cliff-hangers, especially if they contained 'frightening close-ups' or 'over-detailed portrayal of death'. Whitehouse was aware of these guidelines and was able to cite them in relation to *The Deadly Assassin* cliff-hanger.

Curran had no option but to reply to Whitehouse and attempt to mollify her concerns. He pointed out that the cliff-hanger was part of a fantasy sequence (both the Doctor and Goth were in the Matrix), but that 'one or two people… may have imagined that Dr Who's dreams were reality. The head of department [Bill Slater] felt some of the sequences were a little too realistic… Accordingly, several were edited before transmission. The result was reasonably acceptable, although the head of department would have liked to have cut out just a few more frames of action than he did.' The clip showing Baker's head being held under water was removed from all subsequent repeat screenings, although it was reinstated for the 2009 DVD release.

Whitehouse appeared to accept Curran's letter as an admission of a 'mistake of judgement' in a response in the *Daily Telegraph*, and there was no public acknowledgement by the BBC that any further action was to be taken. However, Curran and Slater had apparently decided that *Doctor Who* had gone too far once too often and action was required. The first that Hinchcliffe knew of any change, however, was during the rehearsals for *The Robots of Death* when he and Tom Baker were introduced to a visiting Graham Williams as 'the new producer of *Doctor Who*'. It appears all three were surprised by the change, as Williams had been in development on adult police thriller *Target*, which he'd created and expected to be producing. Instead, management were instigating a job swap, putting Hinchcliffe in charge of the more adult *Target* and parachuting Williams into the *Doctor Who* job. Hinchcliffe later admitted: 'I didn't know I was being replaced until Graham Williams walked in the door.' Williams was not just given stewardship of the show, he was given a definite brief. His instructions were to tone down the horror, reduce the macabre content and remove anything that might be seen by outside critics (especially Mary Whitehouse and her followers) as nasty or objectionable.

Hinchcliffe defends his period on *Doctor Who* to this day, believing that he produced a gripping but grown-up series of stories that were suitable for the audience the show had in the mid-1970s. 'What I tried to do was make the show work,' Hinchcliffe said. 'When I inherited it, it worked very well for the very young audience and the smart 12-year-old, and there was something in it for mum and dad. I think what we did was to increase the appeal, so that it was more compelling. Mum and dad would continue to watch and really believe it and the growing audience of the student generation would also. We wanted to make it more plausible, rather than have people think it was a joke. We treated the stories a bit more seriously in the way that we developed them and handled them.'

Hinchcliffe's time as producer saw *Doctor Who* achieve the peak

.of its ratings and critical success, with each of his three seasons consistently averaging 11.5–12 million viewers, and individual episodes reaching as high as 13 million (the precise number who saw *The Deadly Assassin*, episode three, Doctor drowning and all). With the arrival of Graham Williams and his restrictive brief to remove the horror from the series, *Doctor Who* would have no choice but to move in a new direction. The question was, what would Williams replace the tea-time horror with? The answer was to be humour.

Graham Williams' time on *Doctor Who* started and ended with the show in crisis. Like Philip Hinchcliffe before him, Williams had been promoted to take over the show from a script-editing background (notably on *Z-Cars* and *Barlow at Large*), so he came to it with a great deal of storytelling experience, but virtually no practical producing experience.

The first story on the slate for season 15 was scheduled to be a vampire tale by Terrance Dicks entitled *The Witch Lords*. However, given the controversy over Hinchcliffe's gothic horror legacy, this may have been thought inappropriate and Williams dropped the story. The formal reason offered was that it would clash with the BBC's own 'proper' adaptation of *Dracula* that same year. The story would later be made in revised form in 1980 as *State of Decay*.

The replacement was a hastily written adventure called *Horror of Fang Rock*, also by Dicks. The second-broadcast story *The Invisible Enemy* was made first, but studio space wasn't available at Television Centre when *Horror of Fang Rock* was ready, so the whole production was relocated to BBC Pebble Mill's Birmingham studios. Despite the troubled start to his tenure, viewers would have been hard pressed to see any sign of it when the series debuted in September 1977.

Horror of Fang Rock was not too removed from the gothic thrills of the previous three years. An isolated setting – a Victorian lighthouse – is invaded by the alien survivor of a crashed spaceship.

Survivors from a sunken vessel also take refuge there, only to encounter the shape-changing Rutan creature that has escaped a battle with the Sontarans. The Doctor and Leela arrive and try to protect the lighthouse's new residents as they are picked off one by one by the creature. The story contained much that had worked previously, combining an alien threat with the best period design efforts of the BBC. The script and direction make good use of the limited locations, but, with Robert Holmes continuing as script editor, this is no great surprise. There is, however, little of the literary inspiration of recent tales beyond the poem quoted in the story: *The Ballad of Flannen Isle* by Wilfred Gibson, which tells of strange happenings in a lighthouse. Although almost the entire cast perish, in line with Williams' new 'no-gore' guidelines it's all done with remarkably little bloodletting.

The next story, *The Invisible Enemy*, is notorious for introducing dog-shaped robot sidekick K-9, who was immediately popular with a large proportion of the younger audience, if not with the series' star and production team. Although seen on British TV screens before the 1978 UK release of *Star Wars* (1977), K-9 was definitely inspired by the robotic duo of C-3PO and R2-D2 (as is clear from the name alone). Going further back, the utility droids Huey, Duey and Louie from *Silent Running* (1972) might have been an influence. After the unexpected success of *Star Wars* in the US in the summer of 1977, many space-fantasy movies and TV series followed, and several American shows boasted their own comedic robotic sidekicks, like Twiki in *Buck Rogers in the 25th Century* and Muffit in *Battlestar Galactica*. Having a humorous robot aboard the TARDIS meant that *Doctor Who* was right in the middle of the SF pop-culture mainstream, even if the series had missed the opportunity of having D-84 from *Robots of Death* join the TARDIS crew.

The Invisible Enemy drew much of its inspiration from anticipated medical breakthroughs, especially as depicted in the film *Fantastic Voyage* (1966). The hospital-in-space setting may have been inspired by James White's *Sector General* stories (1962– 99). To battle an intelligent 'virus' that has infected him, the Doctor and Leela are cloned and injected into his own brain. The story even echoes some of the 1970s concern with mankind's effect on Earth (the Gaia theory), extrapolated to a galactic scale as the Doctor likens mankind's expansion into space to a disease.

As with *Horror of Fang Rock*, *Image of the Fendahl* was another throwback to Hinchcliffe horror, having been commissioned by outgoing script editor Robert Holmes. Williams was faced with the challenge of producing a terrifying story of the occult without incurring the wrath of his immediate BBC superiors, Mary Whitehouse and the NVALA. Dennis Wheatley's occult novels were all the rage in the mid-1970s, and *Image of the Fendahl* simply replaced the supernatural with the alien (as *Doctor Who* had done several times before, notably in *The Daemons*). Although Wheatley's best-known works had been written in the 1930s, the 1968 film of *The Devil Rides Out* had brought them new popularity, with well-thumbed paperbacks being swapped in playgrounds nationwide (Wheatley was soon succeeded in the paperback-horror 'nasty' stakes by James Herbert and Guy N Smith). The discovery of the Fendahl skull that begins all the trouble echoes the real-life discovery of the skull of 'Lucy', part of a prehistoric skeleton found in 1974 in Ethiopia that shed new light on mankind's ancient development.

Graham Williams' replacement for the horror content of *Doctor Who* was to be parody and satire, a gambit that only starts to become clear with *The Sun Makers*, by which time Williams was gaining more control over the show and running out of scripts left over from the Hinchcliffe/Holmes period. New script editor Anthony Read was a willing collaborator in Williams' move to produce more parodic, rather than horrific, scripts. This change of direction, however, also allowed star Tom Baker to indulge his more mischievous side (which Hinchcliffe had kept under control). Having four years' experience as the series' lead, Baker could easily ignore Williams' diminished authority, espe-cially as it was already being further undermined by the requirement that he clear scripts with his head of department, Graeme McDonald. It was the beginning of a slippery slope that would pitch the programme in the direction of comedy and see the beginning of a distancing between the programme and its audience.

The Sun Makers had been inspired by Robert Holmes' own prob-lems with the Inland Revenue. The result was a pastiche of out-of-control petty bureaucracy in the far future as Pluto's workers rise up (with a little help from the Doctor) to defeat the evil Company. Beyond Holmes' own personal take on the issue (reflected in a series of script in-jokes), *The Sun Makers* was inspired by a combination of 1970s labour relations in Britain, the 1927 Fritz Lang film *Metropolis* and 1950s comedy movies starring Ian Carmichael, like the Boulting Brothers' *I'm Alright Jack* (1959). That this version of *Metropolis* looks visually far less impressive than the 1927 silent version is down to the budget cuts that Williams was suffering, partly due to Hinchcliffe's profligate overspending on his swan song, *The Talons of Weng-Chiang*, as well as the ever-increasing cost of producing drama at the BBC in the inflationary late-1970s.

If *Horror of Fang Rock* and *Image of the Fendahl* had been Hinchcliffe-style throwbacks and *The Sun Makers* a sign of things to come, *Underworld* can only be explained as an attempt at cost-cutting by using the CSO technology that had so used to excite Barry Letts. Based on the story of Jason and the Argonauts, *Underworld* saw the Minyan spacecraft R1C (captained by 'Jackson') on a quest to recover its race banks from a ship named the P7E. Jackson was Jason, with the race banks replacing the golden fleece, while the P7E was Persephone. Other aspects of the story (from names and settings to lines of dialogue) reflected this source material. Williams encouraged writers Bob Baker and Dave Martin to work this material in, much as he had done with Holmes' Inland Revenue material in *The Sun Makers*.

'That element of sophisticated humour was certainly going to continue for the rest of the time I was doing the series, and that was not accidental,' said Williams. 'I wanted the humour to be there, to add a little bonus without detracting from the story. If people did not get the joke, it should not impair their enjoyment of the show.' Two other stories would mine this seam of Greek myth recast as space opera (*The Armageddon Factor* and *The Horns of Nimon*).

Having built the set of the spaceship featured in *Underworld*, it became clear that the remaining sets would be unaffordable, as would any complicated location shooting. Williams' solution was to fall back on the use of CSO. Instead of filming the heroes traversing sets designed to look like caves, or film them on location in real caves, the choice was made to shoot everyone in front of a studio green-screen and insert background cave photographs to complete the scene. The result is a near-unwatchable visual mess. Despite that, the audience increased across the story from episode one's 8.9 million viewers to episode four's 11.7 million, which just proves that *Doctor Who* is at its best when story driven and character driven, rather than effects driven, and that a discerning audience can ignore poor realisation (or at least they could in the late 1970s) in order to enjoy a well-told story.

Williams and Read also stole another idea from the Barry Letts playbook: they wanted to end their inaugural season with an epic adventure that would have a dramatic effect on the Doctor. The result was *The Invasion of Time*, an inadequately realised story cobbled together in a hurry to replace another, clearly unaffordable and over-ambitious script about killer cats from outer space. Instead, Read and Williams brought the Doctor back to Gallifrey in a sequel to *The Deadly Assassin*, and had him seemingly turn evil by assuming the presidency in order to allow an invasion by the Vardans. Of course, it's all a trap, but the Doctor has been used in turn by the Sontarans, who appear at the climax of episode four, intent on staging their own invasion.

The kind of labour disputes featured in *The Sun Makers* hit the BBC itself and affected the making of *The Invasion of Time*. A scene-shifters' strike caused more of the final episodes to feature outside-broadcast, location-shot footage (including a municipal swimming pool and a disused hospital interior) to represent the deep interior of the TARDIS. The resulting show saw Gallifrey become a Soviet-style society rather than the stuffy English bureaucracy seen in Holmes' *The Deadly Assassin*. The nature of the production, however, did much to sabotage the story (as it had done on almost every story of Williams' first season). This resulted in a meeting between Williams and Head of Serials Graeme MacDonald with a view to figuring out a way of handling the series that would avoid the behind-the-scenes chaos that was beginning to affect the onscreen quality (not the last time this would happen in the series' history). Williams had a plan for the sixteenth season that would address many of the problems. Unlike the season just wrapped, the next would be carefully planned. It would have to be, as the six stories involved would tell one linked story, chronicling the Doctor's search for the Key to Time. This was Williams' first attempt to answer the perceived challenge posed by *Star Wars* and its successors. Audiences were thought to be no longer prepared to put up with poor plotting, and even poorer effects on TV: they wanted *Doctor Who* to match the new breed of television and movie science fiction coming from the US. It would be a challenge the venerable original version of the series could never quite rise to.

Graham Williams saw the Key to Time season as a method of attracting an audience that would stick with the show for a full season, from first episode to last. His previous season had varied widely from a per-story average low of 7.8 million (*Image of the Fendahl*) and a high of 10.5 million (*The Invasion of Time*). Williams' hope was that the ongoing over-arching story, albeit spread across six separate serials, would hold audience attention for a 26-week run.

A three-page document had been drawn up in November 1976 (soon after Williams took the producer's position) outlining his ambitions for what was to become the sixteenth season of *Doctor Who* in 1978. Full of mystical and esoteric-sounding content, the document outlined the forces that balance the universe and introduced the 'Guardians', one representing 'good/construction' and the other 'evil/destruction'. These forces are accessed through the Key to Time, which has been split into six segments and scattered through time and space. The Doctor and his new companion, Time Lady Romana (Mary Tamm), are set the task of finding the pieces, assembling the Key and returning it to the White ('good') Guardian, while avoiding the hindrance of the Black ('evil') Guardian and his agents. An added complication was the nature of each segment: they could change form or be disguised as anything (or anyone). The document included a character profile for the new companion, Romana. 'We decided to do the one big remaining stereotype that had yet to be done,' admitted Williams. 'This was the exact opposite of the savage huntress (Leela), namely the ice goddess.' A long search finally saw Tamm cast as the neophyte Time Lady who was to act as both a companion and conscience for the Doctor.

The six stories were planned as diverse adventures and some had been developed independently of the story arc idea, so the Key had to be inserted into the plot somewhere. This was more successful in some cases than others. Opening tale *The Ribos Operation* pulled off the now established trick of having the design department create a period-costume-drama look representing an alien world. Robert Holmes' script and the look of the story were heavily influenced by the popular movie conception of Russian literature in the *Dr Zhivago* (1965) mould (or *Anna Karenina*, with some of the sets coming from the 1977 ten-episode BBC adaptation featuring Eric Porter) crossed with a heist movie plot. On the planet Ribos, three conmen have tricked the Graff Vynda-K into believing the planet is rich in the mineral Jethryk, used for powering spaceships. In fact, the only Jethryk on the planet is on display in a reliquary and is part of the Key to Time sought by the Doctor. Caught up in the conmen's manoeuvres and the Graff's ambitions, the Doctor also has to recover the Key segment.

The literary games are further played out in later story *The Androids of Tara*, a fun retelling of *The Prisoner of Zenda* in the same future-feudal mode as *The Ribos Operation*, giving the BBC costume designers and set builders a period workout once more. A sword-wielding swashbuckler, with electrically augmented swords and laser-crossbows, *The Androids of Tara* (in which the Key segment is a statue) is an old-fashioned, Errol Flynn-type adventure story given a superficial science-fiction makeover, as *Doctor Who* simply didn't do 'straight' history anymore. That story was preceded by another Hinchcliffe-era horror throwback in *The Stones of Blood*, the first two episodes of which would have fitted very well between the *Jekyll and Hyde*-like *Planet of Evil* and the Hammer Horror-influenced *Pyramids of Mars*. An Arthurian-inspired tale that also draws on the fashionable revival of druidism in the 1970s, *The Stones of Blood* sees the Doctor and Romana tangle not only with the alien Ogri, who resemble standing stones, but also with archaeologist Vivien Fay (really an alien criminal in disguise, an old Hinchcliffe staple) and the Megara, justice machines from the planet Diplos. The Hammer horror vibe is successfully mixed with high-tech SF, and the Doctor discovers the Key segment is Fay's necklace, the Seal of Diplos.

The other three stories (coming second, fifth and sixth in the running order) are varieties of space opera. *The Pirate Planet* (in which the Key segment is the planet Calufax) was a Douglas Adams-written satire that owed a lot to his *The Hitch-Hikers' Guide to the Galaxy* in tone and approach (perhaps due to the fact it was written at the same time). *The Power of Kroll* is another allegory for 1970s Britain's approach to energy policy, but also a critique of the exploitation of 'Third World' resources and people. Searching for the next segment of the Key to Time, the Doctor and Romana land on the swamp moon of Delta

Magna and get caught up in the conflict between native 'swampies' and the giant squid they worship (it has eaten the Key segment!), along with those who administer the local chemical refinery and a mob of gunrunners. Finally, the entire story arc culminates in the six-episode out-and-out space opera of *The Armageddon Factor*, which had two planetary empires – Atrios and Zeos – engaged in perpetual war. The Cold War analogy is not difficult to see, and neither are the Second World War references with a heavy overlay of Greek myth (again from writers Bob Baker and Dave Martin, who'd done the same in *Underworld*). The final Key segment is disguised in the form of Princess Astra (Lalla Ward), who provides the lookalike template for Romana's regeneration at the beginning of the next season. Encouraged to hand over the all-powerful Key to the White Guardian (after a moment's temptation to keep it and rule the universe himself), the Doctor sees through the Black Guardian's disguise and re-scatters the Key. On the run, he must use the Randomiser (a random destination generator now inserted into the TARDIS console) to avoid pursuit by the Black Guardian.

Although deemed to be a critical and ratings success, the idea of a season-long arc story on *Doctor Who* would not be tried again for another eight years, although some seasons would feature related story trilogies or overall themes. The Key to Time season had averaged 8.6 million viewers (consistent with the previous year's 8.9 million average), ranging from lows of 6.5 million for the first part of *The Power of Kroll* to 12.4 million (almost double) for the next part of the same adventure.

The two stories that opened Williams' final season in charge of *Doctor Who* were ratings blockbusters, thanks in large part to a strike that took ITV off air for three months in the autumn of 1979. *Destiny of the Daleks* climaxed with 14.4 million viewers watching, while the following story, *City of Death*, reached a record audience for *Doctor*

Who of 16.1 million (actually coming a week after the ITV strike had ended and broadcasting had resumed).

The return of the Daleks for the first time in four years was event television anyway and bound to draw an audience. It's a shame, therefore, that Terry Nation's final script for the series should be so poor and the resulting production so shabby. Douglas Adams had become script editor, so the series' seventeenth season on air saw the comedy element that had been growing through Williams' period in charge foregrounded even more. *Destiny of the Daleks* sees the Daleks unearthing their creator, Davros, to help them break a stalemate in their ongoing war with the robotic Movellans. Growing awareness of computers and their roles in modern life (especially the military) lay at the root of this story. Superpower stand-offs, like the Cuban Missile Crisis of 1962, are another clear influence on Nation and Adams' thinking, alongside game theory and the doctrine of 'mutually assured destruction', according to which it was believed that no country could initiate a nuclear war due to the fear that instant response would see them destroyed in turn.

The following story, *City of Death*, was the first time *Doctor Who* had been filmed abroad, with the story set in modern Paris (all the location filming was accomplished in a few days, often shooting on the fly on the streets without permits). The disruptive effects of experiments in time see the Doctor and Romana encounter Scaroth, last of the Jagaroth. Splintered through time, the alien has hidden among humanity and financed his temporal experiments to reunite himself through selling art fakes, including the Mona Lisa. It's a light run around, wittily scripted by Adams and Williams (under a false name), with many memorable images and moments, from the unmasking of the alien Scaroth (Julian Glover) to tiny guest appearances by Eleanor Bron and John Cleese as art critics expressing their appreciation of the TARDIS as art object (which it later became thanks to artist Mark Wallinger, who displayed a silver, mirrored TARDIS at the 2001 Venice

Biennale). The complicated time-twisting story is told with an unusual brio, and the story moves at a pace that wouldn't be matched until the 45-minute episodes of the post-2005 series revival.

The remaining stories of Williams' period showed evidence of a series in rapid decline. Although *The Creature from the Pit* was a pastiche of free-market economics, it boasted a central monster that appeared to be a giant inflated green bag. *Nightmare of Eden* had better monsters, in the shape of the Mandrels, and a serious subtext concerning drug-trafficking (the Mandrels can be transformed into deadly addictive drug vraxoin). The cod-disaster-movie setting of two ships that have crashed and merged mid-materialisation is a clever idea, while the Continuous Event Transmuter (a virtual-reality machine) sees the show continuing to experiment with new special-effects technology in the form of the Quantel digital-effects system. Finally, the season ended on a memorably poor note with *The Horns of Nimon*, another parody of a Greek legend set in space, this time Theseus and the Minotaur. Poor production values and over-the-top guest stars served to derail this story, even before the unconvincing, bull-headed Nimon aliens appeared.

Those three adventures suffered troubled production histories as Williams seemed to be increasingly losing control of his show (due to a variety of factors) and was battling with his leading man, who was determined to re-shape the show his way. The culmination of this was the cancellation of what should have been the season-finale story, *Shada*. With 77 minutes of the 132-minute, Douglas Adams-scripted, six-episode story already filmed, the production was abandoned due to strike action at the BBC. It was to be an ignominious end to Williams' troubled time as *Doctor Who*'s producer. It appeared that only a dramatic regeneration could save the series, and that's exactly what incoming producer John Nathan-Turner set out to achieve.

5. TIME LORD ON TRIAL

The 1980s were a turbulent time for *Doctor Who*, as well as socially and politically in Britain (although the series would largely disengage from reflecting this, except perhaps in its own behind-the-scenes turmoil). The 1980s were also a time of increasing postmodernity in pop culture, with self-awareness featuring in a variety of media. A postmodern approach to storytelling came to dominate *Doctor Who*, undermining the audience's long attachment to the show. There was also a boom in nostalgia, with the 1960s in particular coming under the microscope, something the show was only too happy to trade on. This all fed into flamboyant new producer John Nathan-Turner's penchant for event television, a growing aspect of the maturing of the media that he would ruthlessly exploit in the promotion of the show.

With the arrival of Conservative Prime Minister Margaret Thatcher in Downing Street, Britain faced a period of dynamic historical, political and social change through the 1980s. Ruthless modernisation of the economy led to record unemployment and deindustrialisation, which in turn resulted in greater social division and unrest. Privatisation saw many state utilities sold off, while coal mining came to a virtual end as a result of Conservative policies and the controversial (and violent) miners' strike of 1984–85. The country also faced increased terrorist activity on the UK mainland carried out by the IRA as the Irish 'Troubles' continued.

Doctor Who's eighteenth season started the decade with a creative revamp that, nonetheless, saw it receive some of the lowest ratings in its long history. Similarly, the twenty-sixth season also saw a creative renaissance, yet achieved some of the series' lowest ever audience numbers, leading to the end of the show's initial run in 1989. The only common denominator on *Doctor Who* through the 1980s was producer John Nathan-Turner.

Taking over from Graham Williams, John Nathan-Turner had a solid history with the programme, unlike the two previous producers. His connections to *Doctor Who* went back to 1969, as floor manager on the Troughton story *The Space Pirates*. He'd worked on the show throughout the 1970s, most consistently as the budget-controlling production unit manager. Graham Williams had suggested that Nathan-Turner be associate producer, as he was instrumental in getting the programme made on budget. Concern about Nathan-Turner's lack of direct producing experience saw Barry Letts appointed as overseeing executive producer. Through the years, Nathan-Turner became as much of an icon of the show as his leading men, Peter Davison, Colin Baker and Sylvester McCoy. He was a master of publicity, often featuring himself in any coverage as much as the show's stars.

Most of the stylistic changes and format alterations that *Doctor Who* had undergone during its first 17 years were driven by, or identified with, a newly installed producer or production team. From Verity Lambert to Innes Lloyd, *Doctor Who* changed from a serialised exploration of other worlds and strange societies to a series of 'base-under-siege' stories in which the Doctor and his companions confronted marauding monsters. The arrival of Barry Letts and colour brought the show down to Earth for several years, with a gritty, thriller approach.

This changed again with Philip Hinchcliffe and Robert Holmes' 'gothic horror' period, followed by Williams' era of satire and parody.

John Nathan-Turner's decade on *Doctor Who* (from 1980 to 1989) did not feature the same 'producer's mark'. After his initial creative producing in the early-1980s, Nathan-Turner became detached from the show. The decade's stylistic shifts can, therefore, be more easily understood when attributed to changes in script editor. Distinctive periods followed the appointments of Christopher H Bidmead, Eric Saward and Andrew Cartmel as script editors. As the decade progressed, Nathan-Turner was more a practical line producer, bringing the series in on time and on budget, handling internal BBC politics and external promotion. Bidmead and Saward's periods coincided with the departure of Tom Baker (following attempts to tone down his performance) and Peter Davison's arrival, with Saward continuing through the short-lived and controversial TARDIS occupancy of Colin Baker. Finally, Cartmel revitalised the show with Sylvester McCoy as the star, before its cancellation in 1989.

Bidmead and Nathan-Turner set out to make a more serious version of *Doctor Who*. Pastiche and parody were abandoned in favour of serious storytelling and stronger scientific rigour. They paid attention to surface gloss and *mise-en-scène* (the details of sets, costumes) and visual continuity with the series' own past. Their removal of the humour left space for a reliance on 'real science' for story concepts. This led to a dearth of significant social or political content. This new 'hard science' era of the show also drew inspiration from 'new wave' literary science fiction and Hollywood movies, rather than from the political and social realities of the 1980s. Where Letts and Dicks engaged with the contemporary politics of the 1970s (as detailed in chapter three), Nathan-Turner and his script editors were inspired by films like *2001: A Space Odyssey* (1968), *Alien*, *Star Wars* and comic-book superheroes, rather than the politically and socially disruptive rise of Thatcherism.

The problem with this approach was that, instead of being a series with wide appeal and easily accessible to a large casual TV audience, *Doctor Who* became increasingly insular and was widely perceived as a 'geeky' sci-fi show that appealed to a few nerdy obsessives. This style-over-substance approach was suitable for the postmodern 1980s, but it resulted in the series disengaging from its popular audience, turning inwards, becoming self-obsessed and, eventually, losing the support of the majority of viewers, resulting in cancellation in 1989.

The changes to *Doctor Who* were immediately apparent to TV audiences from the first episode of *The Leisure Hive* on 30 August 1980. The blue-tinged, time-tunnel title sequence was gone, replaced by a blast of white light and a starfield that formed Tom Baker's face. This was accompanied by a loud, aggressive, heavily synthesised version of the *Doctor Who* theme. This was *Doctor Who* for the 1980s – slick, glossy, fast paced, loud and brash.

Tom Baker's costume had been redesigned in a deep red that reflected the star's newly subdued, melancholic approach to the role. The Doctor's clothes (and those of his companions) had now become a uniform, in the style of comic-book superheroes. This created an easily recognised silhouette, thanks to the distinctive hat-and-scarf combination. In the past, the Doctor's look could vary from story to story or match a specific theme (like his deerstalker-cap-and-cape affair in *The Talons of Weng-Chiang*). Now the Doctor's outfit (and those of Baker's successors) would rarely change. It was an approach that was much criticised, but it displayed the conceptual thinking that Nathan-Turner (and collaborators) was bringing to the series.

Season 18 was a radical departure for *Doctor Who*. While largely applauded by dedicated fans (see chapter six), it did not find great favour with the vast majority of viewers. This revamped approach resulted in one of the show's lowest-rated periods ever, falling by almost 50 per cent from the previous year. The season averaged 5.8 million, with a low of 3.7 million watching the second episode of *Full Circle*. Viewers were more attracted by the even glossier, easily accessible, action-adventure thrills of the American series *Buck Rogers in the 25th Century*, scheduled opposite *Doctor Who* by ITV. The show, based on the 1929 newspaper comic strip, provided the easy thrills that audiences had come to associate with science fiction since 1977's *Star Wars*. *Doctor Who*, in comparison, seemed low key, domestic (lacking the new-frontier, space-race spirit of the US), limited and old-fashioned, despite Nathan-Turner's drastic reinvention.

The eighteenth season's seven stories featured little in direct political or social commentary. *The Leisure Hive* drew from Francis Ford Coppola's film of Mario Puzo's *The Godfather* (1972), rather than satirising the British holiday business and the growing 'leisure economy' of the 1980s, and rated 5.1 million viewers overall. Only 4.7 million tuned in to the second story, *Meglos*, which saw the Doctor's identity stolen by a cactus-like life form. The story is notable as the first manifestation of Nathan-Turner's interest in the series' own past and his 'celebrity guest stars' policy. Jacqueline Hill, who'd played companion Barbara Wright opposite William Hartnell's First Doctor, returned in a major guest role. This 'stunt casting' would become a regular device used to generate tabloid press coverage.

Bidmead's 'real science' agenda kicked into high gear with the 'E-Space' trilogy. Inspired by the 1978 Key to Time season, Bidmead devised a linked trilogy of stories set in a mini-universe dubbed 'E-Space' (for exo-space). He drafted a memo for the writers, outlining the scientific basis for the trilogy's exotic location, although very little of the divergent laws of physics proposed were realised. The three stories provide a satisfying linked narrative that pays off with the departure of companion Romana and K-9 at the conclusion of *Warriors' Gate*. *Full Circle* is an evolution parable, in which the crew of a crashed starliner discover they're not descended from the original occupants of the craft, but instead from the indigenous 'marshmen' primitives, whom they despise. There's also a critique of animal cruelty in the depiction of the crew's treatment of the Marshman. Filmic influences include *Planet of the Apes* (1968) and *The Creature from the Black Lagoon* (1954), showing the dominance of the visual media in influencing the show, rather than any ideas reflecting the extreme political and social change sweeping Britain in the early-1980s.

The middle story of the trilogy did little to change this: a revival of Terrance Dicks' cancelled 1977 vampire script *The Witch Lords*. In its new form as *State of Decay*, Dicks transported his vampires (ancient enemies of the Time Lords) into E-Space. The result is a New Romantic-inspired, gothic-influenced version of a Hammer film. Bidmead's influence on the story was to make the vampires vulnerable to technology (as they're aliens), rather than anything supernatural. The New Romantic, post-Punk, pop-cultural influence would reach a climax on *Warriors' Gate*, where much of the visual style draws from 1980s pop videos, like Adam and the Ants' 'Prince Charming'. It features elaborate video effects and lashings of stylistic weirdness. Although the story invokes slavery (a big issue, but not particularly contemporary) in the plight of the time-trapped Tharils (the lion-men), the filmic influence this time is Cocteau's 1946 film *La Belle et la Bête*, with the magic-mirror doorway and the look of the Tharils obvious homages. Confirming the dominance of classic filmic culture on this unusual season of *Doctor Who*, it's no surprise that *Warriors' Gate* director Paul Joyce arranged screenings of source films for cast and crew (often done in the feature-film world). Among them was Alain Resnais' *Last Year in Marienbad* (1961, featuring time slippage), Cocteau's *Orphée* (1950, walking through mirrors), and John Carpenter's space comedy *Dark Star* (1974, the blue-collar crew of the trapped spaceship). This primacy given to the 'look' of the show over ideas was a deliberate choice.

The conceptually driven 'E-Space' trilogy held 5.2 million for the first two stories, with a sudden jump to 7.5 million for the third. This appears strange as *Warriors' Gate* is notoriously one of *Doctor Who*'s more 'difficult' stories and is emblematic of Nathan-Turner's consciously challenging approach. The sudden increase in viewers does not denote a sudden awakening on behalf of the British TV viewing public. Realising *Doctor Who* was being slaughtered in the ratings at 6.15pm, the BBC moved the show back to 5.10pm, resulting in a sudden influx of viewers (in an age long before video recorders, time shifting and Sky+).

Season 18 climaxed with a double bill of stories (*The Keeper of Traken* and *Logopolis*) that saw the resurrection of the Doctor's arch-enemy, the Master (Anthony Ainley). The fairytale atmosphere of *Warriors' Gate* continued into the penultimate story, *The Keeper of Traken*. Nathan-Turner carefully structured the end of the season and the beginning of the next to bridge the change of lead actor, fearing that there might be resistance among younger viewers for whom Tom Baker was the only Doctor. New companion Adric (Matthew Waterhouse) had already joined the TARDIS crew in *Full Circle*, and Romana had left, along with K-9, in *Warriors' Gate*. *The Keeper of Traken* introduced Nyssa (Sarah Sutton), orphaned by the Master, but who doesn't opt to travel with the Doctor until the season finale, *Logopolis*. That final adventure for Tom Baker would also introduce the third new companion, Tegan Jovanka (Janet Fielding), an opinionated Australian flight attendant. The biggest change would be reserved for the closing moments of *Logopolis* when Tom Baker's Doctor finally regenerated.

The Keeper of Traken is a 'Garden of Eden' parable (with an atmosphere that echoes Shakespeare's *A Midsummer Night's Dream*, adapted by the BBC that same year), in which a perfectly balanced world is corrupted by the evil Melkur, a long-dormant statue located in a verdant grove. Melkur is revealed to be a TARDIS housing the decaying Master (from 1976's *The Deadly Assassin*). The theme of corruption continued in *Logopolis* as the new Master (having body-snatched Nyssa's father, Tremas) arrives on the title planet, where a society of mathematicians is preserving the universe's harmony through the fundamental manipulation of numbers. The Master's interference disrupts their process and threatens the universe. In defeating the Master, the Doctor falls from a radio telescope to his 'death'. His regeneration is aided (in an echo of the Third Doctor's) by the mysterious wraith-like figure of 'the Watcher' who has been haunting the Doctor throughout. The 21 March 1981 final episode of *Logopolis* was watched by 6.1 million, with the season as a whole averaging only 5.8 million.

The regeneration of Tom Baker's Doctor into Peter Davison, the star of *All Creatures Great and Small* (a show that had John Nathan-Turner as production unit manager) had come at just the right time. The change of time slot had worked, but it was too late to significantly raise the season-average viewing figures. So important was the change of actor after seven years (a generation had grown up knowing no other Doctor than Tom Baker), the BBC scheduled a repeat series showcasing an adventure from each of the previous Doctors in preparation for Davison's debut in 1982. However, the show's retreat from engagement with the realities of the world (filtered through fantasy entertainment) would be a major contributing factor to the decline of *Doctor Who* through the 1980s. The poor viewing figures for Tom Baker's final season meant that Nathan-Turner was aware he would have to do something drastic if he was to win back the popular audience. Part of his new approach would be heavily reliant on the casting of the Fifth Doctor, and for the first time the series cast an already established television star: 29-year-old Davison.

In casting Peter Davison as the Fifth Doctor, producer John Nathan-Turner was looking for a contrast with Tom Baker. Davison's light, straight hair and his youth contrasted hugely with the near-50, dark, curly-haired Tom Baker. While these superficial elements were at the front of Nathan-Turner's mind, he was lucky with his choice. Davison was a rising TV star (with sitcoms *Sink or Swim* and *Holding the Fort*). The change of lead actor and a controversial move from Saturday early evenings to 7pm on Mondays and Tuesdays (in most areas) contributed heavily to the ratings almost doubling over Tom Baker's final year. Davison's first season of stories (the show's nineteenth on air) all averaged around nine million, with atypical period adventure *Black Orchid* reaching ten million. The soap-opera-like cast line-up and scheduling helped *Doctor Who* rise to new levels of success and popularity, even as the show retreated from any popular social or political engagement.

Nathan-Turner, however, appears to have taken the wrong lessons from the failure of Tom Baker's final season with the viewing public. The season had proved a hit with the increasingly vocal and actively involved fan base. The return of the Cybermen and the Master gave Nathan-Turner a taste for reviving monsters and characters from the show's past, a process given more momentum due to the looming twentieth anniversary and growing appetite for nostalgia. Nathan-Turner would continue to exploit the growing cultural and intellectual phenomenon of postmodernism in popular culture. Self-reflexivity became central to narratives in film and television, in which characters would make comments or experience events that seemed to reveal an awareness of their status as fictional entertainments. *Doctor Who* had always enjoyed a loose continuity, but increasingly in the 1980s the show's own narrative history would become central to its storytelling. At first this engaged audiences with a taste for nostalgia, but over the longer run it would become off-putting, with the series perceived as needing a high degree of knowledge of the past to understand it. Nathan-Turner's genius for publicity and PR was also part of this, with narrative developments in the show promoted as event television, or manipulated through the prism of other forms of entertainment (shooting on location for *Planet of Fire*, Davison and Nicola Bryant posed on the beach in a James Bond pastiche, while new companion Bonnie Langford was introduced when she and Colin Baker arrived on a theatre stage suspended by Kirby wires).

The Master was the villain in Davison's first story, *Castrovalva* (a sequel to *Logopolis*), and in the season's climax, *Time Flight*, in which a hijacked Concorde lands on prehistoric Earth. Bidmead continued his exploration of complex mathematics in *Castrovalva*, with a look derived from the work of early-twentieth-century Dutch artist MC Escher. This may have drawn on a then-popular science book, *Godel, Escher, Bach* by Douglas R Hofstadter, which connected music, art and maths, but it was definitely inspired by an Escher print called 'Castrovalva' that was hanging in a BBC office. With modern video effects, the show just about managed to pull off an Escher-inspired environment. The first two episodes (almost entirely TARDIS-set) dealt with the aftermath of the regeneration, before the final two relocated events to Castrovalva, an artificial environment created by the Master as a trap for the Doctor. This story structure made sense in the new twice-weekly transmission slot.

The glamour of filming at Heathrow and featuring Concorde, with the active co-operation of the airport authorities and British Airways, seems to have been enough for Nathan-Turner to commission *Time Flight*. Concluding the series with the unexpected return of the Master was also attractive as a more sophisticated version of Barry Letts' approach to structuring the series (and Nathan-Turner had certainly learned from Letts as executive producer).

Nathan-Turner's recreation of *Doctor Who* was a combination of hard science fiction with game-show or light-entertainment production values. New script editor Eric Saward was keen to build on Bidmead's legacy and push the show in a more ideas-driven direction. Given the political and social upheaval in Britain in the early- to mid-1980s, it is remarkable that this previously socially and politically engaged series should fail to explore this material. Nathan-Turner wanted a new way to engage audiences in an increasingly competitive television environment, and he found it in the combination of Saward's movie-inspired science fiction and an easily accessible visual look that would not be alienating to viewers who experienced *Doctor Who* as part of an evening's television.

Saward would implement Nathan-Turner's idea of event television in the most spectacular way with *Earthshock*. He'd been hired for the job on the back of submitting *The Visitation*, a traditional story that re-tooled classic *Doctor Who* tropes for the 1980s. It featured invading aliens trapped in a historical locale and a notable historical event affected by the Doctor (in this case he's involved in starting the fire of London, after a similar fire-starting experience in Rome during *The Romans*).

Following the ideas-driven double bill of *Four To Doomsday* (a 1960s-throwback political and environmental parable about autocratic rule in which an alien frog god aims for Earth after destroying his own planet's ozone layer) and *Kinda* (a complex Buddhist/colonial parable featuring more pop-video-inspired hallucinations), and the pseudo-historic double bill of *The Visitation* and *Black Orchid* (an Agatha Christie-inspired heritage-house mystery), Saward and Nathan-Turner unleashed *Earthshock*, a story that (for better or worse, often both) was to dictate the style of the series for the rest of the decade.

Doctor Who had always used returning adversaries sparingly in the past, with three exceptions: the Daleks (at the height of 1960s Dalekmania), the Cybermen (in the late 1960s 'monster' season) and the Master (during the early 1970s). This all changed in the 1980s, with the Daleks returning every two years from 1984 and the Master featured as a regular villain during Peter Davison and Colin Baker's time in the TARDIS. Nathan-Turner formulated the idea that exploiting the show's own heritage was a good move following the fan-acclaimed 'Master trilogy'. He went one step further, tapping the postmodern interest in nostalgia by bringing back barely remembered villains like Omega (*Arc of Infinity*), the Black Guardian (*Mawdryn Undead*, *Terminus*, *Enlightenment*), and creatures like the Sea Devils and Silurians (teamed up in *Warriors of the Deep*). The most dramatic return of all, however, was that of the Cybermen in *Earthshock*.

Six years after they were last seen (in *Revenge of the Cybermen*), the cliff-hanger of episode one of *Earthshock* revealed the newly redesigned 'tin soldiers' were back, jolting a nation of fans in surprise. Nathan-Turner had turned down the chance of a *Radio Times* cover announcing their return, preferring to maximise the surprise. This was intended to create word of mouth, turning *Doctor Who* into a must-see event. The intention was to increase the number of viewers for the second surprise, the unexpected (and equally secret) death of the Doctor's companion Adric (Waterhouse) at the climax of episode four (something not seen since *The Daleks' Master Plan* in 1966).

As part of the increasing postmodernism of the show, *Earthshock* features a quick catch-up on Cyber-history when the Cybermen view a selection of clips from past *Doctor Who* adventures. The first time Nathan-Turner had tried this was in a flashback sequence just before the Fourth Doctor fell from the Pharos Project radio telescope in *Logopolis*. This was part of the general nostalgia surrounding the programme as it approached its twentieth year on air, with TV review show *Did You See?* devoting a special report to *Doctor Who*'s past monsters on the back of the return of the Cybermen.

The effect of *Earthshock* on 1980s *Doctor Who* would be profound. Saward would go on to write a series of macho stories full of soldiers, violence and space opera (*Resurrection of the Daleks*, *Attack of the Cybermen*, *Revelation of the Daleks*) that would come to define the decade's *Doctor Who* in the eyes of a dwindling audience. As script editor, he would shape others' work to this template (with other stories modelled after *Earthshock*: *Terminus*, *The Caves of Androzani*, *Vengeance on Varos* and *The Two Doctors*). Each of these stories would (in part) emulate the macho American cinema of the 1980s, drawing on the work of James Cameron and films featuring Arnold Schwarzenegger and Sylvester Stallone. There's a lot of *Die Hard* in the often self-referential tone of much of Saward's work, and it seemed that *Doctor Who*'s mass audience didn't care for it.

From *Earthshock* onwards, Nathan-Turner's *Doctor Who* would be driven by event-television choices. The show's twentieth season saw each story contain a significant element from the series' own past, largely thanks to the influence of fan 'continuity consultant' Ian Levine who was helping the production office keep the show's 20-year-old continuity straight (see chapter six). Each story had a headline-attracting stunt attached, some more than one.

Season opener *Arc of Infinity* combined the return of companion Tegan, who'd been left behind in Heathrow at the conclusion of *Time Flight*, with an encore appearance by Omega, the Time Lord villain who'd appeared in *The Three Doctors*. Adding to the sense of special occasion, the production featured foreign filming (for the first time since *City of Death*) in Amsterdam (a habit that would recur in each of the next two years, on *Planet of Fire* and *The Two Doctors*).

Although there had been a BBC2 repeat of *The Three Doctors* (featuring Omega as the anti-matter villain) as part of the *Five Faces of Doctor Who* season before Peter Davison's debut, *Arc of Infinity* is guilty of assuming detailed knowledge of the show's past. Returning creatures or villains were not effectively reintroduced, other than with a throwaway 'Oh it's X, Y or Z' uttered by the Doctor, and maybe an 'I've met them before' aside to the companion.

The rest of the season would see an encore encounter with the Mara (the dark-side threat from *Kinda*) in *Snakedance* (a spiritual remake of *Planet of the Spiders*); the Black Guardian in the loose trilogy of *Mawdryn Undead*, *Terminus* and *Enlightenment*; and the Master in historical adventure *The King's Demons*. The original plan was for the twentieth-anniversary season to climax with the return of the Daleks in the Saward-scripted *Warhead/The Return* (retooled one year later as *Resurrection of the Daleks*). This reliance on the past allowed for a certain amount of creative reinvention (returning monsters were invariably redesigned), but it satisfied hardcore followers of the show (fans interested in its deep history) at the expense of the wider, casual audience.

The Black Guardian trilogy introduced new companion Turlough (Mark Strickson), an alien masquerading as an English public-school boy, pressured into attempting to kill the Doctor (repeatedly) on the Guardian's behalf. The idea of a traitor-cum-threat within the TARDIS crew was a new one, but old elements of the show continued to recur with an appearance from the Brigadier (replacing the originally planned return of the First Doctor's companion, Ian Chesterton) inspiring another series of nostalgic clips of old episodes built into the narrative. Again, as with *Arc of Infinity*, little care is taken to reintroduce the nostalgic elements to less regular viewers. Showrunner Russell T Davies would better handle the process of bringing back old monsters for the refreshed *Doctor Who*. He would also cleverly rework old plot elements, such as the way David Tennant's Tenth Doctor seemingly began the regeneration process in *The Stolen Earth/Journey's End*, echoing the false regeneration featured in the Davison adventure *Mawdryn Undead*, when the Doctor's companions misidentify a disfigured impostor as the regenerated Doctor.

Big science-fiction ideas feature in *Terminus* and *Enlightenment*. *Terminus* sees the Doctor save the entire universe by ensuring the Big Bang happens in a story that draws heavily from Norse creation myths (mythology that would recur twice more during Sylvester McCoy's time), while *Enlightenment* has the immortal 'Eternals' amuse themselves by racing spaceships disguised as old-fashioned sailing ships. The anniversary season ended with something of a whimper – thanks to the cancellation (due to strike action) of *Warhead/The*

Return – with *The King's Demons*, an old-fashioned historical tale in which the Master attempts to disrupt the signing of Magna Carta. Ratings had averaged seven million viewers for the season, an improvement on Tom Baker's final year, but still falling behind the series highs of the 1970s.

The *Doctor Who* nostalgia boom culminated in a giant, over-subscribed convention at Longleat (see chapter six) in March 1983 and the broadcast, in November 1983, of the celebratory anniversary story *The Five Doctors*. This TV movie was screened as part of 1983's *Children in Need* charity telethon night, two days after the actual twentieth anniversary on 23 November. This was the height of *Doctor Who*'s growing self-awareness, uniting three Doctors (Davison, Pertwee and Troughton), with a stand-in for the late William Hartnell (Richard Hurndall). The Fourth Doctor (Baker) featured in previously unseen material recycled from the incomplete story *Shada*. Opening with a clip of William Hartnell from *The Dalek Invasion of Earth*, *The Five Doctors* encapsulates all the signature traits of *Doctor Who* in the 1980s. The plot – in which various Doctors and companions have to make their way to the Dark Tower in Gallifrey's Death Zone to defeat renegade Time Lord Borusa in his attempts to achieve immortality – comes across as a variation on the Marvel comic-book team-up and a riff on the growing popularity of *Dungeons and Dragons* adventure gaming. It is simply an excuse to pack in as many references to the show's past as possible, and feature characters that ordinary viewers may or may not recognise, but each of whose fleeting returns would be applauded by fans. Various faces from the past were shoe-horned into Terrance Dicks' busy script, with guest villain appearances from a lone Dalek, an army of Cybermen and the Master.

The tendency to recycle and reuse characters and story elements continued into season 21. Facile political commentary crept into underwater, base-under-siege story *Warriors of the Deep*. Pertwee foes the Sea Devils and the Silurians returned in a heavy-handed Cold War analogy thrust forward to the year 2084 (one hundred years after the year in which it was broadcast). Less sophisticated than much of the political content of the show during the early-1970s, it was nonetheless a late – and rare – attempt to re-engage with wider, real-world issues that connected to the larger viewing public. *Warriors of the Deep* was *Doctor Who*'s reaction to the rise of Ronald Reagan, his 'star wars' missile-defence policy, and the Greenham Common protests against the arrival of US nuclear missiles in the UK.

The apparent destruction of the TARDIS in *Frontios* was part of Nathan-Turner's ongoing event-television agenda. The production office had publicly hinted that the police-box shape of the TARDIS might be abandoned and, with the seeming destruction of the ship by a Tractator-manipulated meteor storm, it was plausible that the plan was being enacted. Nathan-Turner would often float these high-concept ideas in press conferences, thereby generating publicity. The idea of an actress playing the Doctor had been used when Baker quit the role, and resurfaced when it was announced that Davison was leaving. The TARDIS replacement idea was given another workout in the opening to *Attack of the Cybermen* when the Doctor (Colin Baker) gets the chameleon circuit working briefly. Despite its originality, *Frontios* also reveals a growing trend in *Doctor Who* stories of the 1980s: it amalgamates elements from various stories from the past. The insect civilisation of the Tractators echoes that of *The Web Planet*, while their plot to pilot the planet of *Frontios* is drawn directly from the Daleks' plan in *The Dalek Invasion of Earth*, and the far-future civilisation seems based upon that shown in *The Ark*.

The next story, *Resurrection of the Daleks*, featured the annual flashback sequence made up of clips from old episodes. The focus this time was on a series of images of the Doctor's companions as the Daleks probe the Doctor's mind (although a production oversight missed out Louise Jameson's Leela). Narratively, however, Saward's script was once again a combination of *Alien* and *Star Wars*, drawing on popular cinematic SF rather than creating any real-life allegory. The nearest *Resurrection of the Daleks* comes to social comment is a Dalek's parting threat that Dalek-hidden duplicates still occupy positions of power in the British Government. The Doctor describes the duplicates as 'less than stable'. Here it is a throwaway line, but Russell T Davies would make aliens-in-government the central conceit of a witty two-part story (*Aliens in London/World War Three*). The story also sees Tegan leave the TARDIS in an abrupt manner when she decides the death and destruction she experiences travelling with the Doctor have become too much. In reality, Fielding, Strickson and Davison were all leaving the show in 1984, so their departures were staggered across several stories. By *The Twin Dilemma*, the entire lead cast of the series had changed.

Nathan-Turner continued playing with icons of the series in *Planet of Fire*. It climaxed with the Master in a no-escape situation (once again), burning in the numismaton flame. He utters the unfinished line (to the Doctor): 'Won't you show mercy to your own…?' Fan speculation had long proposed that the Doctor and the Master were not just Holmes and Moriarty or contemporaries at the Academy on Gallifrey (as the series had established), but might actually be related, even brothers. The line seems to play into that speculation, especially as the story has Turlough discovering his own lost brother. Russell T Davies would play with this speculation in *The Sound of Drums* in 2007, when the Master (John Simm) returns and Martha speculates about his relationship to the Doctor (a family connection dismissed by the Doctor, accusing Martha of watching too many soap operas).

Davison exited the show on a high in Robert Holmes' *The Caves of Androzani*, a morality tale in which the Doctor tries to save his poisoned companion at the expense of his own life, while around him an interplanetary war reaches its climax. While the gunrunning and corporate scheming neatly reflected growing 1980s concerns, even Holmes finds himself falling into the postmodern trap of playing with icons of the past. The semi-sympathetic villain of the piece is Sharaz Jek, a scarred, masked figure who lurks in caves, and is another reprise of *The Phantom of the Opera* (as was Holmes' own *The Talons of Weng-Chiang*).

Unfortunately, the full reveal of Sixth Doctor Colin Baker the following week in *The Twin Dilemma* was a huge step backwards. The regeneration was another big event and, to make it different from any of the previous colour series, Nathan-Turner had the new Doctor debut in the final story of the season. *The Twin Dilemma* was a poorly written and poorly realised adventure, resulting in a controversial debut for a new Doctor whom a lot of viewers professed to dislike. It would be a while before Baker had an opportunity to develop his Doctor and *The Twin Dilemma* left a bad taste with many viewers, one that would be long lasting.

John Nathan-Turner's event-television and publicity strategies came to dominate *Doctor Who* by the middle of the 1980s. Approaching his fifth year in charge – almost all previous producers had moved on by then – Nathan-Turner and his script editor Eric Saward had an uneasy working relationship. While Saward struggled to compile a coherent narrative, Nathan-Turner was on trips to conventions in the UK and US, authorising *Doctor Who* merchandise and creating 'shopping lists' of elements that future stories should include.

The twenty-second season continued to be influenced by big-screen science fiction, but there was at least a theme running through it: loss of identity and physical transformation. New advances in cosmetic plastic surgery and unnecessary operations (especially cosmetic breast enlargements) were often featured in the news or in the growing consumer and 'lifestyle' sections of Britain's expanding newspapers. Each story saw a major character undergo significant physical change, some more permanent than others. About the only character who wasn't physically altered was the one whose physiology regularly allowed for just such transformation: the Doctor.

In *Attack of the Cybermen*, a convoluted, continuity-ridden adventure, the mercenary Commander Lytton (Maurice Colbourne) returns from *Resurrection of the Daleks*, forms an alliance with the Cybermen and is partially Cyber-converted. *Vengeance On Varos*, a smart critique of video violence, saw companion Peri (Nicola Bryant) transformed into a birdlike creature as part of a mad scientist's experiments, while *The Mark of the Rani* had the Master teaming up with villainous Time Lady the Rani (Kate O'Mara) to alter history in nineteenth-century Britain. This tale saw a character transformed into a tree, thanks to a bio-mine. *The Two Doctors* had Troughton's Second Doctor changed into an Androgum, one of a race of hungry carnivores. In *Timelash*, HG Wells joined the Doctor and picked up various story ideas (the very stories that partly influenced the development of *Doctor Who*). The villain was the Borad, a hideous fusion of man and monster. Finally, *Revelation of the Daleks* featured a well-executed scene that saw the father of a young rebel encased in a transparent Dalek frame, mid-conversion, pleading with his daughter to kill him.

The series' format had been transformed, too, from (mostly) serials comprising four episodes of 25 minutes each to two-part stories where each segment lasted 45 minutes (more suitable for transmission on US TV). Previously, *Resurrection of the Daleks*, made as a four-episode tale, had been forced into a 45-minute format due to scheduling problems caused by the BBC's coverage of the 1984 Winter Olympics. In an attempt to update the series to the mid-1980s, it was decided that the entire twenty-second season would be in the 45-minute episode format, so *Attack of the Cybermen* was the first story to be written specifically to this style. It was the first story since *Logopolis* to air on a Saturday, with the BBC abandoning the twice-weekly screenings that had run throughout Peter Davison's three years.

By now, continuity was threatening to swamp original storytelling, and would prove to be a major off-putting factor for the audience as *Doctor Who* entered its declining years. The confusing storytelling of *Attack of the Cybermen* lost the show almost two million viewers between episodes. Serving as a sequel to several stories, notably the Cybermen's debut, *The Tenth Planet*, and *The Tomb of the Cybermen*, *Attack of the Cybermen* was action packed and stylish. However, it was impossible to understand without a crib sheet detailing *Doctor Who* history. Cannibalising its own past, the show featured redone set pieces from previous decades, recast with a glamorous 1980s sheen. Ostensibly set in environments first seen in long-deleted stories like *The Tomb of the Cybermen*, little effort was expended on remaining faithful to the original designs (many reference photos existed, even if the actual episodes were lost).

Attack of the Cybermen was criticised for its gratuitous violence (with many Cybermen dismembered and Lytton's gory conversion). Ironically, *Vengeance on Varos* – the following story – was a critique of video violence and its effects on society (a hot-topic debate in the British media in the early-to-mid-1980s). The 'video nasties' controversy saw movies for home rental subjected to prosecution and eventual classification. This was the subject matter for Philip Martin's tale of a society addicted to watching torture on TV and voting on the outcome. Well in advance of the rise of reality TV and the interactive, participatory television culture of the 1990s and twenty-first century, *Doctor Who* presented a cliff-hanger that relied on a knowing pastiche of television technique. As the Doctor appears to be dying on a video screen, the Varos Governor orders the vision controller to 'cut it, now!' as the episode cuts to the closing titles. The story ends with the Greek-chorus characters of Arak and Etta (who've been watching – and voting on – the action of the story, without ever meeting anyone else involved) deprived of their entertainment and lamenting, 'What shall we do now?'

Rather than feeding off its own narrative past by restaging its greatest hits, or creating sequels and overusing returning monsters, finally the show used its own off-air past and current news headlines (as it had always done previously) to create a truly innovative story. Drawing on the 1970s attacks by Mary Whitehouse (who'd continued to campaign to 'clean up TV' into the 1980s), Martin created a society that used violent imagery to keep the population entertained and sated, thus reducing the likelihood they'd revolt. This was the first *Doctor Who* story for a long time to directly comment on the news headlines. Martin had experienced censorship directly himself when his late-1970s series *Gangsters* was attacked for being too violent. That series also featured several postmodern touches that would recur in *Vengeance on Varos*, including characters commenting on the fiction they were participating in and the creation of the drama being witnessed by the audience (Martin was seen in later episodes of *Gangsters* writing that particular episode's script, while in *Vengeance on Varos* various TV tricks are used to structure the narrative – an idea Steven Moffat would adapt into the 'narrative edits' sequence of *Forest of the Dead* in 2008).

It's a shame that such political commentary did not feature more often during the 1980s, although it could be argued that the following story, *The Mark of the Rani*, dealing with Luddites battling mechanisation, saw the show mirroring the recent industrial turbulence and unrest in Britain. Primarily the story was about the introduction of the Rani, a female equivalent to the Master, and an excuse for more stunt casting by Nathan-Turner, bringing in soap star Kate O'Mara.

Similarly, *The Two Doctors* was entirely constructed around the gimmicks of bringing back Patrick Troughton and Frazer Hines, following their appearances in 1983's *The Five Doctors*, and location filming in Spain (after New Orleans fell through). Additionally, the story featured the stunt casting of *Blake's 7*'s Jacqueline Pearce and the return of 1970s' *Doctor Who* monsters the Sontarans. However, threaded through the story is a vague concern for animal welfare as the origins of human food are considered, with aliens called Androgums (an anagram of 'gourmand') out to sample Earth's finest delicacies. It's hardly a paean to vegetarianism, but it is a theme that runs through several of the season's stories, from the use of people as raw materials (in *Attack of the Cybermen*) and using the dead as the basis of food (in *Revelation of the Daleks*), to cannibalism on Varos and comments from the Rani about the deaths of animals. With vegetarianism becoming a growing 'lifestyle choice' (alongside other 'health' issues) in the mid-1980s, it is no surprise that it should be reflected in *Doctor Who*. The consistency with which the theme is referenced (even if only in passing) would suggest a deliberate policy by script editor Saward or writer Holmes (who was more used to incorporating this kind of real-world commentary in scripts for the 1970s version of the show). The Doctor does turn vegetarian himself as a result.

The poorly written and realised *Timelash* offered a guest-starring role for another of the *Blake's 7* cast: a suitably melodramatic Paul Darrow (who'd appeared briefly in *Doctor Who and the Silurians* in 1970). The season climax saw the return of the Daleks and Davros in a Saward-written story crafted in the style of Evelyn Waugh's *The Loved One*, with a dash of *Soylent Green* (1973). Davros is discovered posing as 'the Great Healer', whose base at the Tranquil Repose funeral home is providing him with all the raw material he needs to feed a hungry galaxy and create a new race of malevolent Daleks. Like *Vengeance on Varos*, the story featured a narrator in the form of Alexei Sayle's radio DJ, commenting on the action before being exterminated.

During the transmission of *The Two Doctors* the BBC announced that *Doctor Who* would be taking a longer break than usual. The unusual announcement sparked a media frenzy, with *The Sun* running a front-page story headlined 'Dr Who Axed in BBC Plot!' The break, as a result of a funding shortfall at the BBC after the launch of daytime TV and *EastEnders*, was seen by those outside the executive floor of Television Centre as cancellation, especially as the show had been criticised from within (mainly by Head of Drama Jonathan Powell and BBC1 Controller Michael Grade) as too violent and having lost its way. The controversy was partially instigated by producer John Nathan-Turner working through 'continuity consultant' Ian Levine, who could plant stories in the press while leaving the BBC producer with a clean pair of hands. Once it was explained that the series would be back after an 18-month break, *The Sun* claimed to have 'saved' *Doctor Who*, even though it appears there was no actual intention of permanently dropping the show.

Nonetheless, when season 23 did air, *Doctor Who* was felt to be on trial, a fear that pervaded the production team. This led to the season-long umbrella theme of the Doctor on trial by the Time Lords. The original plans for the next season were abandoned, even though writers had been commissioned, in favour of four interlinked stories that would be transmitted across 14 episodes under the overall title banner *The Trial of a Time Lord*.

The decision marked the climax of Nathan-Turner's event-television approach: the entire 14-episode season would be the event. The resulting series made many concerned fans and casual viewers wonder what had gone on during the 18-month period the production team had to prepare the show. The growing tensions between Nathan-Turner and Saward were apparent. While Saward had been struggling to find new directions, Nathan-Turner had become increasingly caught up in such extracurricular activities as attending fan conventions (especially in the US), and producing Christmas pantomimes, often starring the main *Doctor Who* cast. Saward had increasing misgivings about the casting of Colin Baker and was extremely worried about the way that Nathan-Turner was running the show, his sixth year in charge (the longest-running *Doctor Who* producer to that date). The casting of child star Bonnie Langford as the Doctor's companion (she'd arrive mid-trial) fuelled Saward's worries.

The Trial of a Time Lord was unrewarding for viewers, despite the gimmick of foregrounding the show's own 'on-trial' status in the onscreen narrative. This took Saward's obsession with Greek choruses (characters within the drama who comment on the action) within the programme (*Vengeance on Varos*, *Revelation of the Daleks*) to a new extreme as the Doctor himself settled down to watch his own adventures on a big screen in the Time Lord courtroom. The trial format – conjured up in a moment of desperation by Saward and enthusiastically adopted by Nathan-Turner – was intended to mirror Dickens' *A Christmas Carol*, with adventures from the Doctor's past, present and future. The opening story (known as *The Mysterious Planet*) was written by old *Doctor Who* hand Robert Holmes to be more humorous following a brief from Grade, but was dismissed by Powell as being 'lightweight'. This contradictory feedback further alienated Saward from the production and would ultimately lead to his acrimonious departure before the completion of the season. *The Mysterious Planet* is a soft *Mad Max* in which mankind has reverted to primitive ways on a planet revealed to be a relocated Earth. It was an inauspicious and low-key re-launch for a series living on borrowed time.

The second adventure (known as *Mindwarp*) provided the highlight of the season, bringing back Sil, the villain of *Vengeance on Varos*, showing the surprising removal of the Doctor from time, and climaxing with the shocking death of companion Peri in a brain-swap operation. A colourful story, *Mindwarp* once again saw *Doctor Who* used as a technical test bed, this time for the HARRY Paintbox digital-effects system, which resulted in Sil's planet boasting a green sky, purple rocks and a pink sea!

Bonnie Langford arrived aboard the TARDIS in the Agatha Christie-style, murder-mystery 'future' segment (known as *Terror of the Vervoids*), set onboard doomed space liner *Hyperion III*. This led into the final two-part wrap-up of the *Trial* season (known as *The Ultimate Foe*, though all these episode titles were not seen onscreen, and only used for novelisations and DVD releases). By the time these final episodes were produced (before the Vervoids story was made), Saward had decided to leave the show. When he quit he gave a scathing interview to SF magazine *Starburst* in which he criticised Nathan-Turner's 'light-entertainment' style of *Doctor Who*, his poor casting decisions and his obsession with peripheral minutiae like merchandising and conventions, rather than well-written scripts or properly thought-out characters. 'I was getting very fed up with the way *Doctor Who* was being run, largely by John Nathan-Turner – his attitude and his lack of insight into what makes a television series like *Doctor Who* work,' said Saward. 'After being cancelled and coming back almost in the same manner as we were before, [with] the same sort of pantomime-ish aspects that I so despised about the show, I just think it isn't worth it.'

As a result of Saward's departure, his original script for episode 14 could not be used, so a hastily created replacement (by Nathan-Turner stalwarts Pip and Jane Baker) was put together. 'When I left, I was writing the last episode,' confirmed Saward. 'We had talked about this ending and he had agreed, in principle, to a hard, cliff-hanging thing. The episode went in and John said, "I don't like the end; we can't go out on that end." He wanted the happy pantomime ending.' As a result, the climax to the 14-week-long trial was an incoherent narrative that only escaped greater criticism because much of it took place in the fantasy environment of the Matrix (*The Deadly Assassin*), so logical storytelling was not a strong point. The conclusion revealed the prosecuting Valeyard (Michael Jayston) to be a future, evil incarnation of the Doctor himself, in collusion with the Time Lords to cover up their criminal actions (which involved the moving of Earth in the opening story, *The Mysterious Planet*). As a result of Saward's walkout, his original cliff-hanger ending – in which the Valeyard and the Doctor tumbled into a 'time vent', their survival (and that of the show itself) uncertain – could not be used. Nathan-Turner felt this ending would be a hostage to fortune, giving the BBC an opportunity to cancel the series. Viewers who had stuck with the trial through 14 weeks would require a satisfactory ending. He didn't quite deliver that, but Colin Baker's Sixth Doctor left the scene intact, along with new companion Mel (Langford).

The Trial of a Time Lord had been a brave experiment, but one that failed to address the criticisms that had resulted in the show being put on hiatus. The behind-the-scenes and onscreen narrative chaos in which the production ended only added fuel to the criticisms, many now voiced by the show's own script editor. Despite the latest of his annual attempts to leave, producer John Nathan-Turner was 'persuaded to stay' as the show's producer, although he had no script editor, no scripts, and was about to lose his leading man. Although the BBC decided to continue with *Doctor Who*, Nathan-Turner was instructed to replace the star, a fact revealed after the broadcast of the final episode of *The Trial of a Time Lord*.

The whole run had averaged only 4.8 million viewers, compared with a previous average of 7.2 million (a remarkably steady figure through the Davison years and into Baker's first season). This dramatic loss of viewers during a serial that was intended as a major re-launch for the show was disappointing, and series star Colin Baker was made the scapegoat. It was felt within the BBC that the only way of revitalising *Doctor Who* was to have a fresh start with a new Doctor.

The casting of Sylvester McCoy as the new Doctor and the arrival of Andrew Cartmel as script editor drew a line under a troubled period in *Doctor Who*'s history and gave the show a new lease of life for the next three years. Nathan-Turner's retreat from many of the show's creative aspects gave Cartmel unprecedented freedom to reinvent the series. He was a young writer and trainee script editor attached to the BBC Drama Unit's scriptwriting workshop. A huge fan of comic books (then in vogue and being taken seriously as literature in the wake of *The Dark Knight* and *Watchmen*), he would bring some elements of comic-book storytelling to *Doctor Who*.

The fresh start saw season 24 open with another Pip and Jane Baker script (commissioned by Nathan-Turner, rather than Cartmel) featuring dodgy science and a return encounter with the Rani (Kate O'Mara). Much like *The Twin Dilemma* before it, *Time and the Rani* proved to be an inauspicious debut for the new Doctor and Cartmel was happy to disassociate himself from it.

Cartmel's time on the show saw the introduction of a host of new, young TV writers, many of whom he'd met while at the BBC's Drama Unit. These new writers had grown up watching *Doctor Who*, would draw on their 'folk memory' of the show, and had a good feel for what worked and what didn't. Several current late-1980s political and social themes permeated the adventures overseen by Cartmel and created by his stable of young writers. After almost a decade, the series finally got around to addressing aspects of Thatcherism, mainly as the writers had come to maturity in Thatcher's Britain. Writing about this came as naturally to them as writing about the mining industry, the European Union or environmentalism did to Letts and Dicks. The writers were Thatcher's children, so a sharp increase in political and social allegory appeared from *Paradise Towers* onwards, although this never came before a need to entertain the audience.

The decline of council estates and the consequences of Thatcher's sell-off of council housing heavily informed *Paradise Towers*. In a time when consumer culture expanded to take in architecture and houses, setting a *Doctor Who* adventure within a run-down, futuristic tower block (perhaps drawn from JG Ballard's *High Rise*) seems obvious. Divisions within society (rich and poor, the suburban and urban communities) had grown throughout the eight years that Prime Minister Thatcher had been in power. Since 1979, her policies had largely increased social division, mirrored in the Kangs (devolved youth subcultures) and the Rezzies (secluded residents of exclusive or 'gated' communities) of *Paradise Towers*. With the Falklands war a strong memory for those who were teenagers or in their twenties at the time (like the writers), the anti-war sentiments of the Towers' 'hero' Pex seem understandable. The satire of dictators was played up by the visualisation of the Caretaker as a Hitler figure, helped enormously by Richard Briers' performance.

Another dictatorial figure emerged in season 26's *The Happiness Patrol*. Helen A (Sheila Hancock) was an obviously Thatcher-inspired ruler, while the story featured elements of Chilean dictator Pinochet's policy of 'disappearance' as a way of dealing with political opponents (the Falklands war saw Thatcher's UK government going easy on Pinochet in return for Chilean support in South America). The visual look of *The Happiness Patrol* – pastel colours and candy-inspired décor – reflected growing 'rave culture' (smiley-face symbols and 'happy' drugs) and the dance-music scene revolving around ecstasy. Kitsch culture was celebrated in the Kandy Man, a robotic creature (chief torturer of the regime) whose look echoed that of Bertie Bassett, a cartoon advertising figure built from sweets and used by Bassett to promote their All Sorts brand. The serious satire may have been buried in the day-glo look, but many viewers were turned off by the superficial impact of the visuals without considering the story's ideas.

Nostalgia, both for *Doctor Who*'s own past and the country's past glories, is another theme running through the final three years of the show. *Delta and the Bannermen* was a fast-moving, three-episode romp from the middle of season 24, set in and around a 1950s holiday camp that is visited by time-travelling tourists, a runaway princess (the last of her race) and a genocidal general (Don Henderson) intent on her elimination. With lots of period music, anachronistic detail and culture-clash humour, the story could easily fit in with the brash approach of some episodes of the most recent version of *Doctor Who*.

Like the twentieth season before it, *Doctor Who*'s twenty-fifth year on air was an excuse for narrative celebration. Opening with *Remembrance of the Daleks* (nostalgically set in 1963, the year of *Doctor Who*'s debut), the season tackled racism and racial purity through the Daleks and the rise of modern fascism. Nazi ideology recurred in *Silver Nemesis*, a Cybermen adventure broadcast around the show's actual twenty-fifth anniversary.

Postmodern pastiche found a new, audience-friendly form during this period too, with characters in *Dragonfire* all named after prominent film theorists, while much of the narrative (including the origins of new companion Ace) mirrored *The Wizard of Oz*. This kind of cultural sampling and remixing was relatively new, but it would go on to become a dominant mode of expression in pop culture. When Ace sees a TV announcer introducing a new programme on British TV in November 1963, only the audience are aware that *Doctor Who* is referring to itself. Self-reflexivity may have reached exhaustion, however, in the cleverly titled *The Greatest Show in the Galaxy*, which saw the Doctor trapped in a psychic circus, battling the gods of Ragnarok. As well as playing with well-worn imagery like scary clowns, haunted circuses and werewolves, this serial featured a character called Whizzkid, an obsessive fan of the circus who has followed its development and collected the associated merchandise. He complains that the circus 'is not as good as it used to be'. This portrait, within the narrative of the show, of a *Doctor Who* fan (referred to disparagingly as 'barkers' by Nathan-Turner, and 'ming mongs' by Russell T Davies) was about as insular as it was possible to get.

Besides new myths, the final episodes also featured new ways of looking at old myths or old stories. Norse mythology was plundered for both *The Greatest Show in the Galaxy* and the final season's *The Curse of Fenric* (set in the Second World War). *The Curse of Fenric* also featured material drawn from Bram Stoker's *Dracula* effectively mixed with the development of British computing and the quest of wartime code-breaker Alan Turing to smash German ciphers. Arthurian tales provided a strong narrative backbone for the final season's opening story, *Battlefield* (nostalgically reviving the Brigadier one last time, and attempting to update UNIT), while female folklore provided a new angle on a traditional good-versus-evil story in *Survival* (written by Rona Munro, the last of a very few female writers for the original series).

Cartmel's interest in comic books played a large part in his development of *Doctor Who*. The Dalek Emperor (really Davros in disguise) portrayed in *Remembrance of the Daleks* was drawn directly from *Doctor Who*'s own comic-book past in the 1960s TV comic, *TV21*. A lot of the absurdist look and feel of *Doctor Who* in the years 1986–9 was in tune with successful British comic *2000AD*, especially stories like *Paradise Towers* and *The Happiness Patrol*. Fan input in the series culminated with a fan writing for the show for the first time since Andrew Smith and *Full Circle* in 1980. Fanzine contributor and aspiring TV writer Marc Platt got *Ghost Light* into production, playing with themes of evolution and change, overlaid with a strong dash of Victorian literature. The haunted-house setting and the confrontation with events in the Doctor's companion Ace's past gave the complicated notions a strong emotional grounding. They also built on a mini story arc for the character that showed her maturing throughout the final year the show was on air. This more proactive approach to a companion would inform Russell T Davies's ideas years later.

Cartmel had a bigger plan in mind when it came to developing the Doctor. He and the group of young writers he was working with were drawing on their own memories of *Doctor Who* in refashioning the show. They all recalled a time when the mystery of who the Doctor was featured regularly, so wanted to return that element, which had been diluted with the addition of Gallifrey and the Time Lords to the programme's growing and increasingly complicated mythology. Cartmel's answer was to graft a new mythology on top of the old, with hints in various episodes that the Doctor was 'more than a Time Lord' pushing the character ever more in the direction of a superhero. Other characters would refer to the Doctor's mysterious origins or claim privileged knowledge of his secrets. These secrets were never divulged to the viewer, and it was not really clear if Cartmel genuinely had a destination in mind when he started this process. Whatever his intention, he did provide fuel for years of fan speculation that would keep *Doctor Who* stories going in other media throughout the fallow period of the 1990s when the series was mostly off air.

Doctor Who's ratings had suffered a terminal collapse from *The Trial of a Time Lord* season onwards. From average highs of 14.5 million for *City of Death* in 1979, audience figures had collapsed within a decade to 3.6 million for *Battlefield*, a fall of over 75 per cent. The failure of the show to engage with the political and social realities of the 1980s, and the producer's interest in pleasing minority fan culture, had turned off the popular audience. *Doctor Who* had become a show made for fans, with many creative decisions serving to alienate the wider audience that the show had succeeded in capturing in the 1960s and 1970s. This loss of popular affection (audiences in the 1980s loved the nostalgic idea they had of the show, but not the version on TV starring Baker and McCoy) led directly to a loss of support for the ageing series within the BBC.

Survival saw out the original series, returning the show to its roots in contemporary London (this time 1989, rather than 1963). This tale of cat people arriving on Earth from their own doomed planet and hunting contemporary teens was full of ambitious ideas (like much of Cartmel-period *Doctor Who*), but was let down by its execution. A final battle between the Master and the Doctor brought *Doctor Who* to a premature close. There were many ideas yet to be explored and many more worlds to visit, but time had been called on a series that had suffered more than its fair share of missteps through the 1980s. The Doctor's future would now be in the hands of his fans.

6. THE FANDOM MENACE

In the 1980s, organised *Doctor Who* fandom became notorious for its involvement in affecting the direction and content of the TV series. Collective, organised fan action has, at different times in its history, both benefited and harmed the show. The twenty-first-century revival of *Doctor Who* may be a popular ratings hit, but it is creatively driven by writers, directors and even actors who grew up as active fans of the original TV series. Writer-producer Russell T Davies was just such an active fan, who went on to write a professional spin-off novel (*Damaged Goods*) while forging a TV scriptwriting career from the early 1990s that led to him reviving the series he loved. Steven Moffat, his replacement after five years, had been just as active in fandom and a regular attendee at London fan pub get-togethers, as well as writer of the affectionate 1999 Red Nose Day *Doctor Who* spoof *The Curse of Fatal Death*. Writers for the new show, like Paul Cornell and Gareth Roberts, cut their creative teeth in *Doctor Who* fandom, while the Tenth Doctor himself, David Tennant, was also a self-proclaimed, knowledgeable fan of the original series whose reason for becoming an actor was to play that role.

These people are the most visible members of a very active and creative group that gathered around *Doctor Who*. More than most media-driven fandoms, the *Doctor Who* fan community has proved to be a creative hotbed that not only provided an outlet for the passions of fans, but kept the series alive when it was off air and created positive new directions for it to move in. While many fans were content to express their own creativity through producing fanzines, fan-made videos or stage productions, and many others were happy simply to participate in the consumption of this material (perhaps contributing through the letter columns), some were driven to pursue professional creative careers, having honed their craft in the worlds of *Doctor Who* fandom. It was a natural conclusion to all this activity that the lunatics should one day take over the asylum, and fans would be in the professional position of producing (and starring in) the show itself.

Doctor Who fandom had its origins in the 1960s. Two years after the series' debut the BBC officially sanctioned the William (*Doctor Who*) Hartnell Fan Club, run by an enthusiastic fan from Stoke-on-Trent. Members would receive signed photos of the cast and an occasional duplicated newsletter. With the change of lead actor to Patrick Troughton in 1966, the organisation became the Official *Doctor Who* Fan Club, but the material it produced continued along the same lines, if slightly more in depth (as would be expected from a growing, more experienced organisation). By 1969, the club was being run by Graham Tattersall, who continued to forge good connections with the *Doctor Who* production office secretaries and developed the club magazine further, expanding it to include coverage of the new show occupying *Doctor Who*'s Saturday time slot, *Star Trek*. As the 1970s dawned, Tattersall found he could no longer afford to devote the time, energy and expense needed to run the club single-handed.

In 1971, an Edinburgh-based fan, Keith Miller, took over the running of the club, producing a revamped newsletter using equipment at his school. When this became impractical, Miller arranged for the *Doctor Who* production office itself (now under Barry Letts) to duplicate and mail out the newsletter to his members. The content of the magazine (called *DWFC Mag* by 1973) developed in sophistication and began to include interviews with the series' cast arranged through the production office. Miller (accompanied by his mother) even visited Television Centre to see the series in production. As the popularity of the show grew, so too did the membership of the club, entering the thousands and spreading worldwide in the wake of the show's overseas sales. Miller found the growing club difficult to manage, and wound it up by mid-1976, moving on to produce his own paid-for 'fanzine' (a 'fan magazine' produced by amateurs, usually on a single topic like a TV show, a football club or a pop band) called *Doctor Who Digest*.

Just as Miller was opting out of his *Doctor Who* activities, the seeds of the *Doctor Who* Appreciation Society (DWAS) were sown in the mid-1970s. The growth of independently produced fanzines (thanks to developments in copying technology) brought together several people who'd previously been part of Miller's growing network, among them *TARDIS* magazine editor Gordon Blows and Jan Vincent Rudzki. The core of the DWAS effectively grew out of a group of *Doctor Who* fans who attended the University of London's Westfield College, combined with some of Miller's most active members. The organisation, officially recognised by the BBC, was founded in October 1975, and was rolled out nationally in May 1976.

Membership grew slowly, with members regularly receiving Society newsletter *Celestial Toyroom*, but the DWAS served as a group around which greater *Doctor Who* fandom could orbit. Independent fanzines flourished in the 1980s (as photocopying and cheap printing made their production even easier, even if circulation only reached a few hundred) and local groups (whether formerly affiliated with the DWAS or not) appeared across the country, holding regular meetings. Being a *Doctor Who* fan moved from being a solitary pursuit to a communal activity, with a growing shared language and set of references.

In 1977, the first *Doctor Who* convention was held in Battersea,

London in a church hall, and gave rise to a regular series of events, each growing in size in terms of venue and attendance. Through the years to come, those running the Society (the self-named 'Executive') would change when their personal lives or jobs changed, giving opportunities to others (usually involved fans who'd managed to make connections with the people already running things). Thus a ready-made chain of succession within organised fandom meant that the DWAS continues to exist today, although it has a far less pivotal role in a much more diffuse, Internet-based fandom.

With the widespread sale of batches of Tom Baker *Doctor Who* episodes to the United States in the early 1980s, fandom took root there as well. Fanzines and conventions flourished on both sides of the Atlantic, and in Australia where *Doctor Who* was regularly screened and gathered a similar active cult following. Stars of the show were encouraged to attend events worldwide by 1980s producer John Nathan-Turner, and the production office was more helpful than ever in facilitating fan access to the show.

Throughout the 1980s, fandom grew, and became more involved in affecting the production of the series itself. One prominent fan, music producer and songwriter Ian Levine, became attached to John Nathan-Turner's production office as an unofficial, unpaid 'continuity advisor'. As previous producers Philip Hinchcliffe and Graham Williams had found, *Doctor Who* had told so many stories over its almost 20 years in production that it was impossible to know everything about them and thus avoid contradicting events in the series' past. Levine had first come to the notice of the production office in the late 1970s when he'd managed to prevent the destruction of key 1960s episodes by the BBC (as part of their ongoing process of videotape recycling). Nathan-Turner came to regard Levine's encyclopaedic knowledge of the show as an asset, so enlisted him to review scripts and make other suggestions regarding continuity issues. As Levine claimed in an online debate in 2008: 'Between

1979 and 1986, I had access to every script and was privy to every decision.'

It is arguable that Levine's influence spilled over from correcting continuity mistakes and making suggestions to actually influencing the approach Nathan-Turner took to producing the show. With Levine working on the inside of the production and vocal fans welcoming the evident 'returning monsters' policy developing through Nathan-Turner's first few seasons, the producer apparently began to tailor the show to appeal to the vocal fan network, while also trying to make a show that would appeal to general BBC1 viewers. More than any previous producer, Nathan-Turner regarded his duties as including attending fan conventions (only Williams had previously attended fan events, being the producer when conventions began to take off). The fan acclaim he received could do no other than colour his production of the series.

However, the insular nature of the later material being created to appeal to fans did not cross over to the larger audience, beyond an initial nostalgia value. The show now often featured obscure continuity, and showcased returning characters and monsters, many forgotten by the more casual mass audience. By the time the show reached *Attack of the Cybermen* (supposedly co-written, or at the very least developed, by Levine) in 1985, the stories being told had become so continuity laden that even actively involved fans had trouble fitting together all the elements.

Fans were not always positive about the programme, even in the early days of organised fandom. One of the earliest reviews published by the DWAS was a scathing assessment of *The Deadly Assassin* (by DWAS organiser Jan Vincent Rudzki) ending with the plea: 'What has happened to the magic of *Doctor Who*?' In later years, Robert Holmes' reinvention of Time Lord society has come to be regarded as a classic, often featuring in the upper reaches of fan-favourite polls. The voices of 1980s fandom quickly turned on Nathan-Turner, even as they continued to enjoy privileged access to the show thanks to his largesse.

Nathan-Turner's 'open-door' policy to fans contributed towards the development of a 'fan hierarchy'. Those who had contacts in the *Doctor Who* production office were privy to advance knowledge that the greater body of fandom was not, and some would use this access to increase their stature within the small pond of fandom.

Small groups of active London fans even secured jobs within the BBC, including in the costume department at Television Centre or even working on the BBC listings magazine *Radio Times*. This afforded them access to information and even to the studio filming of episodes. Small groups of fans – those with BBC passes, their invited friends, and those allowed access by Nathan-Turner or other production-office contacts – were regular attendees at Television Centre studio recordings throughout the 1980s. They were able to watch episodes being recorded in the studio, pick up on behind-the-scenes relationships and politics and even fraternise with cast and crew in the BBC bar afterwards. Part of the reason for *Doctor Who*'s downfall at the end of the 1980s came from this free flow between fans and production personnel, unlike that on any other British TV show – cult, SF, soap or otherwise.

As well as the DWAS newsletter *Celestial Toyroom*, several other prominent fanzines had started up offering a platform for a plethora of critical voices (long before the existence of Internet forums). These magazines offered an outlet for experimentation and created a venue in which aspiring fiction writers and critics could learn their craft. Within this small universe, certain fan names would become well known and their work anticipated, by an actively engaged audience.

Two magazines in particular contributed to the development of *Doctor Who*'s fan culture in the 1980s: the professional *Doctor Who* magazine and the independent and critical *Doctor Who Bulletin*. *Doctor Who* magazine developed from the launch in 1979 by Marvel of *Doctor*

Who Weekly comic. The title would prove to be important to the consolidation of fan identity and community in the UK. Modelled after *Star Wars Weekly*, the comic-strip-led publication was run by *Doctor Who* fans who used the publication's resources and 'official' status to codify the *Doctor Who* canon. This wasn't a deliberate project, but the result of unbridled enthusiasm meeting a welcoming audience. Soon the publication had developed beyond its beginnings as a children's comic and was re-launched as *Doctor Who Monthly* (later just *Doctor Who Magazine*), appealing to an older, teen-and-upwards audience.

The establishment of key agreed facts about the show began in the pages of *Doctor Who Monthly*. Previously, fans had little published material beyond occasional features in the *Radio Times* (including the collectible Tenth Anniversary Special) and other newspapers and magazines, old *TV21* comic-strip adventures and one book, *The Making of Doctor Who* (by scriptwriters Terrance Dicks and Malcolm Hulke), which offered story synopses for the series up to the Tom Baker serial *The Hand of Fear* and some limited behind-the-scenes information. Now, the editors and writers of *Doctor Who Monthly* were able to establish a consensus as to which TV stories of the past were good (dubbed 'classics') and which were poor. Many readers gained an education on how television shows were constructed, with special attention paid to those elements that made *Doctor Who* unique, like special effects or model making. Stories told by cast and crew (often untrue or misremembered) became legends through repetition in the pages of *Doctor Who Monthly*. The publication matured with its audience, becoming *Doctor Who Magazine* and enduring through the years the show was off air (1989–2005), thriving on coverage of fan-produced novels and audio productions, as well as re-exploring *Doctor Who*'s past, often using video or DVD releases as a hook for re-appraising a particular story or era of the show. That *Doctor Who* fandom has a shared language and set of cultural assumptions is largely due to the pervasive influence of *Doctor Who Magazine*.

Within the pages of the magazine, John Nathan-Turner established himself as a larger-than-life personality, one to rival Fourth Doctor Tom Baker. He even had a 'costume' of sorts, often wearing loud Hawaiian shirts in photographs and personal appearances. His was the voice of wisdom; he was the man who held the secrets of *Doctor Who* adventures yet to come and who could explain how fans were mistaken in their view that the 1980s version of the show was not as good as it used to be, due to the fact that 'the memory cheats'. Nathan-Turner developed a series of catchphrases, readily repeated (and eventually mocked), such as 'stay tuned', when promising new developments, and 'I have been persuaded to stay', when fans were desperate for a new producer to take over from 1985 onwards. Nathan-Turner was regularly photographed in the pages of the magazine alongside the series' stars, often wearing those 'trademark' Hawaiian shirts, or a sheepskin coat. His 'cult of the personality' was one that fandom initially fed, before they turned on the monster they'd been instrumental in creating.

A key tool in fan dissent was the maverick *Doctor Who Bulletin* (DWB). *DWB* took issue with the official picture of the series being painted in the 1980s through the pages of *Celestial Toyroom* and *Doctor Who Magazine*. Begun in 1983 as a back-bedroom-produced fanzine, *DWB* would become increasingly professional in its approach and production values as well as function as an outlet for the kind of fan debate not tolerated in the pages of *Doctor Who Magazine*. Pre-Internet, letters-pages debates would rage among fans for months at a time, while editor Gary Levy (later Leigh) built solid contacts within the *Doctor Who* production office. The publication was tolerated by producer John Nathan-Turner until the magazine turned on the show and began to heavily criticise the production and those making it, with much of the criticism seemingly driven by growing personal animosity. With the help of continuity advisor Ian Levine (also an outcast as far as the production office was concerned by 1986), *DWB* chronicled the 1985 cancellation crisis and the reception of the flawed *The Trial of a Time Lord* season in 1986. It gave a voice to increasingly negative fan reaction.

Throughout the 1980s, many of the fans who began as writers for fanzines, or worked on *Celestial Toyroom*, *Doctor Who Magazine* or *DWB*, would become professionals in their fields, shaped by their experiences in *Doctor Who* fandom. Many became writers, whether for magazines or television, while others pursued more technical interests in video production and restoration. Some fans, born in the 1960s, were the right age to find work on the programme itself in its dying days, such as model maker Mike Tucker (who would go on to write official spin-off novels) and mask makers Stephen Mansfield and Susan Moore.

Other events had linked and brought *Doctor Who* fans together, showing isolated, individual fans that they in fact belonged to a large and active subculture. In 1983, to celebrate the twentieth anniversary of *Doctor Who* in advance of that autumn's broadcast of *The Five Doctors*, BBC Enterprises (the publicly funded BBC's commercial arm) arranged an official convention to take place in the grounds of Longleat House in Wiltshire. There had been occasional *Doctor Who* exhibitions and public appearances by the stars before, most notably the ongoing (and constantly changing) exhibition on the sea front at Blackpool and that at Longleat itself. The Longleat event would be different, however. The organisers expected around 50,000 people to attend over the Easter-weekend holiday, drawn by appearances by many of the actors from the show's 20-year history. However, the BBC had underestimated the appeal of *Doctor Who* and the effect of nostalgia. Traffic jams and endless lines became a hallmark of the event, as crowds swarmed to see prop displays, watch old episodes screened in tents and queue for hours to secure autographs from their favourite actors. The enforced waiting in line had a curious side effect: many friendships, some lasting to this day, began in the lines at Longleat. Fan writer Paul Cornell even went on to describe the event as the *Doctor Who* fan equivalent of Woodstock (the 1969 music festival in New York State that many see as marking the end of the 'innocence' of that tumultuous decade).

The unforeseen success of the Longleat event proved at least one thing to the BBC: *Doctor Who* was still as merchandisable a property as it had been during the 1960s at the height of 'Dalekmania'. As a result, the quantity and availability of *Doctor Who* merchandise would rocket, as would products aimed exclusively at fan purchasers. Far from being seen as the creative group they would later be recognised as, the vast majority of fans (those without any privileged access) in the 1980s were largely perceived as an economic construct waiting to be exploited, little more than consumers of merchandise and memorabilia. A plethora of books appeared chronicling the history of the series (not always accurately, as several tomes by Peter Haining showed: it took later writers, who combined their fandom with solid research, to really get the facts on how the show had been created and made from the 1960s to the 1980s). Others had more tenuous links to the programme, such as *The Doctor Who Cook Book* and *The Doctor Who Knitting Pattern Book*.

Fans had been canvassed at the Longleat event to see what story from the past they would like to see released on home video, which was just taking off as a new entertainment format in the early 1980s. The eventual choice would be *Revenge of the Cybermen* (the first choice, the then-lost Troughton serial *Tomb of the Cybermen*, not being available), released in a one-hour, cut-down version for £40. However, throughout the early-to-mid-1980s there was a large fan underground trade in VHS videotapes of many *Doctor Who* stories. Some were sourced from ongoing transmissions of Tom Baker and Jon Pertwee stories in the United States and Australia. Fans with international pen friends would receive copies of off-air VHS video recordings of episodes. These would then be copied further on connected home-videotape machines and redistributed around the UK's fan networks. It was the only way fans gained access to the actual episodes that made up *Doctor Who*'s long history. That lack of access to older episodes of the show was also why the tents at Longleat screening *The Dalek Invasion of Earth* or *The Dominators* proved almost more popular than those boasting appearances by real-life *Doctor Who* actors. Often, small groups of fans would meet in each other's houses (or in rented halls or community-centre rooms if the groups were larger) to watch these fourth- or fifth-generation videotape copies of long-unseen *Doctor Who* stories. It was hardly the ideal way to discover the history of their favourite TV show, but as very little was officially available and repeat screenings on television (limited to just four channels) were almost non-existent, unofficially sourced videotapes were the only way to see vintage *Doctor Who*. Occasionally, fans would gain access to older, black-and-white episodes of the show, clearly not transferred to tape from off-air broadcasts (these were clean copies lacking continuity announcers, onscreen logos or ad breaks). These mysteriously sourced tapes appeared to have come directly from within the BBC archives themselves, and were often copied from film or video versions of the episodes officially on loan from the BBC for screenings at *Doctor Who* conventions. Other material (such as annual gag reels compiled by the BBC's own videotape engineers featuring programme outtakes and often 'adult' humour) found its way into fandom through more nefarious means.

This privileged access to the show's own past was one of the main benefits of being part of *Doctor Who* fandom: beyond the interminably slow official release of the series to home video by the BBC there was just no way to legitimately see episodes. These same fans would later form the core audience for the home-video and (much later) DVD releases of the series, as well as (in many cases) contributing towards the creation of the value-added 'extras' material featured on the DVDs. Fan audio recordings from the 1960s are often the only remaining material from key stories whose videotape recordings had been wiped. These same unauthorised audio recordings of stories like *The Myth Makers* or *Marco Polo* have been audio restored and polished and officially released on CD by the BBC. Efforts by fans of the show, in cases like this, have resulted in the preservation of material that the BBC would otherwise have wilfully destroyed long ago. As of 2008, however, there were still 106 missing episodes of *Doctor Who* (all from the show's earlier black-and-white era), while many of those that have been recovered from foreign broadcasters (to whom they'd been sold for transmission in the 1960s and 1970s) have been found in international searches carried out by dedicated fans.

The problem with this increasing influence of a vocal minority of fans over *Doctor Who* during the 1980s was that it lost its grip on the mass audience. In appealing to vocal fans the programme became more insular (offering more returning monsters and more explorations of the series' fundamental concepts). The irony was that, by the time of the 1985 hiatus, *Doctor Who* was a television show that most fans no longer seemed to like either, at least as far as the current version went. While Nathan-Turner claimed that 'the memory cheats', committed fans actually had contemporary access (through their unofficially circulated VHS videos) to the show's own past episodes and were thus able to make direct comparisons.

Ian Levine was pictured in the press smashing his TV with a hammer in a publicity stunt to protest against the 1985 hiatus. During *The Trial of a Time Lord* season in 1986, he appeared on TV review show *Did You See…?* in a segment entitled '*Doctor Who* in Decline'. Levine voiced the complaints of many fans when he noted that recent years had seen 'a very steep decline in the quality of the show' and that it was now a 'mockery pantomime version of its former self'. Other professional fans (like *Doctor Who Magazine* writer J Jeremy Bentham and later *Doctor Who* novelist Peter Anghelides) appeared to join in the criticism of the in-danger-of-cancellation programme. *Doctor Who* didn't need executive enemies within the BBC – it had 'fans'.

This tension between loving *Doctor Who* but not liking the currently on-air version was unique to the series at the time, but with a rash of 'reinventions' of old formats in recent years, fans of 1970s television series like *Bionic Woman* or *Battlestar Galactica* have found themselves locked into love-hate relationships with the new versions of their old favourites. Production decisions are debated, casting choices bemoaned and alternatives endlessly suggested in Internet forums and chat rooms. This all happened in *Doctor Who* fandom in the 1980s, too, but the media available were the letter columns of fanzines and, eventually, television itself through comment shows like *Did You See…?* or *Open Air* (which saw a group of fans tackle writers Pip and Jane Baker over the faults in the conclusion of the *Trial of a Time Lord* season, including teenager Chris Chibnall, later to become key writer on *Doctor Who* spin-off *Torchwood*).

Through their knowledge of the series, gathered from fanzines and publications like *Doctor Who Magazine* and their viewing of older, generally unavailable episodes, as well as (for the select few who were well connected) their actual involvement with the *Doctor Who* production-office personnel, *Doctor Who* fandom collectively developed a sense of ownership of the show. This perceived ownership reached its height during the aftermath of the 1985 hiatus crisis, and would lead to fan fiction writers 'taking over' the production of *Doctor Who* when the show was off air.

There were benefits to be had from this obsessive attention to a single TV show. As a result of the attention paid to it, *Doctor Who* is the most studied and chronicled television show of all time, and fandom has produced some meticulous and detail-oriented media researchers, key among them being Andrew Pixley. A whole set of professionals all found their initial inspirations and first experiences within the diverse worlds of *Doctor Who* fandom in the 1980s. In this shared vocabulary and set of references, *Doctor Who* fans found a form of discourse that connected them, educated them and equipped them to take over the production of the continuing unfolding text of *Doctor Who* after the BBC had abandoned it, through novels, audio dramas and in-depth research into the making of the programme. Fans became the custodians of the *Doctor Who* legacy, safeguarding it and expanding it until the time was right for the TV show to re-emerge and take its rightful place at the top of the TV ratings.

With the cancellation of the *Doctor Who* TV series in 1989, the range of spin-off novels expanded dramatically beyond the original Target novelisations of television stories. These new *Doctor Who* adventures were largely created by fans who'd cut their fiction-writing teeth on various fanzines, among them new series' scriptwriter Paul Cornell, script editor Gary Russell and showrunner Russell T Davies.

For much of the run of the original show, starting in the mid-1970s and running beyond the 1989 cancellation, Target (initially a subsidiary of Universal-Tandem, then WH Allen) produced an ongoing series of novelisations of the *Doctor Who* television adventures. Many of these slim volumes were written by Terrance Dicks and aimed at younger readers. In a pre-video age, the Target novels were the only way to relive *Doctor Who* adventures (they allowed repeatability through re-reading), with the books and the cover images becoming the defining aspects of certain serials for many fans. It could even be argued that the Target books helped in increasing the literacy of an entire generation. By 1993, when the series of novels adapted from TV episodes finally concluded (four years after the TV series itself had ended, and now published by Virgin), all but a few TV adventures had been novelised (the missing stories were scripts by Douglas Adams and Eric Saward). Spin-offs, like radio serial *Slipback*, TV one-shot *K-9 and*

Company and unmade stories (such as stories from the originally planned version of season 23), were also novelised, bringing the Target total to 157 books.

Once the TV adventures had been exhausted, Virgin extended its official licence for *Doctor Who* novels, splitting the range into two series: New Adventures and Missing Adventures. The New Adventures range (from 1991 to 1997, 61 books) continued, and greatly expanded, the adventures of the Seventh Doctor (as portrayed on TV by Sylvester McCoy), while the Missing Adventures (which ran from 1994 to 1997, 33 books) featured stories for 'past' Doctors, the First to the Sixth.

The first of these fan-authored books consisted of two trilogies: the *Timewyrm* trilogy and the *Cat's Cradle* series. Edited by Peter Darvill-Evans (later replaced by Rebecca Levene and Simon Winstone), the writers included Marc Platt (TV's *Ghost Light*) and Andrew Cartmel (the McCoy years' script editor), in addition to Cornell. The series continued with standalone adventures by writers including Mark Gatiss (later a writer for, and actor in, the revived version of *Doctor Who*), Ben Aaronovitch (writer of *Remembrance of the Daleks*), Gareth Roberts (*The Shakespeare Code, The Unicorn and the Wasp*), Gary Russell (former *Doctor Who Magazine* editor and later a script editor on *Doctor Who* and spin-off *Torchwood*) and even 1980s Cyber Leader actor David Banks, whose *Iceberg* naturally featured the Cybermen.

Heavily influenced by the 'cyberpunk' movement in SF literature, often attributed to William Gibson's *Neuromancer* trilogy of the early 1980s, the New Adventures series was described by Virgin as featuring 'adventures too broad and deep for the small screen'. They were more adult in content than the earlier Target range of novels, reflecting the core audience for *Doctor Who* in the 1990s: men in their 20s and 30s who'd grown up with the programme, but had outgrown the work of Terrance Dicks that they'd devoured in childhood. Sex, violence and strong language all featured – elements that would never have appeared on screen (although the debate about violence in *Doctor*

Who had run for as long as the show was on air). The fan authors took their opportunity to develop the character of Ace, the Seventh Doctor's streetwise 1980s companion, far beyond her origins. Separated from the Doctor for a period of years, she returned to him a somewhat harder and more cynical character than had appeared on TV. This was evidence, along with the harder SF space-opera stories, that the fan writers were using the novel range to produce the kind of *Doctor Who* (heavily influenced by *Star Wars* and the new wave of British space-opera SF authors, including Iain M Banks) they wished they'd seen on TV in the 1980s.

Many elements featured in the spin-offs novels would heavily influence the series when it returned to TV. Throughout the New Adventures novels there is a 'lonely Doctor' motif, a portrayal of the Doctor as alien to human emotions and condemned to remain alone in the universe, despite a series of temporary companions. Pop-culture references abounded within the novels, and would feature heavily in the revived TV show, with the Doctor seemingly very aware of elements of British pop culture (like *EastEnders*, referred to in *The Satan Pit*). Russell T Davies drew on several elements of the New Adventures when formulating the new series, not least of which was his own *Damaged Goods*, set on a grim housing estate. Paul Cornell's *Human Nature* was adapted directly for TV, changing the Seventh Doctor to the Tenth (in *Human Nature/The Family of Blood* in 2007). The novels had an obsession with continuity, inherited from the John Nathan-Turner years, although the novel authors had more justification for this approach as the books were aimed squarely at committed fans, rather than a larger, more mainstream casual audience. A deepening of continuity led to a desire to wrap up loose ends left over from the TV show or blend together previously disparate elements of the series. This process became known as 'fanwank' (a term coined by one-time DWAS co-ordinator and *Doctor Who* novelist Craig Hinton) and was especially visible in the work of Hinton and Gary Russell. New series showrunner Russell T Davies would be accused of 'fanwank' himself, first when he faced off the Cybermen and the Daleks (a long-held fan dream) in *Doomsday* in 2006 and then when he reunited many elements of his own Tenth Doctor continuity in *The Stolen Earth/Journey's End* in 2008 (see chapter seven).

During his time on the show, script editor Andrew Cartmel had developed a vague notion of making the Doctor 'more than a Time Lord' – as revealed in dialogue from a cut scene that didn't see transmission. Fandom developed this into a full-blown 'masterplan' after the series' conclusion. Building on this, the New Adventures continued the Seventh Doctor's manipulative nature, dubbing him 'Time's Champion'. With Cartmel, Platt and Aaronovitch all writing New Adventures novels, there was an obvious temptation to continue to develop the ideas they had envisaged for the TV series in its final days, including making the Doctor more mysterious (and throwing doubt on the few 'facts' the TV series had established about him). The ongoing book series also removed the Time Lords. Russell T Davies built upon these two elements in his version of the revived TV series. As well as exploring the Doctor's character and motivations in the novels, the TARDIS was also expanded with elements such as an alternate console room made of stone. New companions were invented solely for the novels, resulting in characters the like of which would never have been seen in the TV series, as were new monsters and villains, including the Gallifreyan 'gods'. The New Adventures series climaxed with Marc Platt's novel *Lungbarrow*, which explored the Doctor's mysterious origins (linking him to the founding of Time Lord society). The novel explained the Time Lords' non-sexual reproductive system using genetic 'looms'. The final novel, *The Dying Days*, acted as a coda to the range and featured Paul McGann's Eighth Doctor.

The parallel Missing Adventures, written by many of the same professional and fan writers, were freer to draw on the *Doctor Who* canon, providing sequels to several TV stories. Among these were fan favourites *Pyramids of Mars* (which resulted in *The Sands of Time*), *The Talons of Weng-Chiang* (*The Shadow of Weng-Chiang*) and *The Web Planet* (*Twilight of the Gods*). Various characters and monsters were explored in more depth by the Missing Adventures novels, including the Master (*The Dark Path*), the Cybermen (*Killing Ground*), Silurians (*The Scales of Injustice*) and Sontarans (*Lords of the Storm*), among others. Notably absent were the Daleks, due to difficulties in negotiating with the Nation estate. The Missing Adventures could not make the sweeping changes to characters and continuity offered by the New Adventures as they were intended (in theory) to fit into narrative gaps between TV adventures.

In 1997, following the Paul McGann-starring TV movie (see below), the novel ranges were brought in-house by BBC Books and re-branded as the Past Doctor Adventures (76 books) and the Eighth Doctor Adventures (continuing the exploits of McGann's TV movie character, and producing a further 73 books). The Eighth Doctor novels further developed the McGann portrayal and introduced several new companions and new complications for continuity. The arrival of the new TV series in 2005 saw the range of books reformatted to focus on stories featuring the new TV Doctors and characters (and dropping any complicated continuity). Once again, they were aimed at a younger audience, just as the original Target novels had been. The series of novels featuring adventures of past TV Doctors was dropped. The BBC range and those published after the arrival of the new TV series often used many of the same authors who had risen to prominence through the Virgin novels.

The post-Target *Doctor Who* novels showed that the series' concept could thrive in a new medium. They allowed fans – who'd grown up watching the TV series, reviewing, lampooning and criticising it in fanzines and writing their own versions of it in fan fiction – to control the production of official, new *Doctor Who* adventures. Much more so than any other media fandom (even *Star Trek*), *Doctor Who* fans have been heavily involved in prolonging the life of the object of their obsession, ultimately becoming involved in its return to TV. Their work would interrogate and deconstruct the show, in non-fiction and fiction, taking it apart and rebuilding it in their own preferred format. It was an opportunity to (re)create the show they'd watched and the series they wished they'd seen (or hoped to see, with several writers attempting to explore what *Doctor Who* would be like on the big screen or with no budgetary limitations). Some would attempt to reproduce 'traditional' *Doctor Who* stories ('trad' stories, like *The Visitation*), while others explored the more outré opportunities the series offered ('oddball' stories, like *The Happiness Patrol*). This ownership and control of the ongoing narrative by fans would lay the foundation for the triumphant return of *Doctor Who* to television.

Answering a letter in the *Radio Times* in November 1989, The BBC's Head of Series and Serials Peter Cregeen had promised that the Corporation would 'take *Doctor Who* through the 1990s', while warning that 'there may be a little longer between this series and the next than usual'. The series was simply resting, a bit like Monty Python's famous parrot. This uncertainty about the show's future, and the BBC's commitment to it, prevented any effective organised fan outcry. It seems clear that, while they expected the show to take a break, the BBC honestly didn't anticipate the series being off air for 16 years (apart from the one-off McGann TV movie).

In the dying days of the BBC series there had been interest from various parties interested in taking on *Doctor Who* as an independent production, the direction that much television drama was moving in during the early 1990s. Among those either contacting the BBC or simply expressing interest in *Doctor Who* were former scriptwriter Victor Pemberton, one-time series script editor Gerry Davis, Dalek creator Terry Nation (Nation and Davis were presented as a team who between them co-owned the rights to *Doctor Who*'s biggest monsters, the Daleks and the Cybermen), and even CBS Television in the US (thought an attractive option by Cregeen and fronted by *Doctor Who* fan and US TV producer Philip Segal). Also in development at this time (and regular fodder for increasingly speculative tabloid newspaper reports throughout the decade) was a big-screen *Doctor Who* feature film to be produced by Daltenreys (an organisation alternatively known as Coast to Coast and Green Light at various times). Speculation on the casting of a new Doctor for the proposed big-budget movie became a favourite game played by the tabloid newspapers throughout much of the 1990s, and one they found difficult to give up even when David Tennant had played the role for several years.

With no solid developments announced by the BBC during 1990, the eventual fan campaigns against cancellation (including letter writing, phone-ins and even threatened legal action) proved ineffective in securing the early return of the series. At the end of that year, the head of BBC Enterprises (then charged with looking after the show), James Arnold Baker, announced: 'The property is an old one, it's had its day and is no longer commercially viable.' Enterprises rapidly repudiated this view, keen as they were to continue to exploit *Doctor Who* as a licensing property, even if there were no new episodes made. Terrance Dicks, script editor in the 1970s, explained the internal BBC confusion thus: 'Never put down to conspiracy that which can be explained by incompetence.' Later, BBC Drama Publicity spokesperson Alan Ayres stated that a decision had been taken to 'rest the programme for an extended period so that when it returns it will be seen as a fresh, inventive and vibrant addition to the schedule, rather than a battle-weary Time Lord languishing in the backwaters of audience popularity. *Doctor Who* is too valuable a property for us to re-launch until we are absolutely confident of it as a major success once again.' Fans saw these announcements, and the stories of on-again, off-again movies and proposed independent productions, as a series of delaying tactics by the BBC, who hoped that *Doctor Who* could be quietly forgotten. However, it turned out that Alan Ayres' comments on the series' potential were uncannily prescient.

The view of *Doctor Who* as 'battle weary' changed with the approach of the show's thirtieth anniversary in 1993, when the BBC was suddenly keen to mark the occasion. BBC Radio 2 had already committed to a series of *Doctor Who* radio dramas starring Third Doctor Jon Pertwee, alongside Nicholas Courtney as the Brigadier and Elisabeth Sladen as Sarah Jane Smith. Within BBC Home Video (part of Enterprises), there were *Doctor Who* supporters keen to explore the possibility of a straight-to-video newly made drama for the thirtieth anniversary. This led to the early stages of work on a show entitled *The Dark Dimension*, co-scripted by fan writer Adrian Rigelsford with Graeme Harper lined up to direct. The plan was to reunite several past *Doctor Who* leading actors, but with the main role reserved for Tom Baker. The project was reportedly cancelled when the other Doctor actors realised they would be playing supporting roles to Baker, although, later, Philip Segal, producer of the eventual 1996 TV movie, claimed he'd been instrumental in the abandonment of *The Dark Dimension* as he felt it would conflict with his in-preparation comeback for *Doctor Who* as a brand-new, US-focused production.

British-born Segal had been in touch with the BBC since 1989, and had carried his hopes of reviving *Doctor Who* through several jobs in the US, including periods working for CBS/Columbia, ABC and, finally, Steven Spielberg's Amblin Productions. He'd overseen the launch of David Lynch's *Twin Peaks* at ABC and helped develop SF TV shows *seaQuest DSV* and *Earth 2* at Amblin, which involved a co-production deal with Universal. His ability to drop Spielberg's name into conversations with new Controller of BBC1 Alan Yentob (a *Doctor Who* supporter) led to new interest within the BBC about a US-led co-production (so much so that Yentob pulled a Nathan-Turner-style publicity stunt by popping up at the end of a thirtieth-anniversary documentary, *30 Years in the TARDIS*, and dropping tantalising hints that *Doctor Who* may have a definite future after all).

After years of on-and-off negotiations with the BBC, and alongside their own sporadic attempts at reviving the show, Philip Segal was the one who finally secured the rights to *Doctor Who*. Development work started in 1994. A co-production deal was set up between the BBC, Amblin and Universal while a script was written. The initial TV movie was being regarded as a showcase ('back-door' pilot) for any future TV series, while an outline of the proposed series (the 'bible') outlined characters and locations, as well as proposing key stories from the past that could be remade. By 1995, Amblin had dropped out (and Spielberg with it), but Segal had secured Fox as the US broadcaster for a proposed made-for-TV movie. Segal had also dropped earlier draft scripts that set out to give the series a new beginning, deciding instead to tie the proposed new series directly back to the original by featuring Seventh Doctor actor Sylvester McCoy in an opening regeneration sequence (despite worries that this might confuse US viewers new to the show's concept). Matthew Jacobs (whose actor father had featured in the William Hartnell adventure *The Gunfighters*) was hired to write the script, and actor Paul McGann signed on as the Eighth Doctor (after an audition process that had involved Liam Cunningham, Tony Slattery, Mark McGann [Paul's brother], John Sessions and Michael Crawford, among others). The director was Geoffrey Sax, whose previous experience of *Doctor Who* had been directing a sketch parody of the show called 'Dr Eyes' for 1970s sketch series *End of Part One* that had featured Jim Broadbent as the Doctor (he'd reappear in the part – briefly – in *The Curse of Fatal Death* for Comic Relief in 1999).

The TV movie was eventually shot in Vancouver, Canada in January 1996 with the addition of Eric Roberts (brother of Julia) as a new version of the Doctor's arch-enemy, the Master. Also in the cast were

Daphne Ashbrook as surgeon Grace Holloway and Yee Jee Tso as Chang Lee, the TV movie's companion figures. Set in San Francisco, on the eve of the millennium, the Doctor battles the revived Master (following his own regeneration) for control of the Eye of Harmony (the black hole that seemingly powers the TARDIS), to save the Earth and prevent the Master absorbing the Doctor's remaining lives.

The result was a garbled mix-and-match production that slavishly followed 1990s American television norms, while attempting (in Segal's words) many 'kisses to the past' of *Doctor Who* that only hardcore fans would spot or care about. Opening with an info-dump voiceover from McGann, the film introduced Sylvester McCoy's Seventh Doctor at the helm of a vastly redesigned TARDIS (the interior at least; it's still a British police-box exterior), with no explanation offered for the dimensional contradiction between the tiny box shown flying through space and the vast, now gothic-inspired interior). An encounter with an armed gang after an emergency landing in San Francisco in 1999 sees McCoy's Doctor mortally wounded, operated on by a confused Grace Holloway and then regenerated into McGann's Eighth Doctor.

If nothing else, the 1996 *Doctor Who* TV movie proved to many TV-industry sceptics and the BBC that the show could be produced using modern production techniques and appeal to an audience (it attracted over nine million viewers for its UK debut screening, more through the novelty factor as there'd been no new *Doctor Who* for seven years). In the US, the movie attracted 8.3 million viewers (only nine per cent of the available audience), opposite the final episode of venerable sitcom *Roseanne*.

Some of the TV movie's thunder had been stolen by the death of Third Doctor actor Jon Pertwee in the week before transmission. The BBC tagged a dedication to Pertwee onto the UK transmission of the show (Russell T Davies paid similar tribute to *Doctor Who*'s original producer Verity Lambert on the credits of the 2007 Christmas special, *Voyage of the Damned*, following her death that November).

As well as reclaiming the novel range from Virgin, the BBC produced a range of tie-in material to the 1996 TV movie, with *Doctor Who* merchandise being re-branded using the TV movie's logo (itself a reworking of the Jon Pertwee early-1970s logo). They were clearly hopeful that the one-off film would help launch a new TV series starring McGann, but the viewing figures were simply not enough for the American partners to proceed. As a result of the deal, though, the rights to *Doctor Who* were caught up with Universal for many years, hampering additional attempts by the BBC (and even the BBC's film arm) to mount a revival of the show following the McGann TV movie.

It is ironic that Paul McGann's introduction in the 1996 TV movie is in the form of a voiceover, as his role as the Doctor would develop in the audio field rather than on TV. Starting in 1999, a company called Big Finish began producing officially licensed audio adventures (issued on CD and later available as Internet downloads) of *Doctor Who* starring three of the four living original TV Doctors: Peter Davison, Colin Baker and Sylvester McCoy. Tom Baker consistently refused to take part (although he agreed to play the Doctor for BBC audio drama releases in 2009), while, from 2001, TV movie Eighth Doctor Paul McGann brought new depth to his character by featuring in an annual series of audio dramas (many of which were later transmitted on BBC7, giving them an extra seal of authenticity).

Big Finish continues to be a fan-driven (though professional profit-making) enterprise, reflecting its origins as a series of amateur, fan-produced audio tapes from the 1980s called Audio-Visuals. These unlicensed, home-produced audio tapes were the dramatic equivalents of fanzines (there were also non-fiction audiozines available), an outlet for fiction writers who wanted to dramatise their own version of *Doctor Who*. Many of those involved at the time, primarily Gary Russell and Nicholas Briggs, would go on to steer the Big Finish range (and have significant involvement in the TV *Doctor Who* when it returned from 2005). Of the fan-produced 1980s tapes, Russell said: 'We were fans doing some stuff for a handful of people. We never advertised in professional magazines, we kept ourselves to ourselves. In doing so, we broke every copyright rule in the book. [John] Nathan-Turner was certainly aware of us, but he didn't care. Why should he? We were no more [harm] than any other fan product.'

Several of the original Audio-Visuals productions were rewritten and remade for the Big Finish range, including *The Mutant Phase* (featuring the Daleks), *Sword of Orion* (Cybermen), and *Minuet in Hell* (rewritten for Big Finish to incorporate Nicholas Courtney as the Brigadier). The series also featured a variety of companion actors and actresses (with many later featuring in a semi-dramatised audio-book spin-off series dubbed *The Companion Chronicles*), alongside returning monsters and other characters from the TV series' rich history. Additionally, new companion characters were created just for the audio range. These adventures, like the early spin-off novels, were initially designed to fit into narrative gaps between broadcast TV stories. The success of the core range allowed for a series of limited-run spin-offs built around the popular character of Sarah Jane Smith, the complex politics of the Doctor's home world of Gallifrey and the back-story of Dalek creator Davros. One spin-off series even experimented with recasting the central role, allowing other actors (like Derek Jacobi, David Warner and Geoffrey Bayldon) to play alternative Doctors in *Doctor Who Unbound*. Other, more minor characters have appeared in additional spin-off ranges, while yet more were built around the ever-popular Daleks and Cybermen.

From 1999, when the first CD teamed up the Fifth, Sixth and Seventh Doctors in an adventure called *The Sirens of Time*, Big Finish has provided fans with a monthly fix of audio *Doctor Who* adventures. If nothing else, the fact that the range thrived on fan support (with many willing to pay up to £15 for each CD) showed that there was both a significant audience for new *Doctor Who* stories and that the series format itself was far from exhausted. The Big Finish range had more reason than the TV show under John Nathan-Turner to appeal directly to a dedicated fan base. Their audience were the diehard *Doctor Who* fans, rather than the wider casual TV audience, fans who were willing to pay regularly for further *Doctor Who* adventures.

Fan creative activity also extended to consensual retroactive continuity (retcon): fans would spot narrative gaps in the series and fill them (or fix them) with their own explanations. Primary among these was the concept of season 6B, the further adventures of Patrick Troughton's Second Doctor after *The War Games*, but before he changed into Jon Pertwee's Third Doctor. This fanciful notion was based on Troughton's reappearance in *The Two Doctors* as an older version of the Second Doctor: he'd been co-opted by the Time Lords to carry out missions for them, or so the fan theory went. Others investigated the show's past, as with *The Myth Makers* series of interview videos (and later DVDs) with the series' cast and crew or Jeremy Bentham's *In-Vision* series of in-depth 'making of' fanzines. Fan creativity also saw the creation of music videos (cutting images from the series to popular tracks), done by linking two video recorders together in the decades before digital editing and YouTube. Finally, the ongoing comic-strip adventures of the Doctor continued in *Doctor Who Magazine* and would go on to influence the returning TV series.

It wasn't until September 2003 that the BBC realised that there was still a mass audience who'd respond to new *Doctor Who* on TV. Long the subject of nostalgia, jibes about cardboard sets and rubber monsters, *Doctor Who* had survived a decade and a half of being a nostalgic joke to become a postmodern format whose time had come again. Mal Young, the BBC's head of continuing series, announced on 26 September that acclaimed dramatist Russell T Davies (a self-proclaimed fan of the show who'd even pitched how he would bring the series back in the pages of *Doctor Who Magazine* years previously) would be behind the revival: 'It's time to crank up the TARDIS and find out what lies in store for the Doctor, and we're thrilled to have a writer of Russell's calibre to take us on this journey.'

The announcement of the new live-action TV series aimed at a family audience totally overshadowed that same month's launch of an online animated adventure called *Scream of the Shalka* by Paul Cornell and starring Richard E Grant as the 'official' Ninth Doctor (following previous Internet dramas starring Sylvester McCoy, Colin Baker and Paul McGann). *Scream of the Shalka* and Richard E Grant were quickly destined to become interesting footnotes in *Doctor Who* history, the obscure answer to trivia questions about how many actors have played the Doctor. All eyes were now on BBC1 and the 2005 re-launch of the TV series.

7. REGENERATION

Doctor Who returned to BBC1 on 26 March 2005, starring acclaimed actor Christopher Eccleston as the Ninth Doctor and former pop star Billie Piper as his new travelling companion, Rose Tyler. Those who'd re-created the show (now in 45-minute episodes containing stand-alone stories with some two-episode tales, rather than 25-minute four-to-six-part adventures) were unsure what reaction to expect. TV viewers had not seen a regular series of *Doctor Who* since 1989 and the casting was unexpected (and controversial with fans). A whole generation, the producers feared, had grown up knowing *Doctor Who* as something old-fashioned that their parents liked. BBC research, in advance of transmission, seemed to confirm this view, much to the BBC's trepidation.

Showrunner Russell T Davies and executive producers Julie Gardner (head of drama at BBC Wales, where *Doctor Who* was now to be made) and Phil Collinson (the show's practical line producer) needn't have worried. *Rose*, the opening episode, was a rematch between the Doctor and the Nestene consciousness that controlled the plastic-based Autons (previously foes of the Third Doctor). It introduced Rose Tyler (and her mother and boyfriend) and drew an audience of just under ten million viewers. The series was credited with single-handedly reinvigorating Saturday night family viewing, a niche long since believed lost by most broadcasters.

The series – quickly dubbed 'NuWho' by a new generation of fans who saw the Internet and websites like Outpost Gallifrey as their home – was a successful reinterpretation of the classic *Doctor Who* formula, updated for the twenty-first century and carrying an overlay of the contemporary concerns that Davies had incorporated into his previous dramas, such as *Queer as Folk* and *The Second Coming*.

While succeeding as 'family entertainment', this new version of *Doctor Who* still managed to tackle a whole series of social and sexual issues in a way reminiscent of the Barry Letts years, but with the 1980s event-television showmanship of John Nathan-Turner. Over the five years that Russell T Davies would run the revived franchise, *Doctor Who* would delve into politics (right in the middle of a UK national General Election), consumerism (repeatedly used as a front for alien invasions, despite the revived series' own seemingly endless merchandise spin-offs), the media and popular television (satirised several times) and romance and sexuality (the Doctor's relationships with his companions, Rose and Martha, were a little different than those of old, while Captain Jack brought a whole new orientation to the series).

Being *Doctor Who*, and with 40 years of history behind it, the new show could not ignore the series' own past. Major monsters and characters would return over the years to come, but each return was handled in a much more successful and mass-audience-friendly way than any of those attempted by Nathan-Turner. Creatures and characters were rethought so they'd work as new for an audience unfamiliar with them, but would also play to an engaged audience (much like the late-1960s version of the show) who remembered them from first time around or who were familiar with them from satellite TV repeats or DVD releases. However, an in-depth knowledge of the past was not necessary to enjoy the new *Doctor Who*.

Davies could not resist building his own mythology, introducing a series of characters and events that would pay off only at the end of the initial four-year run of the new *Doctor Who*. Seeds sown in *Rose* would later mature in 2008's final regular episode (until 2010), *Journey's End*. This seemingly complicated back-story required little more from a mass audience than an awareness of key characters who'd appeared in the show over the past two to three years and their relationships to each other and the Doctor. Audiences well used to the ongoing developing narratives of domestic soap operas were comfortable with such character recall, so *Doctor Who* fitted right into the modern TV landscape (even if this aspect of the series saw many fans criticise it as 'too soapy').

To many people's surprise, not least some of its most die-hard fans, the new series of *Doctor Who* became the biggest hit the BBC had enjoyed in a long time. It successfully re-energised a timeless format, making it relevant to a contemporary mass audience. It success-fully captured the attention of a whole new generation of young viewers who saw *Doctor Who* as part of an entertainment landscape that included *Harry Potter* and *High School Musical*. In fact, the audi-ence who seemed to be most upset about the return of their favourite show was a sub-section of the series' own longest-serving fans.

During the first season of the new *Doctor Who*, long-term viewers may have felt there was something familiar about the series' satir-ical engagement with contemporary politics. Just as Barry Letts and Terrance Dicks had tackled the contemporary political reality of the 1970s in their fantasy-driven stories, so did Russell T Davies in the 2005 version.

There is much wrong with the new series' first two-part story, *Aliens of London/World War III*. The new production crew had to learn how to make *Doctor Who* after such a lengthy break. However, the satirical engagement with the then-imminent UK General Election was a masterstroke. The story depicted the infiltration of the highest power in the land, Number 10 Downing Street, by the alien Slitheen family in a plot to destroy Earth. The Slitheen were intent on provoking a nuclear conflict and selling off the resulting ruined planet for a profit. The Prime Minister (possibly intended to be Tony Blair) has been killed and key ministers replaced by fat, yellow-green aliens disguised in human 'skin suits' that make them appear to be obese humans. They've additionally faked an alien spaceship crashing into the Thames in order to gather the world's experts on alien life in one place to eliminate them, so they don't uncover the Slitheen plan. The most notorious 'expert' snared by the trap is the Doctor.

These two episodes aired in April 2005, immediately preceding the election of 5 May in which Prime Minister Tony Blair was seeking a third consecutive term in office (something that had previously eluded Labour). One of the main issues was the conduct of the war in Iraq which the US and UK had been engaged in since 2003. Part of the justification for war was Iraq's supposed possession of 'weapons of mass destruction' (primarily taken to mean chemical or biological weapons, and possibly developing nuclear capability), despite the failure of UN weapons inspectors to find any evidence of such weapons on the ground. A government dossier from September 2002 had been compiled to justify the invasion on the basis of weapons of mass destruction that could reach Europe 'within 45 minutes', according to a notorious BBC report. That led to an explosive row between the BBC and the government, resulting in the Hutton Inquiry finding against the BBC in January 2004 and the subsequent resignation of Director General Greg Dyke.

Aliens of London and *World War III* were broadcast in the aftermath of these important political events and in the immediate run-up to an election in which these issues were still playing a major part. The mere replacement of key government figures by corpulent, flatulent aliens may have been an obvious (though no less effective for it) form of satirical caricature of politicians, but Davies went further in his clever script. Dialogue references included comments on the Slitheen plan to use 'massive weapons of destruction' that could be unleashed 'within 45 seconds'. Any alert viewer among the seven million who watched the episodes would have enjoyed a quiet chuckle at these references. This was the kind of thing that *Doctor Who* used to do regularly in the 1970s (often satirising Whitehall), but had abandoned (along with its appeal to the mass audience) in the 1980s. Davies firmly believed that political, social and even sexual comment belonged in a modern version of *Doctor Who*.

Other passing dialogue references contained material aimed at the culture of 'New Labour', who'd been in power since winning the 1997 General Election. *Aliens of London* introduced the character of Harriet Jones, MP for Flydale North (and future Prime Minister), who says of the war, 'I voted against it,' a common refrain from those MPs who opposed the conflict.

The following week saw the broadcast of the episode *Dalek*, reintroducing the Doctor's oldest foes. Mere days before the election, the *Radio Times* combined the return of the Daleks with that week's election coverage in their acclaimed fold-out 'Vote Dalek!' cover, which saw a trio of Daleks patrolling in front of the Houses of Parliament. In September 2008, the cover went on to a surprise win as the best British magazine cover of all time in a poll run by the Periodical Publishers Association. The cover triumphed over 40 other contenders, including striking and influential covers of such top-selling magazines as (among others) *Empire*, *Nova*, *Oz*, *Private Eye*, *The Face* and *Vanity Fair*. One of the magazine professionals who'd nominated the cover was Adam Pasco, editor of the BBC's *Gardener's World* magazine. 'It's May 2005, the General Election is looming, and the public is wondering who to vote for: Labour? The Tories? No – vote Dalek!' He went on to justify his choice: 'This *Radio Times* cover captures the essence of the mood of the nation in a brilliant and original way, and delivers on every level. The cover is totally unexpected and brings a contemporary twist to the iconic image of a Dalek to grab readers of all ages at the newsstand. *Radio Times* really made a statement with this cover that is simple, to the point and encapsulates that quirky British sense of humour.' The *Radio Times* cover, overtly linking *Doctor Who* and national politics (and by implication all that goes with it) was a natural outcome of the fact that the show had returned to serious political engagement for the first time in over 25 years.

Another thematic preoccupation of the new version of *Doctor Who* that echoed concerns from the 1970s version of the show was an interest in satirising consumerism and the influence of big business. Several episodes see giant corporations acting as fronts for various alien invasions, often connected to a consumer product or gadget.

The opening episode, *Rose*, may have missed an opportunity by not returning to the consumerism issues raised by *Spearhead from Space* and particularly *Terror of the Autons*, but plastic was not such a thrilling material in the twenty-first century as it had been in the 1970s. The following story, however, tackled rampant cosmetic plastic surgery. The Doctor and Rose travel to the year five billion in *The End of the World* and encounter the 'last human', Cassandra. All that remains of her is a piece of skin with a face stretched across a metal frame, and her brain contained in a container below. Described as both a 'bitchy trampoline' and 'Michael Jackson' by Rose, it's clear that Cassandra is a satire on modern society's health and beauty concerns, taken to an extreme.

Public health and well-being fads are a recurring theme of new *Doctor Who*, reflecting one of the primary preoccupations of the media in Britain. Celebrity chef Jamie Oliver's campaigns to encourage school children to eat healthily figure in the episode *School Reunion*. The school meal chips (coated in Krillitane oil) are being used to condition the children to solve the Skasis Paradigm. This will allow the Krillitane control over the fundamental building blocks of the universe. While this plot takes a back seat to the nostalgic return (the first of several) of Sarah Jane Smith and K-9, the school meals and poisoned chips element struck a chord with the younger audience (along with the idea that their headmaster and teachers might be aliens, which feels like a story idea *Doctor Who* should have tackled long ago).

Such health issues wedded to big-business exploitation would reappear in the fourth-season premiere, *Partners in Crime*. The Doctor re-encounters Donna Noble (Catherine Tate), his one-off companion from the 2006 Christmas special, *The Runaway Bride*, while investigating Adipose Industries. The company distributes a mass-produced weight-loss pill that, according to their company slogan, sees the 'fat just walk away'. The pills cause human fat to be converted into an Adipose creature, spawning from the dieting human's body. About the size of a bag of sugar, the lard-resembling Adipose simply waddle away from the sleeping human, who appears to have miraculously lost weight in their sleep. The seemingly beneficent company is, in fact, a front for an Adipose breeding programme, operated by the sinister Miss Foster.

Two episodes later, *Planet of the Ood* presented another evil corporation, this time involved in selling Ood creatures into slavery. The episode used spoof advertising to communicate the consumer benefits of owning a domesticated Ood. Where the Adipose breeding programme was getting out of control and threatening to destroy humans by converting them wholesale into new Adipose, the humans running Ood Operations in the year 4126 find themselves coping with an outbreak of Ood 'red eye'. The conditions under which they are being kept (they are telepathic, but have been cut off from their collective unconscious) and their treatment by the humans are turning the normally docile Ood homicidal. Donna's reaction raises the issue of slavery, in addition to the treatment of the Ood as essentially consumer goods (unfeeling domestic aides) rather than living creatures. The Doctor also makes a comparison between the Ood's plight and that of the low-paid and ill-treated foreign workers who make Donna's affordable clothes.

Technology and gadgetry are the satirical focus of other stories. In the two-part adventure *Rise of the Cybermen* and *The Age of Steel*, the Doctor, Rose and Mickey find themselves trapped in a parallel universe in which the Cybermen are just emerging. The population of this world is controlled through the use of Bluetooth-style telephone earpieces. As the latest popular, must-have gadget, everyone has one, so everyone is susceptible to the signal that controls them and makes them head to Battersea Power Station to be converted into Cybus Industries' Cybermen. The conversion is seemingly 'sold' to the population as a desire to 'upgrade', to access the latest life-extending technology. Like Germany during the rise of the Third Reich, the population of this Earth are sleepwalking to disaster through their faith in big corporations and shiny new technology, sold as a way of making their everyday lives easier. The viewing millions would recognise their own world exaggerated for dramatic effect and reflected back at them.

These two episodes also criticised the closeness of industry and government, something repeatedly explored by the 1970s incarnation of the show. The crippled John Lumic, whose personal interest in life extension drives his research into cyber-technology, controls Cybus Industries. Having illegally experimented on the homeless, Lumic knows that Britain's president will not allow him to expand his technology into the consumer arena. He arranges the president's elimination when he is a guest at Jackie Tyler's birthday party, when the new Cybermen attack and 'delete' him. Lumic is then free to initiate his plans for the 'ultimate upgrade' of humanity.

A similar device to the mass-marketed EarPods was used as a front for the Sontaran invasion in the two-part *The Sontaran Stratagem/The Poison Sky*. In this case, it's the ATMOS anti-pollution device, affixed to many cars (an ATMOS sticker can be glimpsed stuck to a taxi in *Partners in Crime*, foreshadowing these two episodes). The story postulates an alien race – the Sontarans returning to *Doctor*

Who for the first time since *The Two Doctors* in 1985 – using a front to sell environmentally friendly devices to a mass population. They are then used to attempt to convert the atmosphere to a more Sontaran-friendly chemical make-up. This time, the must-have gadget is sold on the basis of a pro-environment message to tackle air pollution caused by cars. That the population can be fooled into participating in the downfall of their own planet while thinking they are taking action to save it is a clever twist on the big-business-and-technology theme that recurs in a small-p political way throughout much of new *Doctor Who*. This not very subtle but actually quite clever satire is pitched at just the right level to engage a mass audience. They can be brought into the show through recognition of so much of the contemporary real world, but also enjoy the humour of the political, social and industrial satire that Russell T Davies and his team of writers can work into their *Doctor Who* scripts. If cleverly done, none of this interferes with the straightforward adventure that the younger audience expects.

Another regular target for the new *Doctor Who* is the mass media. Since the twenty-first century is a much more mediated society than even the 1980s (when *Doctor Who* was last in regular production), it was inevitable that the media would feature regularly within the narrative. However, the series has gone one step further and satirised media conventions and organisations.

Many of the (monotonously regular) invasions of Earth in the Russell T Davies period have been communicated to the audience and the characters in the drama through the media. BBC news channels often feature (from *Aliens of London* onwards), covering the events of the story, while the media is also used to give such events a worldwide scale. A seemingly US-based news channel (AMNN) pops up regularly, presented by the same female newscaster in each case (giving an almost subliminal level of continuity). This offers a perspective on each 'end-of-the-world' scenario that is different from that of London (distinct from the approach in the 1970s, when alien invaders seemed to have little interest in anything outside the Home Counties).

Beyond the use of mass media to expand the repertoire of story-telling tools available to writers, media organisations were prime among elements of modern life in Britain satirised by the new *Doctor Who*. *The Long Game* sees Christopher Eccleston's Ninth Doctor and Rose arriving on Satellite Five in the year 200,000, during the time of the 'fourth great and bountiful human empire'. Satellite Five is a news broadcasting station, transmitting 600 channels across the Empire, run by the Editor (Simon Pegg), an almost albino figure, seemingly answerable to a higher power that's manipulating the content of the station's broadcasts. Teaming up with two rebellious journalists, the Doctor investigates the mysterious Floor 500 (perhaps modelled after the infamous 'sixth floor' of BBC Television Centre, notorious among *Doctor Who* fans as the location of the offices of the executives who interfered in, and eventually cancelled, the programme in the 1980s).

This human empire has been manipulated for 90 years by a crea-ture called the Jagrafess, which has used its position of control over the news to create a climate of fear (Davies once again referencing contemporary politics, particularly the fallout from the war in Iraq and 9/11). The Doctor realises that the human race has been enslaved and is not even aware of it, living as it is in a degree of comfort, in a strictly controlled but extremely limited society. Of course, the Doctor defeats the Jagrafess and the Editor and believes he has set the human population back on its correct course to possible utopia.

The title *The Long Game* only becomes meaningful when the Doctor returns to Satellite Five later that same season in *Bad Wolf* (the use of the same space station twice in one season echoes the debut year of Tom Baker's Fourth Doctor). The Doctor, Rose and Captain Jack Harkness (who joined the TARDIS crew in *The Doctor Dances*) are separated and each finds themselves taking part in reality-television shows. Contemporary viewers would recognise *Big Brother*, *What Not to Wear* and *The Weakest Link* as the three TV shows spoofed, along with their iconography and presenters. Contestants are seemingly killed when they are eliminated or 'voted out', including Rose. The Doctor escapes the *Big Brother* 'house' and gains access behind the scenes, only to discover he's back on Satellite Five at a later point in history. Now humanity has a different master: the Daleks!

Led by their Emperor ('the God of all Daleks'), the Daleks have been harvesting humans to boost their numbers. In the opening to the season finale, *The Parting of the Ways*, the Doctor declares these new post-time-war Daleks to be mad, driven insane by self-loathing as they have had to depend upon human organic material to create their new race. Indeed, the Daleks are depicted as a fundamentalist religious group, crying blasphemy when the Doctor suggests they're half-human (this is also a fan in-joke on the part of Davies, as the 1996 Paul McGann TV movie postulated that the Doctor was half-human, a development decried by a subset of online fans as blasphemy). These mad Daleks are limited to their appearance in this one story, but their fundamentalist nature reflects a very precise point in time following the 9/11 attacks on the US in 2001 and terrorist activity in the UK. The episode was broadcast just three weeks before Islamic fundamentalists carried out the 7 July 2005 attacks on transport in London. Religion and the threat posed by its fundamentalist proponents has not often featured in *Doctor Who*, but *The Parting of the Ways* did a fine job of updating Terry Nation's original space fascists to confront one of the most important contemporary issues concerning the mass audience now attracted to *Doctor Who*. Unfortunately, by the time of *Journey's End* in 2008, the Daleks were back to being simple space fascists, an aspect of their character made literally evident by the scene in which the Daleks conquering Earth speak German!

The Daleks' rivals for the position of top *Doctor Who* monster were not about to be left out of the media spotlight. When the Cybermen returned again, in *Army of Ghosts*, their attempts to break through from their universe to ours cause them to appear as ghost-like figures. Once again satirising media conventions, the appearance of these ghosts across the world is shown to be a media sensation. The 'supernatural' events happen at the same time each day, with television providing a countdown. Rose's mum, Jackie, is shown waiting for Rose's dead grandfather to appear during the daily 'ghost shift'. Clips from programmes like soap drama *EastEnders* or talk show *Trisha* reveal to the Doctor how the ghost phenomenon has been absorbed and normalised by the culture. Investigating, the Doctor realises the ghosts are Cybermen, pushing themselves through a breach between universes to become material in our reality. The full materialisation of the Cybermen (represented by reports from Indian, Japanese and French newsreaders) is topped by the opening of the mysterious Void Sphere captured by Torchwood. This reveals four surviving Daleks who escaped the Time War (the Cult of Skaro), setting the stage for a Cybermen-Dalek face-off in the following episode, *Doomsday*.

The uses of, and satirising of, the media has become an intrinsic part of the audience's experience of new *Doctor Who*. With the media forming such a large part of most viewers' lives, its reflection within the narratives of the show and the use of tricks and techniques seen in other media is further evidence of how the series has been success-fully updated to appeal to a new mass audience.

In the 1980s (in response to tabloid speculation), John Nathan-Turner had declared that there would be 'no hanky-panky' in the TARDIS. With an attractive and young cast, and the tendency in the 1980s to dress the female companions in revealing outfits (a situation that reached its climax with Peri's introduction in a bikini and her regular outfit of tight-fitting leotards), it was no surprise that some observers wondered about the Doctor's relationship with his young, female travelling companions.

One of the most radical changes that Russell T Davies brought to the revitalisation of the show was to explore the emotions of the Doctor in relation to his companions. Both the Ninth and Tenth Doctors have enjoyed grand romances, primarily with Rose Tyler, but also with Madame de Pompadour (*The Girl in the Fireplace*) and (when the Doctor is in the guise of human, John Smith) Joan Redfern (*Human Nature/The Family of Blood*). Despite these events, Davies was always keen to return the character to the status of 'the lonely Doctor', as seen at the conclusion of *Journey's End*. He may be interested in his companions and others he meets along the way (dating back to Cameca in *The Aztecs*), but being a long-lived Time Lord (the last remaining, so excluding relationships with one of his own species), he can never sustain a conventional relationship.

Sex has a much more prominent role in the new *Doctor Who* than it ever had in the old show, reflecting the era in which the show is now made. Beyond some sudden and very chaste romances (like those between Susan and David Campbell, and Leela and Andred, concocted as exit strategies for both companions), the original series' approach to sex was simply in the guise of the glamorous assistant or '*Doctor Who* girl' of tabloid fame. Katy Manning (who played Jo Grant) infamously took this one step further by posing naked with a Dalek for men's magazine *Girl Illustrated*, but only after she'd left the show.

Steven Moffat (who took over from Russell T Davies as showrunner for the 2010 fifth season) has paid close attention to the Doctor's love life. The two-part story *The Empty Child* and *The Doctor Dances* introduced both the omni-sexual Captain Jack Harkness (John Barrowman), a time agent from the fifty-first century, and the metaphorical concept of 'dancing' as a family-friendly euphemism for sex. He wrote *The Girl in the Fireplace*, giving the Doctor his first romance other than that seemingly being enjoyed with Rose. Moffat was also the writer of *Silence in the Library/Forest of the Dead*, the fourth-season, two-part story that introduced River Song (Alex Kingston), seemingly a future romantic interest for the Tenth Doctor (strongly hinted at as 'the Doctor's wife', itself a spoof episode title written on an office noticeboard by John Nathan-Turner in the 1980s in an attempt to track down the source of information leaking to fans).

The casting of the young (under 40) and photogenic David Tennant helped build the growing female audience for new *Doctor Who* (the perception being that the audience for the original series was largely male, while the core of organised fandom was largely gay). For his Doctor to be played asexually, as most others had been, would simply not have been possible in a modern television environment. Giving the Doctor an emotional life ensured a higher level of engagement with the series among the casual, especially female, audience that had abandoned the show in the late-1980s. It was the casting of the 'young and dashing' Peter Davison as the Doctor in 1981 that led to the 'hanky-panky-in-the-TARDIS' tabloid speculation. However, Davison's Doctor was never invested with the same emotional range as Eccleston's and Tennant's characters.

Casting a young, attractive Doctor showed that, in many ways, Russell T Davies had learned the right lessons from the misguided 1980s when John Nathan-Turner was producer. Like Nathan-Turner, Davies is a firm believer in event television as part of a strategy to grab a larger-than-usual audience. Likewise, as a longstanding *Doctor Who* fan, Davies was keen on maintaining the series' internal continuity and in refreshing successful elements and characters from the show's past. The new production, however, took a lot more care in reintroducing key things from the past, communicating clearly to an audience who perhaps didn't recognise them why they were important and worth bringing back.

Davies' opening episode had used the Autons, mainly for the recognisable moment of showroom dummies breaking through a shop window (a well-remembered incident from *Spearhead from Space* that was not actually seen on screen, instead being simply heard as a sound effect, an oversight *Rose* rectified).

The big question, in the run-up to the series' debut, was whether the show would feature the Daleks, following a protracted negotiation with Terry Nation's estate. With the rights to the Daleks secured, Davies took a cautious approach to their reintroduction, aware that the Doctor's biggest foes had become the butt of many jokes in the years when the show was off air. Although Daleks had been seen to fly (or hover) twice towards the end of the original series (in *Revelation of the Daleks* and *Remembrance of the Daleks*), they were still considered by comedians and the popular press to be creatures who could be foiled by simply running up a set of stairs. Drawing on a Big Finish audio by Robert Shearman (*Jubilee*, in which a captured solo Dalek is tortured), the episode *Dalek* saw Rose become sympathetic to a chained and abused lone Dalek. The episode goes on to unleash the creature, showing the deadly power it is capable of. The significant 'media moment' the episode builds up to is when the Dalek announces its intention to 'elevate', and is then seen hovering up stairs in relentless pursuit of its quarry.

Audience (and fan) nostalgia also played a major role in *School Reunion*, the episode that saw the return of Elisabeth Sladen as Jon Pertwee/Tom Baker companion Sarah Jane Smith and the robot dog K-9. This was a direct appeal to viewers who remembered the show at its 1970s peak, although Sladen and K-9 were never teamed up on the regular show, only in the 1981 spin-off special *K-9 and Company* (and briefly in *The Five Doctors*). The return of these characters was part of a publicity boost for the series, especially K-9. Davies strongly believed that K-9 would appeal beyond fans and older audiences who remembered him to the new younger audience attracted to the revitalised version of the series. The gambit was so successful that the characters returned again to *Doctor Who* (in *Journey's End*). Elisabeth

Sladen went on to star in her own amazingly successful children's spin-off series called *The Sarah Jane Adventures*, 30 years after she first boarded the TARDIS. The spin-off series is even structured like the original *Doctor Who*, in 25-minute episodes, with each two-part story enjoying an end-of-episode cliff-hanger. The character of Captain Jack Harkness also enjoyed a spin-off series of his own. *Torchwood* saw Jack heading up a team of Cardiff-based investigators who confront alien incursions and other odd occurrences. Both spin-offs would be reunited with the parent show in the two-part, season-four finale *The Stolen Earth/Journey's End*.

Having successfully revived the Daleks, the return of other popular monsters was inevitable. Each season would see at least one prominent monster reinvented for the new show. Season two had the parallel universe Cybermen in *Rise of the Cybermen/The Age of Steel* (again drawing on a Big Finish audio-drama precedent: Marc Platt's *Spare Parts*), with further reappearances in *Army of Ghosts/Doomsday* and the 2008 Christmas special *The Next Doctor*. Season three saw a dramatic reinvention of the Master (John Simm) in *Utopia*. Unexpectedly (for most viewers), Derek Jacobi's mysterious 'Professor Yana' regenerated (in a similar style to the Eccleston/Tennant regeneration in *The Parting of the Ways*, a gambit adopted so viewers would recognise the change that was happening) into Simm's new, younger, more dynamic Master. This led into the two-part season finale *The Sound of Drums/The Last of the Time Lords*, which saw the Doctor and Master fighting for the future of mankind.

Season four's returning monsters were the 1970s clone warriors the Sontarans in *The Sontaran Stratagem/The Poison Sky* (the Sontarans had also recently reappeared in the long-running *Doctor Who* comic strip, another influence on the new TV series). The creatures had a dramatic redesign and their behaviour had changed significantly, with this supposed warrior race attempting to take over Earth by stealth using a front company run by a teenage genius. The end of season four saw the return of Dalek creator Davros (introduced in 1975's *Genesis of the Daleks*) in another two-part season finale, the epic *The Stolen Earth/Journey's End*.

Each of these returns was carefully stage-managed, with publicity stills of the reinvented monsters released to the media long in advance of the episodes, and often accompanied by *Radio Times* covers priming the viewing audience for the episode during the week of transmission. The huge interest in the new *Doctor Who* by tabloid newspapers, once it had proved to be a hit, resulted in several key storylines and character returns leaking (itself sometimes a useful publicity strategy). *The Sun* had reported the Cybermen/Dalek battle almost a full year before the episodes aired, while the returns of both the Master and Davros proved to be open secrets in the world of online fandom long before the characters actually appeared.

The new series also saw dramatic changes in fandom. Printed fanzines were few and far between, as most comment had migrated online in the form of authored blogs or forum postings. Fans participating in *Doctor Who*'s online culture were just as likely to be female now (partly down to the casting of Tennant, but also due to the show's new emotional intelligence). Creating work like music videos illustrated with clips from the new series was far easier than it had been back in the 1980s, and the audiences for such YouTube postings was far larger than local fan groups or conventions. Exhibitions up and down the land attracted families, while a brand-new young audience bought the merchandise (or more likely had it bought for them). The Internet had also created a new fan hierarchy, illustrated by the growing spoiler culture (as wittily addressed by Steven Moffat in his script for *Silence in the Library/Forest of the Dead*). Fans in possession of advance story details, or who were in a position to spread leaked information, became notorious (in both positive and negative senses), while misinformation and rumour was easier to spread than ever before.

The new nature of 'NuWho' fandom, however, had not removed strong fan criticism. In fact, the Internet provided a venue that made such criticism easier (and easier for those who criticise unthinkingly). Accused by fans of recreating *Doctor Who* in the image of a soap opera (by including the companion's families and allowing the Doctor to have emotional involvements), Russell T Davies countered by claiming such things were simply the basis of good modern TV drama. However, Davies set out deliberately to create a new mythology for his version of *Doctor Who*, one that would culminate in *Journey's End*.

Eccleston's Doctor is revealed to be the last of the Time Lords, the sole survivor of a grand 'Time War' that has wiped out his home planet Gallifrey and the Daleks. He's suffering survivor's guilt, and the four years from 2005 to 2008 play out the consequences of his (unseen, offscreen) actions as the Time War is woven into the unfolding narrative of the series. The arrival of each new companion (after Rose there was Captain Jack, Martha Jones and Donna Noble) allowed for the basic set-up to be restated to the audience in a natural and engaging way (a simple trick that the writers and producers of 1986's *The Trial of a Time Lord* totally failed to understand).

Beyond this, there were the storylines assigned to each individual companion. It was always Davies' intention for a version of the Doctor and Rose to end up together, but the first-draft plan saw a split-off human version of the Doctor settling down with Rose following the Tenth Doctor's regeneration (this was somehow tied up with the return of Gallifrey, the resolution of the Time War and the 'human Doctor' storyline of *Human Nature*). Changing production priorities (the departure and return of Billie Piper, uncertainty about when David Tennant would be leaving the role) saw the grand plan revised to become the storyline that unfolded in *The Stolen Earth/Journey's End*.

The final outcome of the relationship was the same, however: a half-human version of the Tenth Doctor ends up with Rose Tyler.

This epic romance defined the other companions. The return of Sarah Jane Smith was played (in soap-opera terms) as the return of an old girlfriend (Rose's boyfriend Mickey calls the meeting between Sarah Jane and Rose a clash between 'the ex and the missus'). Martha Jones' storyline was one of unrequited love: she falls for the Doctor in much the same way that Rose did, but he's not in the right place emotionally to reciprocate (as he's still pining for Rose, trapped in a different dimension after the events of *Doomsday*). Finally, there's Donna Noble, a no-nonsense, older (although possibly less sophisticated) companion who eventually proves to be the most significant companion of all, saving not only this universe but all of reality when caught up in a 'human-Time Lord metacrisis' in *Journey's End*.

Davies' revolving roster of characters included Rose's family members, specifically her dead father, Pete Tyler (who plays a major role in time-travel paradox adventure *Father's Day*, with an alternate-universe version of Pete appearing in *Rise of the Cybermen/The Age of Steel* and *Army of Ghosts/Doomsday*), as well as her mother, Jackie, and her boyfriend Mickey (who also travels with the Doctor, maturing as a character as he does so). Again, Martha's entire family are caught up in the Doctor's world, especially in the 'year that never was' of *The Sound of Drums/The Last of the Time Lords*. While Donna Noble's mother also regularly appears, she is more critical of her daughter than either of the other companions' mothers we see. Donna's significant family connection is to Wilf, her grandfather (played by Bernard Cribbins, whose *Doctor Who* connections stretch back to the second Peter Cushing Dalek movie). The episode *Turn Left* allows audiences to see a version of Donna's life that might have unfolded if the Doctor didn't exist, and how the familiar characters that surround her would react and be changed by events. Cribbins, in particular, is given an opportunity to shine when local people are rounded up for despatch to internment camps and he recalls the similar events of the Second World War (so that old *Doctor Who* standby proves it is still useful).

As well as these characters, who recur on and off throughout the series, providing the audience with an ensemble cast among whom they can choose favourites, Davies also built a mythology set around the year five billion, with returning characters like the Face of Boe, Cassandra, the last human and Novice Hame, one of the cat people. The unfolding stories of these characters, across the first three seasons, provided a more subtle serial narrative that paid off for regular viewers of the series, who could connect episodes across a number of years. The revelation that immortal Captain Jack Harkness would eventually become the Face of Boe (seemingly inspired by fan speculation and intended by Davies as a joke) connected the two ongoing narrative strands together.

Retaining viewers through character loyalty (harking right back to the establishment of the series in the 1960s) was taken to its ultimate extreme in the 2008 season finale *The Stolen Earth/Journey's End*, with the last episode especially extended to 65 minutes to accommodate the story and a huge number of returning characters. These episodes featured all the previous companions from this four-year period, characters from *The Sarah Jane Adventures* and *Torchwood*, and other incidental recurring characters like Penelope Wilton's Harriet Jones, ex-Prime Minister. ('Yes, we know who you are,' say the Daleks, prior to exterminating her, paying off a running joke that began in *Aliens of London*, three years previously.)

This sort of long-term planning (albeit revised, changed and altered as the series developed due to production realities) was a clever strategy, making *Doctor Who* part of a modern TV experience and drawing on the soap-like elements of the twice-weekly Peter Davison episodes and the event-television-driven John Nathan-Turner approach. The difference was that Davies never forgot the mass audience. Where

Nathan-Turner got caught in the trap of pandering to fans, Davies largely ignored the 'ming mongs' (as he rather rudely dubbed engaged *Doctor Who* fandom, of which he had been a very active part in the past) and wrote the new *Doctor Who* for the family audience watching TV at (roughly) 7pm on a Saturday night.

Russell T Davies' reinvention of *Doctor Who* has been an unalloyed triumph. Like it or loathe it (and many dedicated fans seem to alternate between these two positions depending on what's happening on screen in any given week), *Doctor Who* is now one of the BBC's most important programmes. Regularly drawing audiences of between six and ten million, the show has created an entirely new young fan base, while appealing to adults and parents as well as to most fans of the original series. Many of the episodes of the Eccleston- and Tennant-starring series have featured in the week's top ten TV programmes, often only beaten by the daily soap operas. *Journey's End* achieved a first for the show, topping the chart for the first time in the series' 45-year history with 10.57 million viewers.

To achieve this, Russell T Davies brought all his event television tricks to bear on the series. Having hoped to keep the Eccleston regeneration a secret until it happened on air, the high-profile nature of the actor's departure from the series had thwarted that plan. However, at the climax of *The Stolen Earth*, David Tennant's Tenth Doctor is exterminated by a Dalek and appears to begin to regenerate (the dramatic scene was missing from preview discs distributed to the media to preserve the secret). This phenomenal cliff-hanger ending fed into endless media speculation about Tennant's departure from the show, speculation that had started almost the moment he was announced as the new Doctor following Eccleston. That the threatened regeneration was a bluff was not clear to the mass audience until the beginning of the following episode, *Journey's End*. The resolution of the cliff-hanger sees the Doctor's regeneration energy siphoned off into his severed hand (kept in the TARDIS since *Last of the Time Lords*), resulting in the creation of a half-human Doctor that, in turn, allows for the long-running Rose romance story to be paid off. It may have struck many viewers as a cheat. A good proportion of the 11 million viewers (up from 8.7 million for *The Stolen Earth*) tuned in following media coverage during the week solely to see a potential new Doctor revealed (a very similar trick was ill-advisedly used for the 2008 Christmas special, *The Next Doctor*). Whatever the motivation, viewers stuck with the episode through the defeat of Davros and the Daleks to the interminable sequence of goodbyes that saw the long-brewing Rose–Doctor romance finally concluded as she departed back to her alternate universe with a half-human clone of the Doctor.

Just before Hallowe'en 2008, David Tennant finally announced (live on TV, after winning a National Television Award for the third year running) that he would be vacating the TARDIS following the 2009 'specials'. This left the way open for a fresh start to the series by new 2010 showrunner Steven Moffat (winner of three Hugos – science fiction's Oscars – for his acclaimed *Doctor Who* episodes).

Tennant felt he was leaving the show in good shape: 'I think the cross-generational, cross-cultural appeal of *Doctor Who* is pretty unique. I can't think of anything else that has fans who are seven and 70 in almost equal measure.' Russell T Davies had already announced his own departure from the series he'd so successfully reinvented: he'd also step down from the show at the conclusion of the 2009 specials, making his and his star's departures simultaneous. Davies saw this moment of change as a positive step that would help ensure the revived show's long-term future (as if being number one in the ratings wasn't enough in that department). '[Change] is always good for the programme,' said Davies. 'It will keep up a new head of steam and there's lots of excitement about the new *Doctor Who* and that's brilliant. It's still going to be a television programme about a man who fights aliens. It's still going to be *Doctor Who* on a Saturday night, just like it has been for 45 years.'

Doctor Who's forty-fifth-anniversary year was capped with the announcement of a new Doctor, 26-year-old Matt Smith. His surprise casting was revealed in a special episode of *Doctor Who Confidential*, broadcast on BBC1 on 3 January 2009 to six million curious viewers (beating ITV's live coverage of the FA Cup). Speculation about who would win the coveted role had mounted since Tennant's announce-ment, with press coverage suggesting actors as diverse as Paterson Joseph (*Survivors*), Michael Sheen (*Frost/Nixon*), Chiwetel Ejiofor (*Kinky Boots*) and James Nesbitt (Steven Moffat's *Jekyll*). Moffat had previ-ously expressed his own preference for an older actor to play the Doctor, a 'grandfather' figure, so it came as a shock to some fans when he cast the youngest actor yet in the role.

The series' new executive producer Piers Wenger, who made the choice of Smith alongside Moffat, noted: 'It was abundantly clear that he had that "Doctor-ness" about him. You are either the Doctor or you are not.' For his part, Smith was looking forward to working closely with Moffat in developing the Eleventh Doctor. 'The script is where it starts, it's always about the words, and luckily we're in the hands of Steven Moffat, who has this show ingrained in his soul and searing through his blood. We're going to discover it together, who the Doctor is in Steven's mind and words, coupled with pockets of my personality, my history, my life. There's Sherlock Holmes, James Bond, and *Doctor Who*. It has resonance in our cultural fabric.'

As filming began on his first series in July 2009, Smith commented: 'The scripts are brilliant and working alongside Karen [Gillan, new companion Amy Pond], Steven [Moffat] and the rest of the crew is an inspiration because their work ethic and passion for the show is so admirable. I'm excited about the future and all the brilliant adven-tures I get to go on as the Doctor.'

Unveiling the Eleventh Doctor's tweed-jacketed new look, show-runner Steven Moffat recognised the latest instance of renewal in *Doctor Who*'s long and on-going history. 'Here it is, the big moment – the new Doctor, and his new best friend. And here's me, with the job I wanted since I was seven – 40 years to here! If I could go back in time and tell that little boy that one day all this would happen, he'd scream, call for his mum and I'd be talking to you now from a prison cell in 1969. So probably best not then.

'Matt and Karen are going to be incredible, and *Doctor Who* is going to come alive on Saturday nights in a whole new way – and, best of all, somewhere out there a seven-year-old is going to see them, fall in love and start making a 40-year plan...'

Although the new Doctor in the shape of the relatively unknown Smith had been announced in January 2009, excited viewers would have to wait over a year until they got their first glimpse of the new man in action. First there was a year of four 'specials' running throughout 2009, following the regeneration tease of the 2008 Christmas special, *The Next Doctor*.

Repeating the trick pulled on *The Stolen Earth/Journey's End*, Russell T Davies and his crew capitalised on Tennant's announced departure by featuring David Morrissey in *The Next Doctor* as a possible future incarnation of the Doctor in a Victorian-set, Steampunk-tinged romp. The casting seemed plausible to the media and viewers, as it'd be another few weeks before Matt Smith would be named as the genuine 'next Doctor'. In that brief window, with viewers aware Tennant was leaving and a new incarnation was due to arrive, the games played in *The Next Doctor* largely succeeded. The downside was that, following that adventure, and with Tennant still firmly playing the lead, the remaining 'specials' (offered in lieu of a full series of 13 episodes) would appear far less 'special' than promised. For many viewers, Tennant was now yesterday's man and with the announcement of

Smith's casting, there was perhaps an impatience to move on to the real 'next Doctor'.

Tennant's semi-detached status would prove to be a problem for the next two hour-long specials, *Planet of the Dead* (filling the usual new series Easter launch spot) and the downbeat *The Waters of Mars* (airing in November). Despite the doom-laden title, *Planet of the Dead* plays things fairly light, befitting Davies' traditional concept for a season-opener. The first ever episode to be produced in the new High Definition (HD) broadcast standard, it features Michelle Ryan (from *EastEnders* and Steven Moffat's *Jekyll*) as the Lara Croft-like Lady Christina de Souza, a thrill-seeking burglar caught up with the Doctor and a bus load of passengers when the bus is sucked through a wormhole to the barren desert planet of San Helios. Once there, they must save the passengers from the fly-like Tritovores and a horde of flying stingray-like world devourers whose next target is Earth. Once back on Earth, the Doctor refuses to take Christina with him, as the loss of Rose still hurts. Davies co-wrote the episode with Gareth Roberts, but despite the location shooting in Dubai and the incongruity of a London bus stranded on an alien world, the episode disappointed, being some-thing of a mix of styles with no clear 'high concept' for viewers to latch on to. Just over 9.5 million saw *Planet of the Dead*, but various critics viewed the episode as 'hollow', 'predictable' and 'plodding'. Rather than being 'special', it seemed run-of-the-mill.

When *The Waters of Mars* arrived that November (immediately following the animated serial *Dreamland*), it was a far darker tale. With Tennant's Tenth Doctor entering his final days, and Carmen – one of the passengers in *Planet of the Dead* – foretelling his doom ('Your song is ending… he will knock four times'), the autumn special focused on the Doctor's angst more than on thrilling adventures. The Doctor arrives at Bowie Base One, the first human colony on Mars, in 2059. He encounters Captain Brooke (Lindsay Duncan) whom he realises was an important figure in Earth history: the base personnel are due to die that day, but their sacrifice spurs humanity onwards in the exploration of space. Under siege by an 'intelligent water virus' trapped on the planet by the Ice Warriors, the crew struggle to survive while the Doctor must decide whether to leave them to their historically-dictated fate or to intervene and save them... This makes him an impotent figure, a protagonist who refuses to get involved, a bystander to 'history'. Torn by their suffering, the Doctor declares himself to be 'the Time Lord victorious' – able to interfere with history at will now the other Time Lords are dead – and finally rescues Captain Brooke, returning her to Earth. When she discovers that his intervention should never have happened, she kills herself, thus setting history back on the right course. The Doctor is shocked, and realising he has gone too far, feels he must atone. The appearance of an Ood suggests his time has come, but the Doctor attempts to flee in the TARDIS.

The issue of the Doctor's tendency to go too far had been briefly addressed previously by Davies in *The Runaway Bride*, which had temporary companion Donna telling him he should not travel alone as he needed a human perspective to temper his activities. *The Waters of Mars* felt more like a build up to the epic two-part *The End of Time* than a story in its own right, as its main purpose seemed to be to position the Tenth Doctor as a reluctant hero whose time was almost up, consumed with hubris before his fall. Around 10.5 million viewers saw the story, up on the previous episode probably due to the late-autumn scheduling. Critically it was fairly well-received, despite the perceived darkness of a tale that ends in suicide. *The Guardian* liked the depiction of 'a side to the Doctor... we haven't really seen before', while *The Daily Telegraph* delved into 'the murky waters' of just what historical events the Doctor can and cannot interfere with. It was an award-winning show, however, scooping the 2010 Hugo Award for Best Dramatic Presentation, Short Form (previously won by Steven Moffat in 2005 for *The Empty Child/The Doctor Dances*, in 2006 for *The Girl in the Fireplace*, and in 2007 for *Blink*).

*

The departure of the actor playing the Doctor is always a big moment in *Doctor Who* storytelling, but there was none more overblown than the departure of the Tenth Doctor, David Tennant. As showrunner Davies was also leaving (along with other key members of the behind-the-scenes team), he pulled out all the stops to produce an epic two-part regeneration story portentously titled *The End of Time*.

Broadcast on Christmas Day 2009 and New Year's Day 2010, the two episodes were the culmination of the year of 'specials'. Most regenerations in the past had been sudden, unexpected events in the life of the Doctor and his companions. The only one that had made it a feature of the preceding episodes was Tom Baker's swan song, *Logopolis*, in 1981: it was felt that, as the then-longest serving Doctor, something special was needed to mark his departure. Tennant had brought a legion of new fans to the show, especially among women and US viewers, and it was similarly felt that replacing him was more of a test for the reborn programme than even the shock departure of Christopher Eccleston.

Doctor Who took over BBC1 for Christmas 2009, with a series of themed station idents featuring the TARDIS, Tennant and some reindeer. That final story was something of a celebration of Tennant's entire run, with copious shout outs to other eras of the series. Warned by the Ood that 'time itself is ending', the Doctor returns to Earth to confront a reborn Master (John Simm), accompanied by Donna's grandfather Wilf (Bernard Cribbins). The threat is bigger than just the mad and feral Master. Carmen in *Planet of the Dead* had warned the Doctor that 'It is returning', which turned out to be a reference to Gallifrey (the only part of Davies' initial grand narrative plan that had not been included in *Journey's End*). Led by Rassilon (Timothy Dalton), the Time Lords escape the 'time lock' that isolated them from the end of the Great Time War. It was Rassilon who had implanted the sound of drums in the Master's head, driving him mad, but also providing a link that allowed them to escape their imprisonment. In a final confrontation, the Doctor consigns the Master and the Time Lords back into the time lock. However, in order to save Wilf – one relatively unimportant old man – the Doctor must swap places with him in an isolation chamber that results in the Time Lord's exposure to a fatal dose of radiation, kick-starting his regeneration.

Most previous *Doctor Who* stories would have ended there, but Davies and Tennant pushed the boat out, giving the Tenth Doctor an extra 10 minutes above the usual running time for the 2009 specials to go on a farewell tour of the universe saying an emotional goodbye to all his previous companions. It was an indulgence too far, and while it may have worked once in the context of Tennant's departure, it does not stand up well to repeat viewing.

The End of Time, Part One was placed third in 2009's Christmas viewing Top 10, just behind *EastEnders* and *The Royle Family*, with a consolidated figure of 11.57 million (slightly beating the previous Christmas special *The Next Doctor*'s 11.4 million). The second instalment – and Tennant's big farewell episode – was placed first for New Year's Day viewing, with a consolidated figure (including the HD simulcast) of 12.27 million viewers, with an additional 1.3 million viewing requests via the BBC's online iPlayer, an increasingly important part of the show's reach to time-shifting audiences.

The End of Time was fairly well received, although a lot of critics were clearly cutting the show some slack as festive viewing. Bernard Cribbins and John Simm came in for particularly good notices, and Tennant was praised (in *The Guardian*) for bringing 'tragic force' to his exit. The episode ended where the revived series had begun, with Rose (Billie Piper). In his *Guardian* review Mark Lawson noted: 'The final line Davies gives to Tennant was a suddenly regretful "I don't want to go!", and it is likely that, somewhere inside, both actor and writer feel a little like that.'

So ended one of the most successful eras in *Doctor Who*'s history. As the Tenth Doctor told Wilf of the aftermath of regeneration in *The*

End of Time, Part One, '...some new man goes sauntering away'. The slate had been wiped clean, and two 'new men' – showrunner Steven Moffat and actor Matt Smith – would take Doctor Who forward to even greater heights, especially in America.

8. SPACE-TIME FAIRYTALES

The new Doctor arrived at Easter 2010 with a bang, literally, as the action of Matt Smith's 75-minute debut episode *The Eleventh Hour* picks up right where *The End of Time, Part Two* left off. The new Doctor comes crashing to Earth in a wrecked TARDIS in one of the show's most dramatic action sequences. He lands in the garden of a young girl, Amelia Pond – beginning the relationship that would define the majority of Smith's tenure as the Doctor.

The Eleventh Hour had a variety of tasks: introducing the new Doctor and the new companion Amy, played by Scottish actress Karen Gillan, while telling a story aimed at engaging as wide an audience as possible. New showrunner Steven Moffat was, like Russell T Davies, a long-standing fan of the old show who had carved an award-winning career in television encompassing children's shows in *Press Gang*, comedy in *Coupling*, drama in *Jekyll*, and a blockbuster movie in *The Adventures of Tintin* (2011). His knowledge of the show meant he was well aware of previous Doctors' debut episodes, so was determined to avoid howlers like *The Twin Dilemma* or *Time and the Rani*. Moffat used the new companion to introduce a season-long arc story based around a crack in time and space that manifests in Amy's childhood bedroom. Prisoner Zero, an escapee from the alien Atraxi, warns the Doctor: 'The universe is cracked. The Pandorica will open. Silence will fall.' This lays the foundation for a story arc that would reach from *The Eleventh Hour* right up to the show's 50th anniversary in November 2013 and to Matt Smith's own regeneration story at Christmas 2013.

Moffat also took the opportunity of reinventing the series, reducing its logline to the basics of 'a madman in a box', essentially the Doctor travelling the universe in his TARDIS. The rebranding of the new era continued into a new title sequence, a new version of the theme tune, new series logo, and a redesign of both the exterior and interior of the TARDIS. In this way, Moffat put his stamp on the show, positioning it as both a continuation of the reboot begun in 2005 and a fresh start for a new team under new management.

The most important of these new elements was the most visible: Matt Smith. As the youngest actor ever to play the lead – only 26 when cast – and something of an unknown (he'd co-starred with Billie Piper in two Philip Pullman-based TV movies, as well as political drama *Party Animals*), he had a lot to prove. In *The Eleventh Hour*, thanks to Moffat's writing and his own whole-hearted commitment to the role, Smith rapidly became the Doctor, erasing all memory of David Tennant for many viewers.

Moffat made the show new again by taking a fairytale approach, positioning the Doctor – who fell from the sky in a magical box – as an imaginary friend to the young Amelia Pond (Caitlin Blackwood, Gillan's young cousin). This encounter defines his relationship with the adult Amy, to whom he returns after five minutes have passed for him, but 12 years have gone by for her. The 'raggedy Doctor', as she remembers him, has a major impact on her life. In creating a fable around Amy Pond, 'the girl who waited', and in his general take on the Doctor and the universe he now inhabited, Moffat adopted a dark fairytale approach, moving his *Doctor Who* in line with Philip Hinchcliffe's pulp fiction-inspired period of the late-1970s. 'For me,

Doctor Who literally is a fairytale,' admitted Moffat to *The Guardian.*
'It's not really science fiction. It's not set in space, it's set under your
bed. It's at its best when it's related to you, no matter what planet
it's set on. Every time it cleaves towards that, it's very strong.'

With the 'crack in the universe' arc plot in place, the next few
episodes took the usual approach of featuring the new companion
coming to terms with the Doctor and with travelling in the TARDIS.
Amy Pond had an advantage over many of her predecessors in that
she had known of the Doctor since her childhood encounter, while
for the Doctor the relationship is still a new one.

The Beast Below projected the United Kingdom (minus Scotland,
perhaps in a nod to the eventual 2014 independence referendum)
into the far future, reconstituted as a space-faring society (albeit one
with a retro 1950s Festival of Britain vibe) that lives on the back of
a giant 'space whale', unbeknown to the majority of Starship UK (as
they repeatedly vote to collectively forget about their exploitation of
the creature). The social satire is clear, from Moffat (through Amy)
asserting a traditional separate Scottish identity, to the spoof of the
British electorate and their voting habits at successive general elec-
tions. *The Beast Below* sees Amy adapt and employ the Doctor's
methods to solve the problem of this society's cruel reliance on a
trapped sentient creature.

Similarly, in *Victory of the Daleks* (the following episode, a trip into
history), it is Amy's humanity and her heartfelt description of unrequited love that defuses the cybernetic Bracewell (who has become
a Dalek bomb). Summoned by Winston Churchill (Ian McNeice), the
Doctor and Amy arrive in 1940 to discover that the Daleks (described
as 'Ironsides') are masquerading as allies in the British war effort
against Hitler (a reworking of Patrick Troughton's debut story *The
Power of the Daleks*, which also featured deceptively 'friendly' Daleks).
Bracewell (Bill Patterson) is a scientist who claims to have developed
the Ironsides, but the Doctor suspects a different agenda. As soon

as he identifies them as his enemies, their plan kicks into a higher gear. With his acknowledgement of their nature, these Daleks access the 'progenitor' – a store of pure Dalek DNA – and launch a revitalisation of their race, the 'New Paradigm'. This introduced a bold new colourful Dalek redesign, but the multi-coloured 'bumper car' look failed to catch on, and by the 2012 season opener *Asylum of the Daleks*, old and new are happily mixing in the 'parliament' of the Daleks (a way for the production team to stage a graceful climb down and quietly re-introduce the 'classic' look).

The two part *The Time of the Angels/Flesh and Stone* reintroduced the Weeping Angels from *Blink* and Alex Kingston's River Song from *Silence in the Library/The Forest of the Dead* (in which she was uploaded to a computer 'afterlife'). It built on the mythology of the Angels in the same way that James Cameron's *Aliens* (1986) built on Ridley Scott's *Alien* (1979) by multiplying their numbers and giving them new abilities. A ship, the *Byzantium*, carrying River Song and a Weeping Angel, crashes on the planet Alfava Metraxis, reviving a colony of dormant Angels. In an echo of the novel *The Time Traveller's Wife*, Song and the Doctor are meeting out of order, she having met him many times already while for him this is only their second encounter. Her origin and relationship with the Doctor, Amy and Rory would be one of the driving mysteries of the next two years.

Rory – played by Arthur Darvill and introduced in *The Eleventh Hour* as Amy's boyfriend – returned in *The Vampires of Venice*, a parable dealing with questions of immigration and cultural survival. The Saturnynes are fish-like aliens hiding out in Venice in 1580, the last survivors of their world ravaged by 'the Silence'. They arrived on Earth to escape the 'cracks in the universe', and intend to rebuild their race, first by converting the locals (beginning with the girls in the Calvierri school) and then sinking Venice to create a suitable watery habitat. Rather than the vampire story suggested by the title (it is a 'perception filter' that gives the appearance of vampirism to the

Saturnynes – the way things are seen or perceived is a recurring theme in Moffat's *Who*), *The Vampires of Venice* raises the question about an incoming population's right to thrive at the expense of the indigenous inhabitants.

This was ripped from contemporary news headlines in which immigration to the UK was once again a hot button topic. Just as the Gelth in *The Unquiet Dead* could be seen as refugee immigrants struggling for their survival, so too are the Saturnynes, a people severely reduced in numbers and driven to desperate acts justified (they believe) by their self-preservation. This is a theme played up in writer Toby Whithouse's alignment of the 'foreign' invaders with vampire mythology, often itself read as a metaphor for sexually predatory foreign incomers, a 'contamination' entering the world from elsewhere. The episode originally aired just days following the 2010 UK General Election in which immigration had been a factor. The blood-sucking vampire is an old stand-in for the incomer who uses unearned national resources but refuses to adapt or integrate. The Saturnynes are not only intent on converting human women so that they are suitable for reproduction, they are also colonial in intent, aiming to adapt an entire area of Italy to suit their needs, regardless of those who already live there. With the increasing visibility of vampires – in the *Twilight* saga (2008 – 13) and on TV in Whithouse's own *Being Human* (BBC, 2008 – 13) and the American series True Blood (2009 – 14) – *Doctor Who* takes the iconography of one of literature's oldest monsters and moulds it to fit an up-to-date political issue drawn from contemporary concerns.

With Rory firmly on board the TARDIS, the series reverts to the two companions – one male, one female – format it had most recently with Rose and Mickey, but also featured back in the 1970s with Sarah Jane Smith and Harry Sullivan, and in the 1960s, primarily with Jamie McCrimmon and Zoe Herriot. It has been one of the series' most successful formats, second only to the Doctor travelling with a solo female companion.

Amy's Choice saw Rory and Amy deal directly with their perceptions of reality as the Doctor battled the Dream Lord (Toby Jones), a dark aspect of his own personality (an echo of Michael Jayston's Valeyard, the villain of the epic 14-episode *The Trial of a Time Lord* in 1986). The pair are presented with a series of alternate realities (happily married and Amy pregnant, but pursued by monsters; or freezing to death in a seemingly inert TARDIS), with Amy forced to opt for one: but which one is genuine?

Simon Nye's script emphasised relationship issues between Amy and Rory (a focus of the series going forward), played out against a generic *Doctor Who* peril. The Dream Lord is a trickster figure able to articulate the things the Doctor would never say, and he focuses immediately on the uncertainties between Amy and Rory. Rory's perception of Leadworth as their preferred reality (their 'dream', a 'nice village and a family') is disrupted by their regular returns to the possibilities of the TARDIS, and Amy's reluctance to subscribe wholeheartedly to Rory's idyll. The core of the episode is Amy's ultimate decision to abandon any reality that no longer has Rory in it, clearly prefiguring her similarly motivated decision at the conclusion of *The Angels Take Manhattan*, their final episode.

The following two-part tale *The Hungry Earth/Cold Blood* saw the series return to the eco-concerns of the 1970s with an effective re-staging in Moffat's dark fairytale form of the Third Doctor tales *The Silurians* and *Inferno*. A drilling experiment in near-future Wales is disrupted by the re-awakening of creatures hidden below the Earth (like fairytale goblins or gnomes). The newly revived Silurians, believing themselves to be under attack, kidnap a young child – Elliot – and Amy by dragging them through the earth.

The different look of the modern Silurians (represented by two related characters embodied by Neve McIntosh, who'd go on to portray the Silurian character Madame Vastra) is explained by the Doctor as them being 'a different branch of the species'. The story concerns and those of writer Chris Chibnall are the same, however, as the 1970s originals. The ecological threat represented by the drilling project is augmented by the attempted peace brokered by the Doctor between the humans and the Silurians, echoing real-life events between Israel and Palestine.

The end of the story brought the 'crack in space' arc front and centre once more, as the crack claims the life of Rory, erasing him from history and so from Amy's memory. On top of that, the Doctor retrieves a piece of 'shrapnel' from the crack, discovering it to be part of the TARDIS, suggesting it is somehow related to the explosion that created the cracks in time and space. This is a fuller development in the use of arc stories and themes than those achieved during the Davies era (Bad Wolf, Torchwood, Mr Saxon/the Master), and it has a major impact on central characters like Rory, Amy and the Doctor.

The announcement over the end credits of *Vincent and the Doctor* of a helpline number for anyone affected by the 'issues' dealt with by the episode indicates how different it was. Written by Richard Curtis, what starts as a jolly jaunt by the Doctor and Amy to visit painter Vincent van Gogh (where they also save him from a marauding monster) becomes a meditation on mental illness, using van Gogh's well-known depression (depicted with feeling by actor Tony Curran). The result was an appropriately impressionistic (rather than strictly historically accurate) portrayal of the artist, and an unusually moving episode allowing van Gogh to see the acclaim his work is met with in the future. However, there's more than one 'invisible monster' stalking the artist, and while the Doctor can deal with the alien Krafayis, there's little he or Amy can do to help van Gogh cope with his mental anguish.

The serious message was conveyed with a lot of humour and lightness of touch in *Vincent and the Doctor*, an approach even more to the fore in the following 'sitcom' episode, *The Lodger*. Amy is trapped in the TARDIS while the Doctor poses as 'an ordinary human', moving in with Craig (James Corden) while he awaits the resolution of the 'materialisation loop' that has engulfed his time-space machine. This gimmick put Matt Smith's distinctly alien Doctor into a normal domestic situation, while also having him deal with the incursion of a rogue 'time engine' that has caused his own TARDIS to be thrown for a loop. Based on a comic strip from *Doctor Who Magazine* that had featured Tennant's Tenth Doctor, Gareth Roberts' script for *The Lodger* played up the comic culture clash possibilities in the scenario, and was a further indication of modern *Doctor Who*'s willingness to play games with audience expectations. It proved such a successful diversion that a sequel appeared the following year, reuniting the Doctor with Craig in *Closing Time*.

The Lodger was only a pause for breath before the threads of the season were pulled together in the two-part climax, *The Pandorica Opens/The Big Bang*. In not only uniting the diverse elements of the past season (featuring brief returns in the pre-titles sequence for van Gogh, Churchill, and Queen Liz from *The Beast Below*), this epic two-part conclusion explored the back story of Amy, provided a new heroic aspect for the returning Rory, and involved the enigmatic River Song. It rewarded viewers who'd watched the entire season, while also attempting to remain accessible to occasional viewers.

Moffat's script also resolved a long-standing *Doctor Who* question: why do the Doctor's enemies rarely co-operate in order to out-manoeuvre him? In the 1970s, the Master had attempted various ill-fated alien alliances. Russell T Davies had brought the series' two most famous monsters, the Daleks and the Cybermen, together (as mutual antagonists) in *Doomsday*. For his episodes, Moffat created a grand alliance of enemies who have put aside their differences to manufacture a trap, believing that the explosion of the Doctor's TARDIS caused the cracks in space.

This monster mash was a budget-saving move in that it allowed the reuse of a variety of creature costumes, while confronting the Doctor with a formidable array of enemies. It is also a pay off for the fairytale approach that Moffat took: the 'most dangerous being in the universe' is the Doctor himself (as far as his enemies are concerned: he did tell Elliot in *The Hungry Earth* when he asked if the Doctor was scared of monsters, 'No, they're scared of me!'), and they have drawn on Amy's memories to construct their trap (the Roman gladiators and the Pandorica itself come from her childhood reading). The Doctor tells the story of the Pandorica in fairytale terms: 'There was a goblin, or a trickster. Or a warrior. A nameless, terrible thing soaked in the blood of a billion galaxies. The most feared being in all the cosmos. And nothing could stop it, or hold it or... reason with it. One day it would just drop out of the sky and tear down your world.' Little does he realise that *he* is the goblin-trickster-warrior he is describing and the Pandorica is a trap awaiting him. The monsters' alliance and battle with the Doctor has an epic feel, but it also suggests the dark world of fairytales, helped by setting much of the episode in and around Stonehenge (where some actual filming took place, as well as at a partial replica built for the show).

The apocalyptic climax (the end of the universe) follows a series of dire situations: the Doctor is sealed in the Pandorica by his enemies; Amy is killed by the Auton duplicate Rory; and River is trapped in the self-destructing TARDIS. As the stars and planets wink out of existence, the only hope for resolution are the words 'To Be Continued' and the knowledge that there is one more episode to go.

The almost hour-long *The Big Bang* was a low-key follow-up to the epic *The Pandorica Opens*. It reintroduced the young Amelia Pond, in a universe slowly contracting due to the TARDIS explosion. Just as Amy's memories had been used to build the trap for the Doctor, so her memories of the Doctor would ultimately restore him. In between, an out-of-time Doctor gives Roman Rory (dubbed the fairytale-like 'the last centurion') the means to free him from the Pandorica, swapping places with the wounded Amy: the stasis field of the Pandorica keeps her alive until she is in turn freed by her younger self during her visit to the museum in which the mysterious box eventually comes to rest. After River is freed from the exploding TARDIS, the Doctor pilots the Pandorica into the TARDIS explosion where the same 'restoration field' that saved Amy reboots the entire universe, with the cracks in time closing but trapping the Doctor on the other side.

Memory and remembering were fairytale themes running through this series, and it all comes together with Amy's recollection at her wedding of 'something old, something new, something borrowed, something blue' bringing back not just the TARDIS (the ancient-modern blue box time machine that the Doctor 'borrowed' from the Time Lords), but the Doctor himself. In *The Pandorica Opens* he told Amy: 'Nothing is ever forgotten, not completely. And if something can be remembered it can come back.' It was the Doctor who, as his own timeline unravels, sowed the seeds of Amy's recall, travelling back through important moments in the series (including an odd scene already shown in *Flesh and Stone*). There's a pleasingly meta-fictional moment when the Doctor is talking to the sleeping Amy: 'You'll remember me a little. I'll be a story in your head... but that's okay, we're all stories in the end...'

While these fairytale elements are deliberate and run through Moffat's approach to *Doctor Who* stories, *The Pandorica Opens/The Big Bang* also used the audience's expected familiarity with a new strain of television popular science to get across some of its more outlandish moments. At the forefront of this movement was physicist Brian Cox, whose series *Wonders of the Solar System* aired early in 2010. His populist approach to complex ideas prepared British television audiences for the quantum theory notions that Moffat included (Cox would even go on to make a brief appearance during Smith's third series in *The Power of Three*). While the science of *The Big Bang* might be fanciful and outlandish, the work of Cox and other science communicators had paved the way for a general audience to take on board the kind of 'wibbly-wobbly, timey-wimey' complexities, conundrums and paradoxes that Steven Moffat had a taste for.

Moffat's fairytale take on *Doctor Who* exploited a range of childhood and child-like anxieties, often confronted in the guise of children's literature. Classic literature was also the source for the 2010 Christmas special, which wore its influences on its sleeve with the title *A Christmas Carol*. Michael Gambon starred as a miser whose life is reshaped by the Doctor in a Steampunk-tinged imaginative fantasy adventure that relegated the show's science fiction heritage (which in this episode includes cryogenics, and a spaceship flight deck modelled on that of *Star Trek*) to mere background.

Doctor Who was back once more with the first half of Matt Smith's second year in the title role between April and June 2011. In an unusual move, the season was split into two, with seven episodes running from the usual Easter start date, but the remaining six held back for an autumn run. The same would happen with Smith's third season, with an autumn 2012/spring 2013 split. While Moffat attempted to make the best of this stop-start approach to transmission in episodic blocks, it seemed apparent that the scheduling was driven by BBC cutbacks, essentially stretching two years of production over a three-year transmission period. Instead of the 2009 'gap year' strategy pursued by Davies, the Moffat years saw fewer episodes scheduled more regularly but in shorter blocks.

Moffat argued that the new structure gave this run of episodes twice as many launches and twice as many 'season finale' events, building on Davies' own approach to 'event television'. Now in its sixth year on air (considered 'old' by modern TV standards), Moffat realised that *Doctor Who* needed to be kept fresh, so he cleverly structured each batch to emphasise the episodes that gained the show media attention. Unusually he opened the season with a complex two-part tale set (and partly filmed) in America – in itself a hook for a news item. *The Impossible Astronaut* opened with the apparent death of the Doctor at the hands of a mysterious figure in an Apollo-era space suit, before an earlier Eleventh Doctor gets involved with the Silents/Silence and the 1969 moon landings. Amy, Rory and River Song having witnessed the Doctor's presumed 'death' struggle to keep the information to themselves. There are other mysteries, such as the status of Amy's suggested pregnancy and the appearance of an eye-patch wearing figure observing her.

The Silents (connected to the 'Silence will fall' voice) were another ingenious Moffat monster creation. The gimmick was that if you see them, you instantly forget, making their covert infiltration of mankind possible. Thematically they fitted well with the ongoing theme of 'remembering', and proved to be a formidable opponent, difficult to combat if their very presence is instantly forgotten.

The complexities surrounding the Doctor's apparent death would not be resolved until the autumn, so it was a deliberate ploy to follow up a dense pair of episodes with two somewhat lighter stories. *The Curse of the Black Spot* took *Doctor Who* into *Pirates of the Caribbean* territory (with the fourth movie in the franchise, subtitled *On Stranger Tides*, released shortly after this episode aired), playing out both as a traditional tale of pirates and their treasure and something more like science fiction (even if the eventual reveal that the menace here is simply an automated system gone wrong echoes past stories such as *The Empty Child/The Doctor Dances* and *The Girl in the Fireplace*, all written by Moffat).

Doctor Who has done pirates before, whether in 1966's *The Smugglers* (featuring the same real-life Captain Avery as this episode), or the space variety in *The Pirate Planet*, or even the Tennant-starring animated spin-off *The Infinite Quest*. What should have been a fun, stand-alone light romp was undermined by the need to include the series-long arc elements (eye-patch lady reappears) and a heavy-handed father-son relationship, something Moffat (himself a man with a young family) has brought to the show (a motif later repeated in *Night Terrors*).

Comics scribe Neil Gaiman – a self-described *Doctor Who* fan – delivered a love letter to the series in *The Doctor's Wife*. The title, provided by Moffat rather than Gaiman, came from a fake episode posted on 1980s producer John Nathan-Turner's office noticeboard as a way of tracing the source of leaks about upcoming episodes. Family (beyond friends and companions) had never been central to *Doctor Who* beyond the existence of his granddaughter Susan, but it had often been referenced or recreated in the revived series. The relationship between the First Doctor and his granddaughter was never explored in any depth, to the extent that she often became just another companion, the original model for the young female companions who followed. Although it has connections to the overall season story arc (Amy is still concerned about her foreknowledge of the Doctor's death, while the future is hinted at when Rory is told that 'The only water in the forest is the river...'), it integrates them with far more success than *The Curse of the Black Spot*. Littered with shout outs to *Doctor Who*'s own on-screen history (Time Lord cubes, deleting TARDIS rooms, the ringing Cloister Bell, Artron energy), *The Doctor's Wife* is built around one key conceit: the way the Doctor has often anthropomorphised his relationship with the TARDIS, frequently calling it 'old girl'.

The TARDIS arrives upon a junkyard asteroid outside the known universe after the Doctor receives a Time Lord psychic message cube, suggesting there may be other survivors of the Time War. Upon arrival, the 'soul' of the TARDIS is removed and 'downloaded' into a young woman called Idris (Suranne Jones). The asteroid contains a malevolent intelligence called House that has been feasting on the Artron energy of captive TARDISes, killing the Time Lord occupants – it is now starving due to the demise of the Time Lords, so plans to use the Doctor's TARDIS to escape into the 'real' universe.

The heart of the episode is the relationship between the Doctor and his now human TARDIS in the female-shaped person of Idris. Arguing like an old married couple, the TARDIS reveals that it was she who stole him from Gallifrey, and not the other way around – although Moffat's later *The Name of the Doctor* complicates this matter... It is also suggested that what the Doctor took to be random wanderings that always landed him in trouble may have been, partially at least, guided by the TARDIS. All this was like catnip to long-term fans, but it also resonated with casual viewers, with a final consolidated rating of almost eight million.

Following that, the two-part meditation on identity *The Rebel Flesh/The Almost People* was a come down, even if, like *The Hungry Earth/Cold Blood* before it, it contained strong echoes of the Pertwee period in its make-up. Arriving on a remote island on 22nd century Earth, the Doctor, Amy and Rory become involved with the maintenance crew of a toxic acid factory where 'Gangers', or doppelgangers, of the real crew made of an artificial substance called 'the flesh' (a type of programmable organic matter) do all the dangerous work. A 'solar tsunami' disrupts the plant, and leads to the Gangers gaining sentience and a sense of self-preservation, causing them to rebel against their 'creators'. While much heavy work is made of telling the real crew from their Ganger doubles, the story also throws in a Ganger double of the Doctor (allowing Amy to admit her knowledge of his impending death to the real Doctor under the impression she is talking to the Ganger) and a climactic revelation that the Amy who has been travelling with the Doctor and Rory is also a Ganger 'flesh' duplicate. The real Amy, whose pregnancy is well advanced, is held prisoner by eye-patch lady. The result is an uneven, artificially extended (at two episodes) tale that serves as little more than a background explanation for the presence of the duplicate Amy on board the TARDIS and a possible way out for the Doctor when it comes to his 'death' at Lake Silencio.

As well as the Pertwee era notions of pollution and the care and handling of hazardous chemicals, these episodes share some affinity with the Pertwee period plastic Autons. Issues of identity, memory and humanity all come into play, but none are developed enough to make the story compelling beyond a simplistic Frankenstein metaphor. There are echoes of big screen science fiction, such as the 'skin job' Replicants of *Blade Runner* (1982), the genetic 'spares' from *Never Let Me Go* (2010), or the disposable duplicate manual labourers of *Moon* (2009). Dominated as it is by the need to build to the cliffhanger as the lead-in to the mid-season finale of *A Good Man Goes to War*, the detail of *The Rebel Flesh/The Almost People* is all but obliterated, dulling its impact.

A four-month break followed *A Good Man Goes to War* before the series returned, so a lot of questions had to be answered and a dramatic hook provided to ensure audiences would return for the rest of the ongoing story. This was both the danger and the opportunity of the split-season scheduling that Moffat had no choice but to embrace in his storytelling strategies.

A Good Man Goes to War sets up a new format for the show that would be explored further. It gave the Doctor a 'gang' of friends instead of one or two companions, comprising the Victorian Silurian crime fighter Madame Vastra and her servant Jenny, the Sontaran nurse Strax, and Dorium Maldovar, the rotund blue chap briefly seen in the opening sequence of *The Pandorica Opens*. Although that episode saw characters from earlier in the season collectively helping the Doctor, they never worked together, unlike those featured here and in the later *Dinosaurs in a Spaceship* (in which the Doctor openly declares 'I've got a gang now...'). Moffat couldn't have known the eventual popularity of Vastra, Jenny and Strax, leading to him re-using the characters frequently next season (in *The Snowmen*, *The Crimson Horror* and *The Name of the Doctor*).

The 'gang' come together to help the Doctor rescue Amy from

her incarceration at Demon's Run, a fortified asteroid, where she is being held by Madame Kovarian (Frances Barber), the mysterious eye-patch lady. Throw in a brief appearance by the Cybermen and a Silurian army, and this episode presents a more cleverly conceived monster team-up than *The Pandorica Opens* achieved. Again, the aim is the budget-saving re-use of available costumes, but Moffat approached the challenge by creating a core group of characters that unexpectedly struck a chord with viewers.

Although full of action and incident, *A Good Man Goes to War* was actually about a fundamental change in the Doctor (one followed up at the end of this series and the beginning of the next). He comes to realise that his victories have resulted in him gaining a reputation, one that has caused opponents to preemptively strike at him. Kovarian and the Clerics have set out to create a human-Time Lord mix to give them a controllable weapon: the result is River Song, revealed at the climax to be the lost-in-time daughter of Amy and Rory. Born at Demon's Run, the baby is kidnapped by Kovarian (suggesting the changeling myth in Scottish folklore or the kidnapped/abandoned children of many fairytales), raised in the orphanage seen in *The Day of the Moon*, who then escapes and regenerates into River Song (a scene revealed in the next instalment, *Let's Kill Hitler*). Eventually, it is she who ends up in the Apollo-era space suit and is seen to kill the Doctor. This was Moffat talking his 'timey-wimey' storytelling to the max, and hoping that viewers would be able to keep up with him. Douglas Adams, script editor on the series in 1979, once described his job as making the show simple enough for adults and complicated enough for children. It was an approach with which Moffat concurred: 'We haven't actually had any complaints from the general audience at all,' Moffat told the *New York Magazine*'s Vulture website. 'Not one single bit of audience feedback has even mentioned complexity. *Doctor Who* can be complicated at times, it absolutely can be – but it's supposed to be. You're supposed to pay attention. I'm also addressing children, hugely the case in the UK, and children are demanding of complexity. I think we do some complicated stories, [but] we also do incredibly simple stories. I always think this: I don't care if it's complicated or too scary or too grown-up or too childish or whatever they are saying this week, so long as they never say it's too boring. If anyone says "Oh, it was a bit dull this week" [that] is when the show will start to die.'

Just over 7.5 million saw *A Good Man Goes to War*, and the following instalment attracted 8.1 million to further discover the answers to Moffat's complex and teasing questions.

9. HALF-CENTURY HERO

The hook to bring viewers back to *Doctor Who* in the autumn of 2011 was what showrunner Steven Moffat termed the 'slutty' title of *Let's Kill Hitler*. The episode introduced Mels, a newly revealed 'best friend' of companions Amy and Rory: they'd all grown up together, as shown in an increasingly amusing series of flashbacks. Having accosted the Doctor in a cornfield, Mels announces 'You've got a time machine, I've got a gun. What the hell, let's kill Hitler', explaining the title as the show launches into its regular title sequence.

Although the TARDIS crew arrive in Berlin 1938, the encounter with Hitler is brief and comic (and allowed Rory to cement his new hero status by knocking him down with a single punch – similar to the treatment meted out to the dictator in US wartime comic books, such as on the cover of *Captain America*#1 in March 1941). The war and its real-life consequences are not a topic for this show. Instead, Hitler is relegated to a cupboard for the rest of the episode, as the narrative latches on to the far more interesting story of Mels regenerating into River Song (the weapon Kovarian has bred to kill the Doctor), and her role in saving her ultimate target. Here the show is playing with some of its core ideas in depicting another regeneration (the newly regenerated River goes through the same inspect-appearance/select-costume routine as every new Doctor), and builds on the idea from *Journey's End* that 'regeneration energy' can be used to save the poisoned Doctor. The episode also features the Teselecta, a humanoid robot piloted by a miniaturised crew that dispenses justice to war criminals. As a get out to explain the death of the Doctor witnessed at the opening of *The Impossible Astronaut*, the Teselecta couldn't be more obvious (although Moffat had already seeded 'the flesh' as an alternative explanation).

Fatherhood and relationships were the theme for the next three episodes: *Night Terrors*, *The Girl Who Waited*, and *The God Complex*. In *Night Terrors* the object of the Doctor's aid is a frightened little boy called George, eventually revealed to be an alien cuckoo in the nest (a Tenza), but one still in need of his father for protection. Along the way, the Doctor, Amy and Rory find themselves trapped within a doll's house, haunted by clothes peg dolls. It's a surreal fairytale image, an approach extended further when the trio are hunted by a minotaur (explained as a relative of the Nimon, last seen in 1979's *The Horns of Nimon*) in the hotel setting of *The God Complex*. Similarly, *The Girl Who Waited* featured Moffat-style time warped storytelling (Amy and Rory enter a medical facility and find themselves on different time tracks, so she ages more rapidly), but still depends upon the relationship between the pair for its emotional climax. Their marriage – seen in *The Big Bang* – is central to their remaining time on the show, an unusual depiction of a long-term romantic and domestic partnership on *Doctor Who* (and the nearest concession Moffat makes to Davies' previous 'soap opera' approach). The hotel in *The God Complex* features rooms containing each individual's 'greatest fear': Amy's sighting of a Weeping Angel in one room is a neat foreshadowing of her (and Rory's) eventual fate.

The sentimental conclusion of *Night Terrors* has Daniel Mays, as George's father, express his love for the alien boy, thus saving the day. Similarly, the penultimate episode, *Closing Time* (the sequel to last season's *The Lodger*), has Craig defeat the Cybermen through the power of his love for the son he's previously failed to bond with. These family and relationship dramas (the group trapped in the hotel in *The God Complex* have to work together to survive) reflect Moffat's status as a father with young children.

The season reached its climax with *The Wedding of River Song* at the beginning of October 2011, an episode that had much to do in terms of wrapping up disparate running stories. It revolved around the enigma of River Song (Alex Kingston) and her out-of-sequence relationship with the Doctor. In this one all of history appears to be happening at once (resulting in, among many other things, Charles Dickens – Simon Callow from 2005's *The Unquiet Dead* – appearing on Breakfast TV promoting his Christmas special, a neat series in-joke). Ian McNiece was back as a Roman emperor-style Churchill, ruling over a historically mixed-up Britain in which the Doctor ('the soothsayer') is held prisoner. This reality is a consequence of River attempting to prevent the Doctor's death in Utah, so causing time to stop and history to become confused.

Thanks to the crack in time manifested in her bedroom, Amy still remembers the Doctor, even if she's fuzzy on who exactly Rory is. Along with captive Silents, whose stated aim is to destroy the Doctor, Area 52 holds Madame Kovarian, who masterminded the assassination plot using Amy and Rory's child, Melody/River Song. The surprise is that although this all sounds incredibly complicated, picking up on story strands that stretch not only back to the start of the season but beyond to the previous year, the episode itself is a fast-moving and entertaining piece that connected with the viewing audience, as indicated by the final figure of 7.67 million.

The Doctor cannot escape his death as it is a 'fixed point' in time and therefore unalterable – however, he is able to cheat a little. Using a Teselecta in the shape of the Doctor, he is able to meet his destiny, fool the universe into believing he is dead, and continue his travels in space and time unhindered. There's one catch: there's a prediction from the still-living severed head of Dorium Maldovar of the Doctor's future. 'On the fields of Trenzalor, at the fall of the Eleventh, when no living creature can speak falsely or fail to answer a question will be asked – one that must never be answered. And Silence *must* fall when the question is asked.' By the end of the episode it is clear that the question is that which has haunted the series from its very beginning: 'The first question! The question that must never be answered! Hidden in plain sight! The question you've been running from all your life! Doctor *who*?' The answer would be central to the finale of the following series, tantalisingly entitled *The Name of the Doctor*, and would be the cue for the regeneration of Matt Smith into his replacement in the 2013 Christmas special.

Riffing on well-loved stories once more, Moffat wrote the 2011 Christmas special *The Doctor, The Widow, and The Wardrobe* (loosely modelled after elements of CS Lewis's *The Lion, the Witch and the Wardrobe*), finally free of the arcing plot elements that had dominated the previous two years. The feel-good episode attracted 10.77 million viewers on Christmas Day, and in its smaller scale, the characters of the wooden king and queen, and its environmental message, it continued the fairytale focus of recent years.

With the next season's start delayed until Autumn 2012, and the first batch consisting of only five episodes before the next Christmas special, Moffat took the opportunity to wrap up the Pond story arc. Across the five episodes that made up the first part of the show's seventh full series, he wrote out Karen Gillan and Arthur Darvill's characters – two of the longest running companions in the series history – while pulling off a major surprise with the early introduction of the Doctor's next companion Clara (played by Jenna-Louise Coleman) in season opener *Asylum of the Daleks*.

Selling the show with the publicity hook of 'Every Dalek ever' Moffat re-introduced the classic gold Daleks, pushing his own *Victory of the Daleks* iteration – which had gone down badly with fans and the public – to one side, as just one among many variants. It was only the fourth time that *Doctor Who* had opened with a story featuring the Daleks (*Asylum* aired 33 years to the day after season 17's *Destiny of the Daleks*, while previous Dalek season openers had been 1972's *Day of the Daleks* and 1988's *Remembrance of the Daleks* – each of those returns had followed a significant period of time since the Daleks had last appeared). The other approach Moffat took to the new series was to downplay the fairytale tropes he'd been employing and instead adopt a 'movie poster' pitch for each instalment (the deliberate removal of two-part stories made this possible), with each episode accompanied by a stylish image incorporating the main characters, setting or mood.

Asylum of the Daleks opened with Amy and Rory (their marriage having broken down) kidnapped, along with the Doctor, to carry out a mission the Daleks will not undertake themselves. They need the Doctor to infiltrate their Asylum planet (depicted almost as a fairytale haunted house) where they have imprisoned their damaged and rogue brethren. There he must deactivate the force-shield so the Daleks can destroy it. The trio discover Oswin Oswald (Coleman), a human prisoner who has been converted into a Dalek, although she has retreated into a fantasy world to preserve her own sanity. With Oswin's help, the Doctor hacks the Daleks' database deleting their knowledge of him. That leaves the Daleks questioning his identity at the episode's end, with the phrase from *The Wedding of River Song* recurring: 'Doctor who?'

Moffat successfully gained the collusion of the press and preview audiences in keeping Coleman's early appearance a secret after her casting had been announced to the press in March. Her character would not return until the 2012 Christmas episode *The Snowmen*, but the showrunner was clearly intent on building a mystery around her. An audience of 8.33 million viewed *Asylum of the Daleks*, so would hopefully be hooked by the on-going mystery of Clara...

With *Asylum of the Daleks* meeting Moffat's stated aim of making the Daleks scary again, the following episode was a straightforward populist romp. *Dinosaurs on a Spaceship*, written by Chris Chibnall, did exactly what it said on the tin (with advanced CGI dinosaurs making up for the largely inert plastic models of 1974's *Invasion of the Dinosaurs*). The Doctor and his 'gang' – this time consisting of Egyptian queen Nefertiti and the British big game hunter John Riddell – pick up Amy, Rory and (inadvertently) Rory's dad Brian (Mark Williams) on the way to investigate a rogue asteroid threatening to crash to Earth. The asteroid is a disguised spaceship – a Silurian ark – that has been infiltrated by black market trader Solomon (David Bradley), who saw the value in the ship's cargo of dinosaurs but had no qualms about killing its crew of Silurians. While fending off the dinosaurs, the Doctor causes the Earth missiles aimed at the asteroid to destroy Solomon's fleeing ship instead. This is the best example of Moffat's 'movie poster' approach, and it prioritises visual spectacle above any outward connection to real-world events. Despite that high concept approach, the heart of the tale is a variation of the father-son relationship, albeit a mature one between Rory and Brian.

Shooting in Spain had afforded *Asylum of the Daleks* its snow-bound location for the Dalek Asylum planet, but the main reason the cast and crew had travelled there was to use the standing Western set at Almeria (seen in many classic spaghetti Westerns, including *A Fistful of Dollars*, 1964) for the third episode, *A Town Called Mercy*. The episode was the first time *Doctor Who* had attempted a Western-themed instalment since the 1966 story *The Gunfighters* – which featured the series' lowest-ever audience appreciation scores – and this one proved to be just as unsuccessful in execution, despite being the highest rated of these five autumn episodes at 8.22 million viewers.

Couched as a moral debate around the Doctor's actions when he comes between Jex, an alien war criminal, masquerading as a town doctor in the wild west and the justice cyborg send to kill him, the

Toby Whithouse-scripted episode manages to waste decent guest stars like *Farscape*'s Ben Browder in disposable roles of little consequence. The location rarely comes across as little more than a relatively empty movie set, and the moral debate about whether the Doctor should abandon Jex to his fate seems like a leftover from an old Tenth Doctor story, rather than something fitting the newest incarnation.

Any mis-steps taken by *A Town Called Mercy* were more than made up for by *The Power of Three*, the second of two great scripts by Chibnall (a writer who had previously rarely impressed on this show or *Torchwood*). Celebrating the relationship between Amy, Rory and the Doctor it chronicles 'the year of the slow invasion' when the Earth is inundated with billions of mysterious little black cubes (treated by the population as collectible consumer items, the latest must-have but useless high-tech gadget). The Doctor lives with the Ponds in order to observe the cubes. It introduced Jemma Redgrave as the Liz Shaw-like Kate Stewart, the daughter of Brigadier Lethbridge-Stewart, and UNIT's current commander – and the character would make a return appearance in the show's 50th anniversary special, so honouring the late Nicholas Courtney.

As the episode dealt so well with the soon-to-be-departing companions, it can perhaps be forgiven (more than the previous instalment) for a somewhat garbled and easy solution to the problem of the cubes (they're analysing humanity to discover their weakness so alien 'pest controllers' the Shakri can eliminate them) and for doing little with guest star villain Steven Berkoff. The central concept and the character comedy it allowed powered the episode along, with Chibnall's script recalling some of the tropes of the Davies era including the modernisation of UNIT (and their Tower of London HQ), and the use of famous faces (physicist Brian Cox, and Lord Alan Sugar from *The Apprentice*) and multi-media populist coverage to comment on the arrival of the black cubes. The meat of the episode, however, was in comparing the Ponds' humdrum domestic home life with their exotic adventures with the Doctor, and how they were now mature enough to settle for the former. The hyper-activity of the Doctor, now confined to the 'slow path' taken every day by the Ponds, nicely contrasts with the mature commitment of Brian, Rory's dad, in observing the cubes across days of inactivity. His observant nature is key in him realising that his son and daughter-in-law have actually been gone for some time with the Doctor during mere moments at a Christmas party. The Ponds' three years or so of on-screen time with the Doctor has actually been about a decade in their 'real life' character time.

That was simply preparing the way for the mid-season finale (all five of these episodes aired during September 2012). *The Angels Take Manhattan* featured the end of the Ponds' story, and the return of River Song and Moffat's trademark monsters, the Weeping Angels. After an atmospheric run-around in 1930s New York (partially filmed on location in the city, a move reflecting the increasing popularity of the Matt Smith series in the US, and including the Statue of Liberty as a giant Weeping Angel – an idea that doesn't entirely make sense, but makes for a great visual), the story saw Amy resolve to follow Rory (who has been the victim of a Weeping Angel) back to a time-locked version of 1930s New York (caused by the interaction of the Angels and the TARDIS), meaning that the Doctor can never re-visit them. It is perhaps the ultimate happy ever after dark fairytale ending that Moffat has been building to since *The Eleventh Hour*. In choosing this exit strategy for the characters, Moffat wisely avoids killing them off, but also handily prevents their easy return (a criticism made regarding Billie Piper and Catherine Tate's reappearances after their 'final' stories). It was a point reinforced by Karen Gillan in interviews: 'I want the impact of the Pond era to remain strong. I don't want to spoil it by coming back a few episodes later to say "Hello!"' Ending with a brief flashback to young Amy from *The Eleventh Hour* (truly, 'the girl who waited'), the climax brings her story full circle and provided one of the most moving and satisfying companion departures on this long-running series. An emotional 'postscript' scene (entitled *P.S.*) that had been written but never filmed was released on the BBC's official *Doctor Who* website depicting (through illustrated storyboards and an Arthur Darvill voice-over) Brian, Rory's father, receiving a letter explaining their disappearance. *The Angels Take Manhattan* cleared the slate for a new take on the Doctor and the (re)introduction of a new companion in the Christmas episode, *The Snowmen*.

The 2012 Christmas special *The Snowmen* was more relevant to the on-going storylines of the series than most (in fact, the most relevant since the first Christmas Special, *The Christmas Invasion*). Not only did it re-introduce 'new' companion Clara (and promptly kill her off again), but it also re-introduced a long-dormant antagonist, the Great Intelligence. Not seen since the series' fifth year on air (Patrick Troughton's second season), the Great Intelligence was portrayed as an disembodied alien evil that acted through others. It first appeared in *The Abominable Snowmen*, using robotic yeti in Tibet, and again in *The Web of Fear*, the sequel that same season, in which the yeti invaded through the London Underground.

In *The Snowmen*, Moffat created both a sequel and a prequel, bringing back the Great Intelligence (voiced by Ian McKellen, with Richard E Grant as its human puppet, Dr Simeon, the embodiment of the cold-hearted Victorian capitalist) and providing it with an origin story set in Victorian London. Having isolated himself after the loss of the Ponds, the Doctor is a recluse living in the TARDIS hidden on an invisible cloud high above the city (yet more fairytale elements), despite the entreaties of Madame Vastra, Jenny and the Sontaran Strax. The Doctor encounters Clara, a Mary Poppins-style governess (also mirrored in the dead governess that the Great Intelligence intends to use as a DNA template for its ice army) who occasionally works in a bar. He is initially unaware of her resemblance to Oswin (only having heard her voice). They are all caught up in the plan of the Great Intelligence to use psychic 'memory snow' to create an army of snowmen to conquer the planet. It is only after the defeat of the Great Intelligence and the death of Clara that the Doctor realises he has encountered her before.

The Snowmen also introduced a brand new version of the title sequence and the theme music that would run throughout the series' 50th anniversary year of 2013. These new titles were a deliberate and triumphant celebration of everything that had gone before. Presented as a journey through time and space, the titles incorporated the TARDIS, clouds and galaxies of the Hartnell and McCoy titles, planets and nebulae in a swiftly spinning tumble, the Doctor's face forming from the clouds (like Troughton's – Matt Smith's inspiration), and the logo breaking apart to unleash an up-to-date CGI version of the classic Tom Baker slit-scan time tunnel (albeit in red hues). It was an effective encapsulation of the show's potential, capturing perhaps for the first time the true time and space traversing nature of *Doctor Who*.

The episode also introduced a new console room interior for the TARDIS, the third since the new series began. Unlike the previous two that adopted a whimsical attitude to the controls, the new version (from new production designer Michael Pickwoad, whose father had acted in the Hartnell serial *The War Machines*) reverted to the original style for the console established by designer Peter Brachacki in 1963. Looking more like a functional machine than at any time since the series was revived, the interior of this new TARDIS would be more fully explored in the episode *Journey to the Centre of the TARDIS*.

The mystery of Clara was followed up in the first episode of the second part of season seven, broadcast in the traditional 'new season' Easter slot in early 2013. *The Bells of Saint John* reintroduced Clara as a contemporary character in a story about wi-fi and internet usage ripped from contemporary headlines (the first in quite a while to be so direct about its relevance to the contemporary lives of viewers). As worries about the time spent online by children and adults alike increased, and the growing reliance of people on the internet to conducted everyday tasks from grocery shopping to paying bills, became ever more evident, so Moffat wrote a contemporary thriller based on the concept that 'there's something lurking in the wi-fi'. Moffat's departure from Twitter after complaining that it took too much time away from his scriptwriting duties may also have been an inspiration.

An organisation – led by guest star Celia Imrie – run from one of London's newest iconic buildings, The Shard, is harvesting minds via the wi-fi and internet, but they are defeated when the Doctor and Clara turn their 'spoonhead' remote robotic technology against them. The Great Intelligence (briefly portrayed by Richard E Grant) is behind the plot and accepts defeat, but comments 'I have feasted on many minds. I have grown', setting the character up as a recurring antagonist once again.

Contemporary fears about the interface between technology and the personal – from Facebook privacy controls to 'big state' snooping on emails – inform *The Bells of Saint John* (the title is a reference to the TARDIS telephone, which rings for the first time since Moffat's *The Empty Child*). Miss Kizlet's (Imrie) control over her employees through hacking their personalities (she can increase or decrease their paranoia, obedience or intelligence – among other attributes – at the slide of a finger) highlights worries about decreasing worker rights in the 'new Victorian' age of austerity under the coalition government. In technological terms, there's also the issue of how big business reduces people to mere data. Other sly contemporary references slipped in include the summer riots of 2011, and concerns about cattle and Burger King that coincidentally followed recent news about horse-meat in burgers. Additionally, the power of 'crowd sourcing' and the surveillance possibilities of the internet are co-opted by Kizlet to find the Doctor and the TARDIS.

Re-encountering Clara once more makes the Doctor determined to solve her 'mystery', feeling her repeated existence through time and space and her multiple deaths make her 'impossible'. The next few episodes would, as well as being stand-alone adventures, revolve around the Doctor's search for answers about Clara's true nature as 'the woman twice dead'.

Neil Cross – a writer new to *Doctor Who*, but known for *Spooks* and *Luther* – was responsible for *The Rings of Akhaten*, and although it was his second script for the series it was screened first. It fell to Cross to provide some backstory for Clara, with the opening few minutes depicting her parents' history and her early years, under the watchful eye of a curious Doctor. By the end, Cross has cleverly used the leaf that provided the 'meet-cute' moment for Clara's parents.

The challenging *The Rings of Akhaten* was disliked initially by many fans (although a significant number seemed to revise their opinions after rewatching). It was an example of the kind of format-breaking 'oddball' story that populated the Sylvester McCoy years when Andrew Cartmel was script editor. It's that rarest of beasts, a *Doctor Who* story driven by music. In an echo of *The End of the World* and *The Beast Below*, the Doctor takes his new companion somewhere exotic to display the possibilities of travel in the TARDIS, in this case a fractured planetary system known as the Rings of Akhaten. Amid a menagerie of bizarre creatures (more than have ever been seen in a single *Doctor Who* episode before), Clara hooks up with Merry (Emilia Jones, daughter of singer Aled Jones) who is due to sing at a huge public event to pacify a legendary god. Cross explores the foundations of religion in myth and legend, while depicting a parasitic 'god' (perhaps modelled by Cross on Marvel comics' Galactus, Devourer of Worlds) that feeds on memories. This echoes the strange barter system of the planet, where goods and services are swapped for items of sentimental value, imbued with meaningful memories. When the song is interrupted, the 'angry god' is awakened. The Doctor confronts it (it takes the form of the system's sun), but even his copious experience fails to sate its hunger – only Clara's leaf, containing as it does not only her memories of her late mother, but the 'infinite potential' that her mother failed to live, destroys the menace. With a pyramid, an ancient mummy, sun worship and a planet name based on pharaoh Akhenaten, it is clear Cross drew much of his inspiration from Egyptian mythology. Several times in the episode Clara states her disbelief in ghosts, but Cross's next script, *Hide*, would bring her face-to-face with one.

The return of a classic monster has been a frequent hook for *Doctor Who* since its return in 2005. However, having tackled the Daleks (successfully in their 'bronze' variety, unsuccessfully with their *Victory of the Daleks* revamp), the Cybermen, and the Sontarans most of the 'core' monsters (those remembered by casual viewers, as opposed to fans) had been done. Second tier creatures – the Silurians and Autons – had also been reinvented for modern viewers. Even some more obscure creations had featured, such as the Macra in *Gridlock*. Two returns had been long awaited: the Ice Warriors and the Zygons (who would crop up in the anniversary special).

Writer Mark Gatiss answered many of the questions about the Ice Warriors (originally created by Brian Hayles) arising from their four previous appearances. They'd been seen twice with the Second Doctor plus a brief cameo at the climax of *The War Games*, and twice with the Third Doctor following a similarly brief cameo in *The Mind of Evil*. A variety of spin-off novels and audio dramas had kept the memory of the iconic Martians alive for fans.

Gatiss had pitched the return of the Ice Warriors to Moffat several times, but the showrunner had constantly declined fearing they were (as Gatiss noted to the *Radio Times*) 'the embodiment of the slow-moving *[Doctor] Who* monster of legend'. Pitching a story that trapped a lone-but-powerful Ice Warrior (an approach that had worked well to re-introduce the by-then much-mocked Daleks in 2005) on a 1980s'

Russian submarine, Gatiss had his story, but he also had to supply 'something new'. That turned out to be an exploration of just what the Ice Warriors were like under their iconic reptillian armour (Hayles had provided some explanations in his novel of *The Ice Warriors*, but nothing had ever been seen on screen). *Cold War* gave the Martian marauders a new lease of life.

In 1983, a Russian nuclear-armed submarine has unearthed a frozen 'something', quickly thawed out (recalling Howard Hawks' *The Thing from Another World*, 1951) and on a rampage. The Doctor and Clara, expecting Las Vegas but finding themselves trapped in *Das Boot* instead, take charge of the situation with the Doctor identifying the thing as an Ice Warrior, a preserved survivor of a once noble race.

The remainder of the episode essentially riffed on the 1979 Ridley Scott film *Alien*, with various crewmembers falling prey to the Ice Warrior – identified as Grand Marshall Skaldak, a warrior not unlike the Russian submarine commander. Skaldak escapes his bio-mechanical armour and is able to secret himself about the submarine, striking at will – and allowing modern CGI to show what the Ice Warriors look like under their armour (with a face resembling the Martians of *The War of the Worlds*, 1953, and claws that recall the 'face hugger' creatures of *Alien*).

With modern international tension as high as ever and a more complex geopolitical world, even though the cold war is only a memory, this episode showed that weapons of mass destruction were just as bad an idea in the 21st century as they had been in the 20th. At the time of broadcast in April 2013, it was North Korea that had taken the role of the world's nuclear bogeyman, threatening the US with radioactive destruction. For all its nostalgia, both for the mid-1980s and for an old style of 'base under siege' *Doctor Who, Cold War* revealed itself to be as chillingly relevant to the present day as any far-future set parable of mankind's end.

Clara's lack of belief in ghosts came back to haunt her in Neil

Cross's *Hide*. Channelling Nigel Kneale's *The Stone Tape* (1972), Cross adopted shades of Kneale's Professor Quatermass for Dougray Scott's Professor Alec Palmer. It's 1974, and Palmer and psychic Emma Grayling (Jessica Raine, who would go on to portray *Doctor Who's* original producer Verity Lambert in the celebratory drama *An Adventure in Space and Time*) are attempting to summon the ghost of 'the witch in the well'. The Doctor discovers that the 'ghost' is a trapped time traveller whom he must rescue from a 'monster' menacing her in a pocket universe. When he becomes trapped there, Clara must commandeer a seemingly-reluctant TARDIS (the 'sentient' ship has been consistently difficult with Clara) to rescue him. The Doctor realises that the 'monster' in the house and its counterpart in the pocket universe are a couple, trying to be reunited. At the climax, the episode effortlessly switches genres from ghost story to love story. Only at the end is it revealed that the Doctor came to this time and place so that the psychic Emma could evaluate the 'twice dead girl', Clara Oswald.

That the solution to what appears to be a supernatural problem (a ghost) turns out to be science fiction (a time traveller) should be no surprise to viewers of *Doctor Who*, or fans of Nigel Kneale whose *Quatermass and the Pit* (BBC, 1958-59) took a similar stance. The rise of 'parascience' in so-called 'reality' TV shows such as *Most Haunted* (2002–13) would have appalled Kneale, but it is through the context of such shows (or hit movie series like *Paranormal Activity*) that most viewers experienced *Hide*, even if the 1974 setting puts the events in a pre-digital world of magnetic tape and photochemical film.

The TARDIS itself became the focal point of *Journey to the Centre of the TARDIS*, an area ripe for exploration during the show's 50th anniversary year. The activities of the Van Baalen Brothers salvage crew, determined to extract anything of value from the Doctor's disabled space-time machine, recalled news reports of metal thefts during the economic downturn. Beyond that, the episode is a love letter to the Doctor's vehicle, albeit in a very different style to Neil Gaiman's *The Doctor's Wife*. There's more than a hint of *Alice in Wonderland* in Clara's recursive wanderings of the TARDIS corridors. From its first appearance in *An Unearthly Child* the TARDIS had been a point of fascination for fans and general viewers alike. While occasional dialogue would explain attributes of the vehicle or would anthropomorphise it, very few episodes dealt with the ship as a focal point. *The Edge of Destruction* was the first serial to explore the TARDIS and its nature in any depth. *The Time Monster* and *Logopolis* both featured the TARDIS as central to their stories, and companions' living quarters were a recurring element of the 'soapy' 1980s episodes, while *The Invasion of Time* depicted much of the interior as an unimaginative 1970s leisure centre (where the story was actually shot, due to industrial action at the BBC). For *Journey to the Centre of the TARDIS*, the production were able to depict more diverse rooms than ever before, not only the swimming pool and library (both referenced in *The Eleventh Hour*), but also a dramatic re-imagining of the Eye of Harmony (featured in the 1996 Paul McGann TV movie) and the heart of the vehicle itself.

While some of these vistas were fan-pleasing and spectacular (such as the tree-like 'architectural reconfiguration system' and the Apple-iMac style blown-apart engine room), in the end the episode fails to fulfill its promise, despite raising questions around fate and identity. Audio quotes from past characters are lost in the noisy sound mix, while the characters of the scavengers were underdeveloped (with even the reveal that the 'android' of the trio is no such thing falling flat). The 'monster of the week' time zombies were also explained in a rush, and – perhaps worst of all – the story adopted a 'magic reset button' (literally labelled as a 'big friendly button') to eliminate almost all that happened, although elements would later be recalled by Clara...

The next episode – *The Crimson Horror*, the new series' 100th instalment – was the second this season from Mark Gatiss and a riff on some classic *Doctor Who* settings and characters. For the first time, someone other than showrunner Moffat got to write for the Victorian 'Paternoster gang' of Silurian Madame Vastra, housekeeper Jenny and Sontaran 'butler' Strax, and the first 15 minutes almost function as a pilot for a spin-off series as it takes that long for Matt Smith's Doctor to appear. Investigating a strange idyllic community established in Yorkshire in 1893 by Winifred Gillyflower (Diana Rigg), the Doctor has managed to get himself immobilised as a victim of 'the crimson horror'. Exploiting the 'deplorable excesses of the Penny Dreadful', Gatiss conjures up a mock Victorian world familiar from many *Doctor Who* episodes.

In an episode verging on Steampunk, Gatiss spoofs the Victorian 'social improver' in Mrs Gillyflower, who has developed Sweetland (a new Jerusalem – they even sing the hymn) in the mould of real world Victorian model villages like New Lanark in Scotland, where workers lived next to the factory (although the one here consists of nothing more than gramophone records playing sound effects) in a crude form of theoretical utopian socialism. Her evangelising on the coming apocalypse has provided a steady stream of recruits, but only the best survive the 'preservation' process (and are stored under giant bell jars awaiting reawakening). The rejects – those seen by the area's mortician as suffering from the inexplicable 'crimson 'orror' – are cast into the canal, stiff and red skinned. It's in this form – but still alive – that the Paternoster gang discover the imprisoned Doctor.

There's more than a touch of Mary Shelley's *Frankenstein* in Mrs Gillyflower's daughter Ada (Rigg's own daughter, Rachael Stirling) and her naming of the captive Doctor as 'my monster' (and in Matt Smith's distinctly Karloffian performance). Ada's blindness (a result of her mother's experimentation) relates to other notions of sight and seeing in the episode, from the optogram (the last vision preserved in a dead man's retina), and the cod-silent movie flashback explaining the Doctor's prior involvement with Sweetville, through to her mother's vision of a new world in a 'shining city on the hill'. This phantasmagoria of an episode turns on Mrs Gillyflower's plan to poison the Earth by launching a rocket loaded with venom derived from her symbiote, Mr Sweet (a prehistoric parasite familiar to Madame Vastra), and repopulating the new world with her preserved morally upright recruits.

The Crimson Horror is an unashamed grand guignol genre mash-up, drawing as much on Victorian archetypes (filtered through film and television recreations) as on Doctor Who's own preferred form of storytelling in the past. Mrs Gillyflower's mad scheme is just the kind of thing a Doctor Who villain of the 1960s or 1970s might have dreamt up, with her happily confessing that the weapon the red leech's venom represents has indeed fallen into the wrong hands: hers. In its joyful excess, in storytelling and visual realisation, The Crimson Horror is a throwback in more ways than one to classic Doctor Who (in a very different way to Gatiss's Cold War), and a fitting episode to feature in the show's 50th year on air.

The same could not be said for the return of the Cybermen in Neil Gaiman's Nightmare in Silver, a disappointing attempt to trade on key icons from the past. While the Cybermen are suitably 'upgraded', it is only through the acquisition of old tricks, such as bullet time movements (from 1999's The Matrix) and on-the-fly upgrading (from Star Trek: The Next Generation's Borg, first seen in 1989's 'Q Who?', a Cyberman rip-off themselves). The story is set in a rather cheaply realised futuristic theme park called Hedgewick's World (recalling the Dickensian 'Fantasy Factory' from The Trial of a Time Lord, episodes 13–14) which quickly falls – despite the presence of a platoon of military rejects – to an army of reborn Cybermen, while the Doctor engages in a battle of wits (expressed through a chess game, shades of The Curse of Fenric) within his own mind against the Cyber Planner. The only really new element here is the reconfiguration of the old Cybermats (recently seen in *Closing Time*) into suitably miniaturised Cybermites. There are nostalgic shout outs to the Cybermen of the past in the Cyber Planner (last heard of in the Troughton story *The Wheel in Space*) and in cleaning fluid (*The Moonbase*) and gold (*Revenge of the Cybermen*, *Earthshock*, and *Silver Nemesis*) being fatal to Cybermen's health. The sets in the Cyber-army's lair recall those of *The Tomb of the Cybermen* much more directly than anything in the supposedly direct sequel *Attack of the Cybermen*. However, Gaiman's reconfiguration of the Cybermen does much to remove their original role as a form of upgraded humanity, as explored in *Rise of the Cybermen* and *The Age of Steel* and in their original 1960s stories.

Instead, the story explores the relative morality of war (drawing on recent conflicts in Iraq and Afghanistan, as well as the 'war on terror' rhetoric) and the danger of becoming too like your aggressor in order to defeat them (an issue raised almost simultaneously in cinemas in *Star Trek Into Darkness*). Emperor-in-disguise Porridge (Warwick Davis) relates the history of the Cyber-wars and how trillions had to die to save billions. 'I feel like a monster sometimes,' he confesses, as he was the 'poor blighter who had to press the button to blow it all up'. This theme takes precedence over any ideas of the Cybermen as updated automata or the occasionally uncanny nature of sideshows, circuses, freak shows and fairs represented in Hedgewick's World.

The 50th anniversary run of stories culminated in *The Name of the Doctor*, a season finale truly wrapped up in the show's own history (a dangerous area for the series after its failures of the 1980s). It opened with the instigating incident for the whole *Doctor Who* mythology in which William Hartnell's First Doctor steals/borrows/liberates a TARDIS on Gallifrey. Cleverly reconstructed using CGI and colourised clips from the original series, the pre-titles sequence teases the mystery of Clara (whose 'I don't know where I am' phrase is repeated from *The Bells of Saint John*, along with the leaf motif from

The Rings of Akhaten) as she is seen to interact with several past Doctors.

The Doctor's tomb (a giant version of the Police Box TARDIS) has been discovered on Trenzalore, and his friends have been kidnapped, so the Doctor must go where he should never go: the end of his own timeline. This somewhat sombre and funereal, rather than celebratory, episode was an unusual way to lead in to the show's 50th anniversary special that November. The episode ties in to the Trenzalore warning delivered by Dorium in *The Wedding of River Song* (and she make a muted spectral appearance), and hints at the Doctor's greatest secret. After the mystery of Clara is resolved – she's been splintered in time, repeatedly 'born to save the Doctor' and to undo the damage done by the Great Intelligence when it (in the form of Richard E. Grant) has invaded the Doctor's past, turning all his victories into defeats – the Doctor's secret is revealed, kicking off a new wave of fan and viewer speculation. His 'secret' is a previously unknown incarnation, played by John Hurt, the guest star in the anniversary special rather portentously unveiled at the cliffhanger climax. Matt Smith's Eleventh Doctor refers to him as 'the one who broke the promise' inherent in the Doctor's choice of title. Hurt's one line is the mysterious: 'What I did I did without choice… in the name of peace and sanity'. Frustrated viewers would have to wait until November to have those new mysteries resolved.

However, a mere two weeks after transmission of the season finale came the sudden announcement that Matt Smith was leaving the series. With recent speculation about his increasing US profile and career ambitions – and given Dorium's comments two years earlier that '…the fall of the Eleventh…' would take place on Trenzalore – fans were perhaps not too surprised. Once again, media speculation became rife as to who would be cast as the Twelfth Doctor.

With *The Name of the Doctor* Moffat's dark fairytale had reached its climax. The Christmas episode *The Snowmen* and the eight episodes aired in the show's 50th anniversary year of 2013 each contained key elements of Moffat's approach to *Doctor Who* as an imaginative fantasy for family viewing. While overnight ratings had fallen a little through the run, time-shifting (which continued to increase as the show was transmitted earlier and earlier on Saturday evenings) easily brought the overall average ratings up to the approximate 7.5 million viewers each year had reached since 2005.

The appearance of John Hurt at the conclusion of *The Name of the Doctor* may not have been a complete surprise. His casting in the 50th anniversary special had been announced weeks before the episode aired, although his precise role was still a secret. The only clue had come from Hurt himself, who in a newspaper interview described his part as 'an aspect of the Doctor'.

Moffat's run on the series had done much to foreground the role of the Doctor as a character in a fairytale story or legend. Davies began it with Eccleston and Tennant, making their Doctors legendary figures which monsters should fear. Moffat turned the character into an imaginary friend for young Amy, and he's brought back into existence through her remembrance of him as a storybook figure. With Clara, she is tasked with saving the Doctor by actually jumping into his 'story', his timeline, in *The Name of the Doctor* in order to save him and – in turn – be saved by him. Moffat's meta-textual take on *Doctor Who* had reached its heights by the 50th anniversary, suggesting that the Twelfth Doctor might benefit from a 'back to basics' storytelling approach to the series.

To the disappointment of some fans, the 2013 anniversary special did not take the approach of previous anniversary shows *The Three Doctors* and *The Five Doctors* in reuniting all the still-surviving actors to have played the series' title role. Moffat's solution had been the inclusion of past doctors in *The Name of the Doctor*.

With Christopher Eccleston having declined to take part, Moffat instead wrote an episode that revolved around Matt Smith's current

Eleventh Doctor and included the reappearance of David Tennant's still popular Tenth Doctor, alongside Billie Piper as Rose Tyler. Both had only been absent from the show for three years, but the producers knew their return would attract additional viewers when the special aired on 23 November 2013, exactly 50 years to the day since the first episode of *An Unearthly Child*.

Filmed between 2 April and 5 May, the episode entitled *The Day of the Doctor* was written by Moffat, shot in 3D and featured the return of the Zygons (who appeared only once before in 1975's *Terror of the Zygons*), alongside the obligatory appearances by Daleks and Cybermen. Returning from *The Power of Three* was Kate Stewart, played by Jemma Redgrave, with Joanna Page appearing as Queen Elizabeth I.

The celebratory epic episode was not the only way that *Doctor Who*'s 50th anniversary was marked. Alongside a documentary on the show and many other news reports and special programmes, a drama entitled *An Adventure in Space and Time* recounted the early days of the programme. Written by Mark Gatiss, it starred David Bradley as William Hartnell and dramatised the key moments and personnel who were instrumental in the creation of the iconic series. Fittingly, it was one of the final programmes to record at Television Centre, where much of *Doctor Who* was made in the 1970s and 1980s, before the BBC vacated the distinctive building.

The introduction of the twelfth actor to play the Doctor became a sensational media event in itself. Topping the 2009 instalment of *Doctor Who Confidential* that had introduced Matt Smith, the 2013 special live broadcast *Doctor Who Live: The Next Doctor* was a global phenomenon, transmitting simultaneously in the UK, America, Canada and Australia (at 4am!). In the days before the 4 August transmission, speculation as to who had won the part was rife in newspapers. Among the suggested candidates were comic actor Chris O'Dowd, stand-up Chris Addison and BAFTA-winner Daniel Rigby, all actors in the now expected 30–40 age range.

To the surprise of many, though not all as his name had featured prominently in the previous week, the role went to the 55-year-old star of *The Thick of It*, Peter Capaldi. Fittingly for the 50th anniversary, Capaldi was the same age as William Hartnell when he first took on the role in 1963. Like David Tennant before him, Capaldi was also a life-long fan of the show having been involved in the Official Fan Club when a teenager in the 1970s. He'd had a letter about the show published in the *Radio Times* in 1973. Capaldi had also previously appeared in the *Doctor Who* episode *The Fires of Pompeii* (2008) alongside Tennant, as well as in a major role in the Torchwood mini-series *Children of Earth* (2009). Almost seven million viewers watched the live reveal on BBC1, with a further 1.5 million watching in the US, Canada, and Australia.

Capaldi said of winning the role: "It's so wonderful not to keep this secret any longer, but it's been so fantastic… Being asked to play the Doctor is an amazing privilege. Like the Doctor himself I find myself in a state of utter terror and delight. I can't wait to get started." For Moffat, the choice had been reasonably simple. "One of the most talented actors of his generation is about to play the best part on television. We made a home video of [Capaldi] being the Doctor and I showed it around and everyone said 'Yes, that's the Doctor'. There was a shortlist of one: Peter Capaldi."

Capaldi would be the first Oscar-winner to take the role (he won in 1994 as the director of the Best Live Action Short for *Franz Kafka's It's A Wonderful Life*), as well as the first established writer-director. He was the third Scottish actor to play the part, following Sylvester McCoy and David Tennant. Of his take on the Doctor, Capaldi said: "Even though I'm a lifelong *Doctor Who* fan I haven't really played *Doctor Who* since I was nine... So as an adult actor I've never worked on it, so what I did was I downloaded some old scripts from the Internet and practised those in front of the mirror. I'm surprised now to see *Doctor Who* looking back. You look in the mirror and suddenly, strangely, he's looking back and he's not me yet – but he's reaching out, and hopefully we'll get it together..."

Beyond the 50th anniversary *Doctor Who's* future looked secure. A Christmas special was scheduled for the end of 2013 and production was due to resume on an eighth series with Jemma Louise-Coleman set to return alongside Capaldi's Twelfth Doctor. With ratings fairly steady across the first seven series of the revived show, continually increasing iPlayer viewing figures, a higher profile in the US – where the series now aired on BBC America the same day as in the UK – and a host of peripheral spin-off sales, from DVDs to action figures, there seemed little reason why *Doctor Who* in its newest, refreshed form with a new leading actor would not celebrate its own 10th anniversary in 2015.

Across its 50 years on television, *Doctor Who* has become a part of the folklore of British culture. Every so often it might disappear for a while, but it will always return, refreshed and renewed (regenerated, you might say), as it has the most flexible format of any show, anywhere: a mad man in a magical box that can travel anywhere in space and time. No wonder it endures.

Steven Moffat – lucky enough to be the showrunner during *Doctor Who's* pivotal 50th year – had his own views on why the series succeeded: 'Imagine the sheer nonsense of devising a show, one of whose mission statements was to terrorise eight-year-olds! I'm not sure we could pitch it now. *Doctor Who* isn't just Hammer Horror or sci-fi. It's also a little bit *The Generation Game*, a little bit showbiz. It's a weird show. It's half scary Gothic castle, half shiny floorshow. Any show can be one or the other, but *Doctor Who* manages to be both. It's great – the most entertaining thing that British television has ever done.'

The newest incumbent of the 50-year-old part of the Doctor agreed. Peter Capaldi said on *Doctor Who Live: The Next Doctor*. 'I think *Doctor Who* is an extraordinary show and the thing that strikes me about it is that it's still here after all this time. And the reason that I think that it's still here is because of the work of all the writers and the directors and the producers who've worked on the show, and the actors – and I don't just mean the fabulous actors who've played the Doctor, but all those actors who've sweated inside rubber monster costumes and those who wear futuristic lurex catsuits. But the real reason – the big reason – that *Doctor Who* is still with us is because of every single viewer who ever turned on to watch this show – at any age, at any time in its history and in their history – and who took it into their heart because *Doctor Who* belongs to all of us. Everyone made *Doctor Who*.'

RESOURCES

EPISODE GUIDES

Through to the 2013 Christmas Special, *Doctor Who* had racked up 800 individual episodes. That's far too many to list here with associated credits (there are entire books that do little else), so this 'resources' section will direct readers to useful *Doctor Who* guides hosted on the Internet. Be aware: the Internet is dynamic and constantly changing, so the following URLs could be subject to change.

OFFICIAL BBC EPISODE GUIDES

Classic Series (1963-89, 1996):
http://www.bbc.co.uk/doctorwho/classic/episodeguide/

New Series (2005-onwards):
http://www.bbc.co.uk/programmes/b006q2x0/episodes/guide

BOOKS

A selection of titles consulted in the writing of this book and recommended for further reading on key topics and issues raised.

Bignell, Jonathan and Andrew O' Day. 2004. *Terry Nation*. Manchester: Manchester University Press.

Booy, Miles. 2012. Love and *Monsters: The Doctor Who Experience, 1979 to the Present*. London: IB Taurus.

Britton, Piers D and Simon J Baker. 2003. *Reading Between Designs: Visual Imagery and the Generation of Meaning in The Avengers, The Prisoner and Doctor Who*. Austin: University of Texas Press.

Britton, Piers D. 2011. *TARDISbound: Navigating the Universe of Doctor Who*. London: IB Taurus.

Burk, Graham & Robert Smith. 2012. *Who is the Doctor: The Unofficial Guide to Doctor Who, the New Series*. Toronto: ECW Press

Chapman, James. 2006. *Inside the TARDIS: A Cultural History of Doctor Who*. London: IB Taurus.

Clapham, Mark, Eddie Robson and Jim Smith. 2005. *Who's Next: An Unofficial and Unauthorised Guide to Doctor Who*. London: Virgin.

Collins, Frank. 2010. *Doctor Who: The Pandorica Opens – Exploring the Worlds of the Eleventh Doctor*. London: Classic TV Press.

Cornell, Paul (ed). 1997. *License Denied: Rumblings from the Doctor Who Underground*. London: Virgin Publishing.

Cornell, Paul, Martin Day and Keith Topping. 1995. *Doctor Who: The Discontinuity Guide*. London: Virgin Publishing.

Gillatt, Gary. 1998. *Doctor Who from A to Z: A Celebration of Thirty-Five Years of Adventures in Time and Space*. London: BBC Books.

Howe, David J, Mark Stammers and Stephen James Walker. 1992. *Doctor Who: The Sixties*. London: Virgin.

Howe, David J, Mark Stammers and Stephen James Walker. 1994. *Doctor Who: The Seventies*. London: Virgin.

Howe, David J, Mark Stammers and Stephen James Walker. 1997. *Doctor Who: The Eighties*. London: Virgin.

Miles, Lawrence and Tat Wood. 2004. *About Time 3*. New Orleans: Mad Norwegian Press.

Miles, Lawrence and Tat Wood. 2004. *About Time 4*. New Orleans: Mad Norwegian Press.

Miles, Lawrence and Tat Wood. 2005. *About Time 5*. New Orleans: Mad Norwegian Press.

Miles, Lawrence and Tat Wood. 2006. *About Time 1*. New Orleans: Mad Norwegian Press.

Miles, Lawrence and Tat Wood. 2006. *About Time 2*. New Orleans: Mad Norwegian Press.

Miles, Lawrence and Tat Wood. 2007. *About Time 6*. New Orleans: Mad Norwegian Press.

Newman, Kim. 2005. *BFI TV Classics: Doctor Who*. London: BFI.

Segal, Philip, with Gary Russell. 2000. *Doctor Who: Regeneration*. London: Harper-Collins Entertainment.

Sleight, Graham. 2012. *The Doctor's Monsters: Meanings of the Monstrous in Doctor Who*. London: IB Taurus.

Tulloch, John and Henry Jenkins. 1995. *Science Fiction Audiences: Watching Doctor Who and Star Trek*. London and New York: Routledge.

Walker, Stephen James. 2012. *Cracks in Time: The Unofficial and Unauthorised Guide to Doctor Who 2010*. London: Telos.

Wood, Tat. 2009. *About Time 3: The Unauthorized Guide to Doctor Who* [Expanded 2nd Edition]. New Orleans: Mad Norwegian Press.

DVD

As the list of available Doctor Who stories on DVD is constantly changing, the web is again the best place to obtain an up-to-date list of what's available.

Stories Available on DVD List:

http://en.wikipedia.org/wiki/Doctor_Who_DVD_releases

DVD Restoration Team:

http://www.restoration-team.co.uk/

SELECTED OFFICIAL/LICENSED RESOURCES

Big Finish Productions (Audio Dramas):

   http://www.bigfinish.com/

Doctor Who Magazine (4-Weekly Magazine):

   http://www.paninicomics.co.uk/Home.jsp

Character Options (Action Figures):

   http://www.character-online.com/

DOCUMENTS

The Genesis of Doctor Who

After years of previously only being accessible to researchers, the BBC have made a collection of documents (some referred to in chapter one) about the creation of *Doctor Who*, available for all via their online archive.

http://www.bbc.co.uk/archive/doctorwho/index.shtml

REFERENCES

CHAPTER ONE

'Up to the age of 40…', Sydney Newman. Interviewed by Auger, David & Stephen James Walker. *Doctor Who Magazine*, issue 141. October 1988. London: Marvel.

'When Donald Wilson and I…', Sydney Newman. Howe, David J, Mark Stammers and Stephen James Walker, *Doctor Who: The Handbook – The First Doctor, The William Hartnell Years: 1963–1966*. London: Virgin Publishing Ltd, 1994.

'She had never directed…', Sydney Newman. Howe, David J, Mark Stammers and Stephen James Walker, *Doctor Who: The Handbook – The First Doctor, The William Hartnell Years: 1963 –1966*. London: Virgin Publishing Ltd, 1994.

'I think it just looked so very strange…', Verity Lambert. Tulloch, John and Manuel Alvarado, *Doctor Who: The Unfolding Text*. London: Macmillan, 1983.

Donald Bull, Alice Frick and John Braybon, Internal BBC Reports on Science Fiction, April–July 1962.

CHAPTER TWO

Newsom, John (Chair). *The Newsom Report (1963), Half Our Future: A report of the Central Advisory Council for Education (England).* London: Her Majesty's Stationery Office, 1963.

'I was intent upon it containing...', Sydney Newman. Howe, David J, Mark Stammers and Stephen James Walker, *Doctor Who: The Handbook – The First Doctor, The William Hartnell Years: 1963–1966.* London: Virgin Publishing Ltd, 1994.

'We were going backwards and forwards in time...', Verity Lambert. *Doctor Who Magazine*, issue 234. January 1996. London: Panini.

'We have in mind...', Sydney Newman. Howe, David J, Mark Stammers and Stephen James Walker, *Doctor Who: The Handbook – The First Doctor, The William Hartnell Years: 1963–1966.* London: Virgin Publishing Ltd, 1994.

'He works very well for us...', David Whitaker. Howe, David J, Mark Stammers and Stephen James Walker, *Doctor Who: The Handbook – The First Doctor, The William Hartnell Years: 1963–1966.* London: Virgin Publishing Ltd, 1994.

'...it is slightly tongue-in-cheek...', Verity Lambert. Howe, David J, Mark Stammers and Stephen James Walker, *Doctor Who: The Handbook – The First Doctor, The William Hartnell Years: 1963–1966.* London: Virgin Publishing Ltd, 1994.

CHAPTER THREE

'I thought, "That's a great start..."', Terrance Dicks. Howe, David J, Mark Stammers and Stephen James Walker. *Doctor Who: The Sixties*. London: Virgin, 1992.

'If you're doing a science fiction serial set on Earth...', Terrance Dicks. Howe, David J, Mark Stammers and Stephen James Walker. *Doctor Who: The Seventies*. London: Virgin, 1994.

'By the time we were doing it...', Barry Letts. 'What Lies Beneath', *Doctor Who: Beneath The Surface*, DVD Box Set. London: 2Entertain, 2008.

'*Doctor Who* always tended to deal with fairly serious matters...', Terrance Dicks. Howe, David J, Mark Stammers and Stephen James Walker. *Doctor Who: The Seventies*. London: Virgin, 1994.

'It seemed to him...', Salman Rushdie. *The Satanic Verses*. London: Viking Press, 1988.

'We always used to try and think of a gimmick...', Terrance Dicks. Howe, David J, Mark Stammers and Stephen James Walker. *Doctor Who: The Seventies*. London: Virgin, 1994.

'One of the first things I did...', Barry Letts. 'Prime Time', *Dreamwatch Magazine* #117, July 2004. London: Titan Magazines.

'*Doctor Who* is the only prison...', Terrance Dicks. Howe, David J, Mark Stammers and Stephen James Walker. *Doctor Who: The Seventies*. London: Virgin, 1994.

'It is wrong to have a greed for knowledge…', Barry Letts. Howe, David J, Mark Stammers and Stephen James Walker. *Doctor Who: The Seventies*. London: Virgin, 1994.

CHAPTER FOUR

Philip Hinchcliffe quotes from a personal interview with the author, originally published as 'Gothic Shock', *Dreamwatch Magazine*. London: Titan Magazines.

'…more than anybody else…', Mary Whitehouse. Dennis Barker, 'Mary Whitehouse: Self-appointed campaigner against the permissive society on television', *Guardian*, Saturday 24 November, 2001. London: Guardian Media Group.

'…strangulation – by hand, by claw, by obscene vegetable matter – is the latest [*Doctor Who*] gimmick…', Mary Whitehouse. *Screen Violence*. French, Karl (ed). London: Bloomsbury, 1996.

'At a time when little children are watching…', Mary Whitehouse. Letter to Director General Charles Curran, quoted in: Gillatt, Gary. *Doctor Who from A to Z: A Celebration of Thirty-Five Years of Adventures in Time and Space*. London: BBC Books, 1998.

'One or two people…', Charles Curran. Gillatt, Gary. *Doctor Who from A to Z: A Celebration of Thirty-Five Years of Adventures in Time and Space*. London: BBC Books, 1998.

'That element of sophisticated humour…', Graham Williams. Howe, David J, Mark Stammers and Stephen James Walker. *Doctor Who: The Seventies*. London: Virgin, 1994.

'We decided to do the one big remaining stereotype...', Graham Williams. Howe, David J, Mark Stammers and Stephen James Walker. *Doctor Who: The Seventies*. London: Virgin, 1994.

CHAPTER FIVE

'I was getting very fed up...', Eric Saward. *Starburst* #97. 1985. London: Visual Imagination.

CHAPTER SIX

Howe, David J, Mark Stammers and Stephen James Walker. *Doctor Who: The Seventies*. London: Virgin, 1994.

Cornell, Paul (ed.). *License Denied: Rumblings from the Doctor Who Underground*. London: Virgin Publishing, 1997.

'We were fans...', Gary Russell. Gary Russell talks about the Audio Visuals. *Sonic Screwdriver*. 1998. Victoria, Australia: *Doctor Who* Club of Victoria.

Robb, Brian J. Interview with Philip Segal. *Dreamwatch* #15, November 1995. London: Gary Leigh.

Robb, Brian J. Various fanzine/magazine features. *The Highlander. Celestial Toyroom. Doctor Who Bulletin. Dreamwatch. Doctor Who Magazine*. 1986–90.

DWB/Dreamwatch (1983–2007)
Doctor Who Magazine (1979–present)
Doctor Who Appreciation Society (1976–present)

CHAPTER SEVEN

'It's May 2005...', Adam Pasco. *Magazine Week*, 29 September–5 October, 2008. http://www.magazineweek.net/cover-debate/22/read/

'I think the cross-generational...', David Tennant. Interview, BBC Television, 30 October 2008. London: BBC.

'[Change] is always good for the programme...', Russell T Davies. WalesOnline.co.uk, 31 October 2008. Cardiff: Media Wales Ltd.

Matt Smith, Piers Wenger and Steven Moffat quotes from BBC Press Releases.

INDEX